Alternatives to Multilateralism

Earth System Governance

Frank Biermann and Oran R. Young, series editors

Oran R. Young, *Institutional Dynamics: Emergent Patterns in International Environmental Governance*

Frank Biermann and Philipp Pattberg, eds., *Global Environmental Governance Reconsidered*

Olav Schram Stokke, *Disaggregating International Regimes: A New Approach to Evaluation and Comparison*

Aarti Gupta and Michael Mason, eds., *Transparency in Global Environmental Governance: Critical Perspectives*

Sikina Jinnah, *Post-Treaty Politics: Secretariat Influence in Global Environmental Governance*

Frank Biermann, *Earth System Governance: World Politics in the Anthropocene*

Walter F. Baber and Robert B. Bartlett, *Consensus in Global Environmental Governance: Deliberative Democracy in Nature's Regime*

Diarmuid Torney, *European Climate Leadership in Question: Policies toward China and India*

David Ciplet, J. Timmons Roberts, and Mizan R. Khan, *Power in a Warming World: The New Global Politics of Climate Change and the Remaking of Environmental Inequality*

Simon Nicholson and Sikina Jinnah, eds., *New Earth Politics: Essays from the Anthropocene*

Norichika Kanie and Frank Biermann, eds., *Governing through Goals: Sustainable Development Goals as Governance Innovation*

Oran R. Young, *Governing Complex Systems: Social Capital for the Anthropocene*

Susan Park and Teresa Kramarz, eds., *Global Environmental Governance and the Accountability Trap*

Teresa Kramarz, *Forgotten Values: The World Bank and Its Partnerships for the Environment*

Lena Partzsch, *Alternatives to Multilateralism: New Forms of Social and Environmental Governance*

Related books from Institutional Dimensions of Global Environmental Change: A Core Research Project of the International Human Dimensions Programme on Global Environmental Change

Oran R. Young, Leslie A. King, and Heike Schroeder, eds., *Institutions and Environmental Change: Principal Findings, Applications, and Research Frontiers*

Frank Biermann and Bernd Siebenhüner, eds., *Managers of Global Change: The Influence of International Environmental Bureaucracies*

Sebastian Oberthür and Olav Schram Stokke, eds., *Managing Institutional Complexity: Regime Interplay and Global Environmental Change*

Alternatives to Multilateralism

New Forms of Social and Environmental Governance

Lena Partzsch

The MIT Press
Cambridge, Massachusetts
London, England

This book was supported by the German Federal Ministry of Research and Education (project no. 031B0235A).

This book was set in ITC Stone Serif Std and ITC Stone Sans Std by New Best-set Typesetters Ltd.

Library of Congress Cataloging-in-Publication Data

Names: Partzsch, Lena, 1978- author.
Title: Alternatives to multilateralism : new forms of social and environmental
    governance / Lena Partzsch.
Description: Cambridge, Massachusetts : The MIT Press, [2020] | Series:
    Earth system governance | Includes bibliographical references and index.
Identifiers: LCCN 2019049226 | ISBN 9780262539227 (paperback)
Subjects: LCSH: Business logistics—Standards—Case studies. | Business
    logistics—Government policy—Case studies. | Social responsibility of
    business—Case studies. | Trade regulation—Case studies. | Globalization—
    Economic aspects.
Classification: LCC HD38.5 .P365 2020 | DDC 338.6—dc23
LC record available at https://lccn.loc.gov/2019049226

Contents

Series Foreword

Humans now influence all biological and physical systems of the planet. Almost no species, land area, or part of the oceans has remained unaffected by the expansion of the human species. Recent scientific findings suggest that the entire earth system now operates outside the normal state exhibited over at least the past five hundred thousand years. Yet at the same time, it is apparent that the institutions, organizations, and mechanisms by which humans govern their relationship with the natural environment and global biogeochemical systems are utterly insufficient—and poorly understood. More fundamental and applied research is needed.

Such research is no easy undertaking. It must span the entire globe because only integrated global solutions can ensure a sustainable coevolution of biophysical and socioeconomic systems. But it must also draw on local experiences and insights. Research on earth system governance must be about places in all their diversity, yet seek to integrate place-based research within a global understanding of the myriad human interactions with the earth system. Eventually, the task is to develop integrated systems of governance, from the local to the global level, that ensure the sustainable development of the coupled socioecological system that the Earth has become.

The Earth System Governance series is designed to address this research challenge. Books in this series will pursue this challenge from a variety of disciplinary perspectives, at different levels of governance, and with a range of methods. Yet all will further one common aim: analyzing current systems of earth system governance with a view to increased understanding and possible improvements and reform. Books in this series will be of interest to the academic community but will also inform practitioners and at times contribute to policy debates.

This series is related to the long-term international research program called the Earth System Governance Project.

Frank Biermann, Copernicus Institute of Sustainable Development, Utrecht University

Oran R. Young, Bren School, University of California, Santa Barbara

Earth System Governance Series Editors

Preface

This monograph developed in parallel to several research projects, through which I was funded over the last years. Writing a monograph as a side activity allowed me to be completely free in terms of its content. I was able to develop a deeper interest in and understanding of the issues at stake. While I started with the idea of studying ways to address blood consumption, I became more and more aware of new tricky types of regulation that allow the EU and the United States to govern outside their own territory. At the same time, I have increasingly scrutinized conventional understandings of power in international relations (IR), and I wanted to contribute to developing the concepts *power to* (empowerment and resistance) and *power with* (cooperation and learning). If we want to understand change, it is not enough to study gridlock. Rather, we need to look for and learn from the possibly rare but existing transitions to greater social justice and environmental sustainability in IR.

I am especially grateful to Beth Clevenger, Frank Biermann, and Oran Young, the editors of the MIT Press book series. They asked the right questions and very much encouraged me to find my own voice.

Moreover, I would like to thank all my Freiburg colleagues. Warm thanks for research assistance to Miriam Beulting, Laura Kemper, Frank Neto, Hannah Robinson, and Haley Wilhelm. Hannah Robinson proofread the entire manuscript, and I am especially grateful to her. When I was drawn into my intellectual work, my colleagues constantly reminded me to take care of my physical and emotional needs too. One of the most frequent phrases I heard over the last years was: "Like in an airplane, put on your own oxygen mask first before trying to help others—or save the world."

I cooperated with a range of colleagues all over the world for this book and I am very grateful to Abebe Beyene, Atakilte Beyene, Basil Bornemann,

Katharina Glaab, Sara Geenen, Aarti Gupta, Agni Kalfagianni, and Sara Stattman. Sara Hughes was the one who recommended submitting my manuscript to MIT Press. Eva-Maria Nag gave me feedback on the first version of my book proposal and stayed supportive throughout the revision process. Thank you both so much!

In addition, I would like to thank my students in Freiburg, Leipzig, and Münster, who participated in courses that I developed in parallel to the research on this book. I felt very privileged to be able to work closely in Freiburg's Master of Environmental Governance program with students from all over the world, including from the case study countries. Our exchange nourished the empirical chapters of this book. In this context, I also would like to thank all interviewees and people who helped with my field work for their time and trust. Universities can provide unique spaces of mutual exchange, and I hope that present and future generations are able to defend these spaces against corporatization.

Last but not least, warm thanks to my family and friends for sharing my enthusiasm about this project. I am very fortunate in so many ways (including having access to an "oxygen mask" whenever I need it), and I hope to be able to help others and contribute to protecting the earth with what you hold in your hands.

Lena Partzsch

Erfurt, October 2019

Figures

Tables

Abbreviations

3T&G	Tantalum, tin, tungsten, and gold
ADF	Allied Democratic Forces
AFP	Analytical Fingerprint
AMDAL	Indonesian Environmental Feasibility Assessment
ARM	Alliance for Responsible Mining
ASI	Aluminium Stewardship Initiative
ASI	Accreditation Services International
BCI	Better Cotton Initiative
BMGF	Bill and Melinda Gates Foundation
BSP	Better Sourcing Program
BV	Bureau Veritas
CAN	Climate Action Network
CFSP	Conflict-Free Smelter Program
CFTI	Conflict-Free Tin Initiative
CITES	Convention on International Trade in Endangered Species of Wild Fauna and Flora
CLAS	Certisource Legality Verification System
CmiA	Cotton made in Africa
CoC	Chain of custody
COFO	Committee on Forestry
COP	Conference of the Parties
CPOPC	Council of Palm Oil Producing Countries
CTC	Certified trading chains
DFID	Department for International Development (United Kingdom)
DRC	Democratic Republic of the Congo
EC	European Commission

ECPGEA	Ethiopian Cotton Producers, Ginners, and Exporters Association
EIA	Environmental Investigation Agency
EPFL	École polytechnique fédérale de Lausanne
EPRM	European Partnership for Responsible Minerals
EU	European Union
EUTR	European Union Timber Regulation
FAO	Food and Agriculture Organization
FFL	Fair for Life
FFP	Forest Peoples Program
FLA	Fair Labor Association
FLAG	Field Legality Advisory Group
FLEG	Forest Law Enforcement and Governance
FLEGT	Forest Law Enforcement, Governance, and Trade Action Plan
FLO	Fairtrade Labelling Organizations International
FONAP	Forum Nachhaltiges Palmöl (Forum on Sustainable Palm Oil)
FPIC	Free, Prior, and Informed Consent
FSC	Forest Stewardship Council
FTUSA	Fair Trade USA
FVLC	(Woodmark) Forest Verification of Legal Compliance
FWF	Fair Wear Foundation
G20	Group of Twenty
G7	Group of Seven
G77	Group of Seventy-Seven
GAIN	Global Alliance for Improved Nutrition
GAPKI	Gabungan Asosiasi Pengusaha Kelapa Sawit Indonesia (Indonesian Palm Oil Association)
GATT	General Agreement on Tariffs and Trade
GDP	Gross domestic product
GHG	Greenhouse gas
GM	Genetically modified
GMO	Genetically modified organism
GOTS	Global Organic Textile Standard
GTAS	Grain and Feed Trade Association Trade Assurance Scheme
GTP	Growth and Transformation Plan
HCV	High conservation value
HVO RD	HVO Renewable Diesel Scheme

ICC	International Criminal Court
ICGLR	International Conference on the Great Lakes Region
ICME	International Council on Metals and the Environment
IFAT	International Federation of Alternative Traders
IFOAM	International Federation of Organic Agriculture Movements
ILO	International Labor Organization
ILPA	Illegal Logging Prohibition Act
ILUC	Indirect land use change
IPM	Integrated pest management
IPOP	Indonesian Palm Oil Pledge
IR	International relations
IRMA	Initiative for Responsible Mining Assurance
ISCC	International Sustainability and Carbon Certification
ISD	Institute for Sustainable Development
ISPO	Indonesian Sustainable Palm Oil
ITRI	International Tin Research Institute
iTSCi	ITRI Tin Supply Chain Initiative
IVN	International Association of Natural Textiles
JOCA	Japan Overseas Cooperative Association
LHV	Legal Harvest Verification
LS	LegalSource Standard
LTPA	Legal Timber Protection Act
LVS	Legal Verification Service
MECNT	Ministry of the Environment, Nature Conservation and Tourism (DRC)
MEDD	Ministry of Environment and Sustainable Development (DRC)
MFA	Multi Fibre Arrangement
MoA	Ministry of Agriculture of the Republic of Indonesia
MPOB	Malaysian Palm Oil Board
MSPO	Malaysian Sustainable Palm Oil
NEPCon	Nature Economy and People Connected
NFP	National Forest Program
NGO	Nongovernmental organization
NOP	National Organic Program (United States)
NPE	Normative power Europe
Npr-PPM	Non-product-related production process method
NTA	Netherlands Technical Agreement

NTAC	Never Trust a COP
OCS	Organic Content Standard
OECD	Organization for Economic Cooperation and Development
OGF	Observatoire de la Gouvernance Forestière
OI-FLEG	Independent Observer of Forest Law Enforcement and Governance
OLB	Origine et Légalité du Bois (Origin and Legality of Wood)
OTA	Organic Trade Association
PAN	Pesticide Action Network
PASDEP	Plan for the Acceleration and Sustained Development to End Poverty
PEFC	Programme for the Endorsement of Forest Certification
POME	Palm Oil Mill Effluent
PPM	Production process method
RBSA	RED Bioenergy Sustainability Assurance
RED	Renewable Energy Directive
RFS	Renewable Fuel Standard (United States)
RMAP	Responsible Minerals Assurance Process
RMI	Responsible Minerals Initiative
RRN	Réseau Ressources Naturelles
RSB	Roundtable on Sustainable Biofuels
RSPO	Roundtable on Sustainable Palm Oil
SAI	Social Accountability International
SCIE	Sustainable Cotton Initiative Ethiopia
SCS	Scientific Certification Systems
SEC	Securities and Exchange Commission (United States)
SFM	Sustainable forest management
TLTV	Timber Legality & Traceability Verification
TMN	Transnational municipal network
TNC	Transnational corporation
UCIRI	Union of Indigenous Communities of the Isthmus Region
UK	United Kingdom
UN	United Nations
UNCED	United Nations Conference on Environment and Development
UNDP	United Nations Development Programme
UNEP	United Nations Environment Programme

UNFCCC	United Nations Framework Convention on Climate Change
USA	United States of America
USDA	United States Department of Agriculture
VLC	Verification of Legal Compliance
VLO	Verification of Legal Origin
VPA	Voluntary Partnership Agreement
WFTO	World Fair Trade Organization
WRI	World Resources Institute
WTO	World Trade Organization
WTP	Wood Tracking Program
WWF	World Wide Fund for Nature

1 Introduction

Globalization has lost its shine. Social inequalities are pervasive. Pressures on the environment and natural resources have increased dramatically. Although the worldwide integration of markets has drained political control from individual nation-states, they have failed to collectively coordinate their responses to global challenges. Multilateralism is either focused on declarations or completely missing. There is an objective to create inclusive economic growth that provides sustainable jobs and promotes equality, and yet 42 percent of the population in sub-Saharan Africa continues to live below the poverty line (UN SDG 2019). Furthermore, the international community has declared its intent to keep the global temperature rise below 2 degrees Celsius above preindustrial levels and to pursue efforts to limit the temperature increase even further to 1.5 degrees Celsius, but measures to mitigate greenhouse gas emissions are largely delayed or absent (UNFCCC 2019).

In the following section, I explain, on the one hand, why social and environmental governance is so challenging in a globalized world. On the other hand, I highlight that alternatives to multilateralism do exist. These alternatives are private forms of governance (in particular, certification programs), public supply-chain-related laws, and hybrid forms of public-private governance. Each alternative was initiated in the Global North and has resulted in different power dynamics in global supply chains. This book discusses these dynamics by shedding light on the most affected exporting states in the Global South. In the next section, I explain the three alternative forms of regulation and introduce my case studies in more detail. This is followed by a section outlining my research methodology and the book structure.

1.1   Why This Book: Globalization and Governance

The effects of globalization on governance are complex and uncertain. Fewer and fewer products that we, as citizens of one country, consume are produced in the same country in which we reside. Economic exchanges occur between an increasing number of actors over ever-increasing distances. For example, the production and sale of a single cup of Starbucks coffee can depend upon as many as nineteen different countries for its ingredients (including the coffee beans, milk, sugar, and paper cup; see figure 1.1). The United States alone imported 728 million tons of commodities worth USD 377 billion in 2016 (Chatham House 2019). At the same time, governments are increasingly unable to track these trade flows and enforce rules outside of their own jurisdictions. There is hence a need for new types of regulation.

Friedmann (2000, 8) defines globalization as "the inexorable integration of markets, nation-states and technologies to a degree never witnessed before—in a way that is enabling individuals, corporations and nation-states to reach around the world farther, faster, deeper and cheaper than ever before." Figures show that the world economy became more systematically open to global trade from the 1970s onward. In particular, from 1995 to 2001, the world trade system experienced fairly strong growth, followed by a boom from 2002 to 2008. Since the financial crisis in 2008, there has been a recovery in recent years, and the volume of world exports has continued to grow (WTO 2018).

Increased trade of goods over time has consistently been spurred by technological innovations and sharply reduced transportation and cross-border communication costs (Ruggie 2013). These factors also affect cultural integration through the spread of digitized images (Bleiker 2018; Nygren 2015). Today, images portraying tragedies such as the collapse of the Bangladeshi Rana Plaza factory building in 2013 or the displacement or extermination of the Bornean orangutan due to the expansion of oil palm plantations in recent years proliferate around the world. In consequence, Western consumers are becoming increasingly more aware of the burden shifting associated with international trade and the need for regulation in global supply chains (Haufler 2010; Gupta and Mason 2015; van der Ven 2019a).

Regulation refers to a set of rules that are defined by an actor or a group of actors and followed by the same, a different, or a broader set of actors.

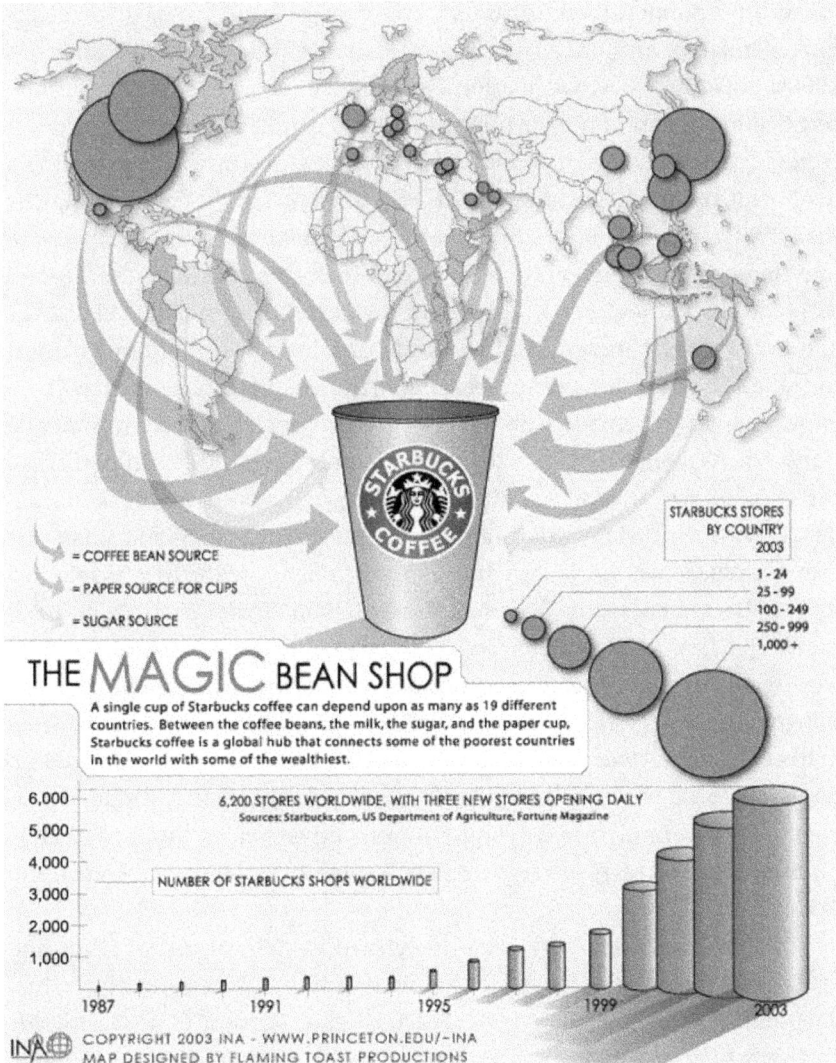

Figure 1.1
Global ingredients of a Starbucks cup. *Source:* International Networks Archive 2003.

Classically, public actors including governments and other state actors have regulative authority over a defined nation-state territory. Since the 1990s, however, private regulation has garnered recognition and voluntary certification has become an increasingly integrated part of many market sectors (Green 2013; Mattli and Woods 2009). Governments promoting a neoliberal model of governance, in which states take a "steering" rather than "rowing" role, ultimately constrained themselves by signing onto free trade rules when joining the World Trade Organization (WTO) and its predecessor, the General Agreement on Tariffs and Trade (GATT). GATT and WTO restrict trade rules that create discriminatory nontariff barriers to trade. They do not preclude all import restrictions, as evidenced by a growing body of research on WTO-compliant social and environmental standards (Gabler 2010; Jakir 2013; Morin and Jinnah 2018). In particular, the WTO allows private regulation, although in many instances such standards that are officially voluntary are in fact de facto mandatory because they have become an industry norm, or compliance with them is required for suppliers to access the proprietary value chain of transnational corporations (TNCs) or large retailers (Du 2018; Shaffer 2015). In such cases, those who regulate progressively are nonstate actors, which include TNCs and nongovernmental organizations (NGOs). TNCs generate an income from markets in more than one country, whereas NGOs' activities are based on donations and public funding (with a few exceptions). Nonstate actors have adopted, implemented, and enforced private rules in an increasing number of countries (Dauvergne 2018b; Ruggie 2013; Schleifer, Fiorini, and Auld 2019).

The *supply* or *commodity chain* is defined as "a network of labor and production processes whose end result is a finished commodity" (Hopkins and Wallerstein 1986, 159). The upstream portion of global supply chains, which is where the production flow starts, and is mostly located in the Global South (and China),[1] has gained particular attention. NGOs often blame TNCs' greed for profit for tragedies like the Rana Plaza collapse, for example, whereas others call upon consumers to take responsibility, join a "fashion revolution" (Armedangels 2016), and put an end to "dirty" and "cheap" clothing production (Brooks 2015; Hoskins 2014). In response to the Rana Plaza tragedy in particular, voluntary initiatives renewed their impetus for developing private standards in the global garment industry (Jacobs and Singhal 2017). Today, certified textiles have a market share of almost 20 percent (BCI 2018). As companies disclose information and guarantee compliance with specific standards, such as minimum wages or prohibition of toxic pesticides and fertilizers, consumers are increasingly willing to pay a higher price for clothing, as well as a range of other products (Bartley 2018; Bloomfield 2017; Schleifer, Fiorini, and Auld 2019).

The first qualitative case study in this book sheds light on the effects of private regulation by examining cotton certification in Ethiopia, a country now becoming known as the "new Bangladesh" (Donahue 2018). There is some literature on downstream textile certification (Bartley 2007, 2018; Macdonald 2014); however, for most certified textiles, production circumstances have been improved only in the upstream part of the supply chain, especially in cotton production, and scholars have widely neglected certification efforts at this stage (for an exception, see Sneyd 2011, 2014, 2015). At the same time, international trade of cotton clearly demonstrates the shifting of both environmental and social burdens by textile consumers in the Global North to producing countries in the Global South (Brooks 2015; Donahue 2018). In Ethiopia, with regard to environmental problems, the introduction of Bt cotton, a genetically modified organism (GMO), and the expansion of irrigation for cotton cultivation are the most controversially debated topics (Beyene and Sandström 2016; Fikade 2018). At the same time, there is a range of social problems; for example, cotton field workers receive as little as USD 0.60 per day, and child and young adult labor is very common in the industry (Donahue 2018; Schoneveld and Shete 2014). Private regulation attempts to address these challenges and change respective power dynamics in global supply chains (see chapter 3).

More recently, building upon new and emerging forms of private regulation, the EU, the United States, and other consuming countries have adopted public supply-chain-related laws. Specifically, companies now face mandatory requirements for imports of potential conflict minerals and timber or timber products (Sarfaty 2015; Bartley 2014). The US Dodd-Frank Act Section 1502 targets the Democratic Republic of the Congo (DRC). Although Section 1502 is no longer enforced under the Trump administration, it requires "due diligence" checks on importers of tantalum, tin, tungsten, and gold (3T&G) to stop the financing of armed groups through the trade of these minerals in the DRC and the African Great Lakes region (Sarfaty 2015, 427). In parallel, since 2010, the EU and the DRC have been negotiating a Voluntary Partnership Agreement (VPA; EU FLEGT 2018). The EU Timber Regulation (EUTR) prohibits EU operators from plac- ing illegally harvested timber and timber products on the EU market. A VPA aims to ensure that all timber exports comply with the relevant laws of the exporting country and hence the EUTR (Fishman and Obidzinski 2014; Leipold et al. 2016). In this book, the DRC serves as a second qual- itative case study on the impact of public supply-chain-related laws (see chapter 4).

Finally, a hybrid approach that combines mandatory requirements with voluntary certification emerged with the introduction of the EU Renew- able Energy Directive (RED),[2] which in part regulates biofuels, includ- ing palm-oil-based diesel (Ponte and Daugbjerg 2015). RED requires that at least 20 percent of total energy must come from renewables by 2020, of which at least 10 percent must come from renewable transport fuels. Biofuels are seen to be instrumental in reaching this 10 percent target but may only count if they meet certain sustainability criteria (Renckens, Skog- stad, and Mondou 2017; Kemper and Partzsch 2018). The EU prescribes a meta-standard by which biofuel producers can demonstrate compliance through private certification (European Commission 2009). Currently, 20 percent of palm oil worldwide is certified by the Roundtable on Sustain- able Palm Oil (RSPO), in addition to other certification schemes (Efeca 2016, 2). Indonesia, which has become the largest exporter of palm oil to the EU with a share of 23 percent (European Commission 2018b), is most affected by RED. The Indonesian government adopted its own palm oil certification system, the Indonesian Sustainable Palm Oil (ISPO) program, in response to RED. Indonesia therefore serves as a third qualitative case study in this book to illuminate the impacts of hybrid forms of regula- tion (Mukama, Mustalahti, and Zahabu 2012; Silva-Castaneda 2012; see chapter 5).

The emergence of new forms of regulation in global supply chains raises questions about the withdrawal of the state, potential environmental and social implications, North–South asymmetries, and whether "ethical" or "normative" power exists in the transnational sphere (Diez and Manners 2007; De Zutter 2010). Scholars have shown that new forms of regulation emerged from a neoliberal agenda and have remained cautious about the intended impact of these regulations in the Global South (Hilson 2014; Levidow 2013; McDermott, Irland, and Pacheco 2015). By understanding power as *power over* (coercion and manipulation)—that is, the capability of dominant actors, structures, and discourse over others—scholars have demonstrated why positive change, such as a fashion revolution, has *not* happened yet (Partzsch 2017b; Partzsch and Kemper 2019).

Only a few scholars have considered the possibility that new forms of regulation are pioneering change with regard to environmental and social issues (Risse, Börzel, and Draude 2018; Ruggie 2013). Most have remained skeptical (Bartley 2018; Dauvergne 2018b; Levidow 2013; Sneyd 2014, 2015). Complementing these studies, I make a strong claim in this book for acknowledging *power to* (empowerment and resistance) and *power with* (cooperation and learning; Allen 1998; Partzsch 2017b). *Power to* corresponds to the ability of agents "to get things done" (Parsons 1963, 232)— for example, the ability of actors in the Global South to develop sustainably despite structural constraints. *Power with* refers to collective empowerment through convincing and learning with and from one another. It refers to processes of developing shared values, finding common ground, and generating collective strength (Partzsch 2017b). In this sense, actors may overcome the artificial divide between consumers (in the Global North) and producers (in the Global South) and take joint action.

For the first time, this book sets out different types of private (voluntary), public (mandatory) and hybrid (public-private) regulation for global supply chains in a cross-sectoral comparison. Simultaneously, it includes new and timely cases, studying their on-the-ground impact in selected countries of the Global South—specifically, Ethiopia, the DRC, and Indonesia. Each of these cases is highly relevant to the new form of regulation studied in each respective chapter. The overall objective of the book is to understand the potential that new forms of social and environmental (re-)regulation have against a backdrop of power dynamics in global supply chains. The book addresses three fundamental questions:

1. Do new forms of regulation increase private *power over* nation-states, and does this power shift support or undermine environmental and social considerations?

2. Do new forms of environmental and social regulation allow actors in the Global South to exercise *power to* develop sustainably?

3. Do new forms of regulation enable processes of *power with* others to pursue collective norms and ethical values?

1.2   Research Methodology and Book Structure

The book is based on liberal institutionalism and informed by political economy and constructivism. I use a supply chain approach to track state and nonstate actors that are linked in the globalized economy. My research strategy is to first explore power dynamics in global supply chains based on literature review. Chapter 2 lays the theoretical and empirical grounds for the study. Here, I formulate three dominant perspectives regarding the consequences of economic globalization for political power in current IR research debates. These three perspectives concern public-private relations (Fuchs 2007; Green 2013), asymmetries between the Global North and South (Brooks 2015; Quark 2013), and universal norms and ethical values in international relations (Diez 2013; Manners 2015). The appendix provides an overview of the three perspectives.

Methodologically, the three perspectives build the core of my analytical framework for conducting my comparative research. I operationalize the perspectives by structuring them into analytical questions, which allow me to study (code) my empirical material (Kelle 2007). The appendix provides a list of these analytical questions. The three new forms of regulation—private (voluntary) regulation, public supply-chain-related laws, and the hybrid governance approach—stand at the beginning of a causal chain (independent variable), at the end of which we can observe either power dynamics as assumed in the literature or something else (dependent variable). When studying power perspectives similar to hypotheses, however, I am mainly interested in understanding processes. I assume that actions and developments overlap and complement each other to avoid applying a purely positivistic research approach. I am interested in more than confirming or rejecting monocausal hypotheses. Therefore, narrative elements are also important to provide comprehensive explanations (Kelle 2015; Kelle and Kluge 1999).

The three power perspectives and the respective framework bridge the theoretical and empirical parts of the research and the book. The goal is to zoom in close enough to examine how alternative forms of regulation are put into practice while still being able to compare the different forms of regulation more broadly. The analytical questions essentially serve as a means to compare and study the alternative types of regulation in light of broader research debates on power in global supply chains and world trade. In consequence, the book represents neither purely theoretical nor empirical research. Instead, theory and empirics are brought together in a theoretical sampling (Kelle and Kluge 1999, 44–46).

I conduct three case studies to assess the impact of each of the three new forms of regulation. In each case, I chose the most illustrative country concerning the relevance of the alternative form of regulation on which I focus in the chapter. The case studies are as follows: first, cotton certification and Ethiopia; second, public timber and minerals supply chain laws and the DRC; and third, palm oil and Indonesia.

For the first case study, I decided to focus on cotton supply chains due to the garment industry's campaigns in response to the Rana Plaza event. I detected a research gap regarding the very upstream portion of (cotton) textile supply chains, which is directly related to the private regulation of cotton production. At the same time, the case of cotton illustrates well both environmental and social burden shifting through international trade. Ethiopia recently witnessed a cotton revival and is often considered the next Bangladesh (wages are lower than in Southeast Asia; see Brooks 2015; Donahue 2018; Schoneveld and Shete 2014). If certification has an impact, Ethiopia should suffer less from foreign textile investments than Bangladesh did, and still does, with regard to social and environmental issues. Therefore, the country makes an excellent case through which to examine the impact of private regulation (voluntary certification) and its ability to contribute to the prevention of tragedies like Rana Plaza.

Second, public supply-chain-related laws do not exist for many sectors (Sarfaty 2015). During negotiations on the EU Conflict Minerals Regulation, the mining industry argued that mandatory due diligence checks for minerals would cause rebels to shift their business to the timber sector with the result of increasing deforestation in conflict regions (Partzsch 2018). This argumentation piqued my interest in dynamics between the two sectors. As the US Dodd-Frank Act's Section 1502 focused on the DRC, and the EU has been busy negotiating a VPA on timber imports with the DRC, I selected conflict resources and DRC for the case study on the impact of public supply-chain-related laws in the Global South.

Third, palm oil production in Indonesia serves as a case study for the hybrid governance approach. Palm oil production in this country is by far the most affected by the EU-RED hybrid regulation (Silva-Castaneda 2012; Ponte and Daugbjerg 2015). There are ongoing controversies at the diplomatic level between the European Commission and the Indonesian government regarding the extension of the hybrid approach after 2020 (when RED expires; see European Commission 2018b). Despite criticism and scholars querying the normative intention behind the request for sustainability (Dauvergne 2018a; Dauvergne and Lister 2013; Levidow 2013), the European Commission (2016) has proposed to increase the overall required share of renewables from 20 percent to 27 percent by 2030. In response, the European Parliament voted in favor of excluding biofuels produced from palm oil from being counted toward this target. This would have created a de facto embargo on Indonesian palm oil, of which 15.6 percent is currently exported to the EU, with a foreseeable drop in prices and slump (European Commission 2018b; Chatham House 2019). Therefore, I selected this case to study the impact of the RED hybrid approach in the Global South.

Chapters 3–5 are empirical chapters. Each of the empirical chapters starts with a background section in which I describe a particular form of regulation, including its origins, the current state of the research, and debates on its impact in the Global South. This section is essentially based upon literature review and document analysis. In a second section of each empirical chapter, I conduct the country study with a qualitative case study approach. In addition to reviewing the literature, I collected empirical material for this purpose. The means of data collection are outlined in more detail in the beginning of each chapter. Policy documents published by governments and other state actors, including the European Commission, were an essential source. In addition, I collected documents published by nonstate actors, such as self-portrayals on homepages, flyers, and so on. I also considered relevant news articles and private reports.

Semi-structured interviews and participatory observations helped me to complement and verify information. My sampling strategy aimed to maximize potential diversity among actors in terms of their interests and roles in the supply chains and their regulation, but my main aim was to close information gaps. In total, I conducted more than sixty-five semi-structured interviews with key informants all along the various supply chains, including smallholders, certifiers, retailers (merchants, manufacturers, etc.), government officials, and NGOs. In Ethiopia and Indonesia, I also organized several group discussions during field visits in 2017 and 2018. All interviews and discussions lasted between thirty minutes and three hours. The interviewees insisted on anonymity because they revealed sensitive economic and political information. Therefore, I use initials when quoting interviewees in the book.

Moreover, I used notes from participatory observations. These participatory observations were conducted in Germany, a key consuming country with regard to certification and new types of supply chain regulation (many voluntary certification initiatives are headquartered in Germany, including the Fairtrade Labelling Organizations International [FLO] and Forest Stewardship Council [FSC], both in Bonn), as well as in Ethiopia and Indonesia, key producing countries. For example, I used notes from participatory observations at a Fairtrade Fair in Freiburg, Germany, in May 2017, and I visited certified cotton farms close to Arba Minch, Ethiopia, in September 2017. By comparing three different types of regulation used in different sectors and their impacts on countries situated upstream in the supply chain, an understanding of the world system as a whole could emerge. This comparison allows me to trace the power dynamics as well as normative convergence between actors at the same node—for example, between organic movements in Germany and cotton producers in Ethiopia.

In the final chapter, I compare the findings on each new type of regulation and draw some general conclusions. We will see, first, that new regulative approaches underline the withdrawal of the state, although this does not necessarily undermine environmental and social considerations (Gabler 2010; Jakir 2013; Morin and Jinnah 2018). Governments shackled themselves to the World Trade Organization (WTO). This means, first, that the WTO has *power over* individual states, particularly states of the Global South (Azubuike 2018; Widiatedja 2019). Second, the WTO gives private actors a new power over all nation-states (Bartley 2018; Du 2018). Due to WTO rules, all forms of regulation are essentially based on the principle of disclosure—that is, greater transparency improving circumstances of production, instead of prescribing specific rules (Haufler 2010). However, on the one hand, an increasing number of standards has emerged since the 1990s (Bartley 2018, 8). Early regulative initiatives, such as organic and fair-trade certification, were initiated out of political motivations to provide greater environmental sustainability and social justice. On the other hand, one of my essential findings is that most new regulative approaches are guided by state regulation, and their content and outreach are limited. As new—private, mandatory, and hybrid—regulatory approaches are essentially shaped by state regulation and do not operate in "empty spaces" (Bartley 2018, 34), they fail to change mainstream markets. However, there is a considerable power shift (Mathews 1997). Complementing other research that emphasizes the new "business power in global governance" (as described in the book by that title, Fuchs 2007; see also Dauvergne 2018b), I highlight the new significance of NGOs in governing supply chains. Alternative forms of regulation require NGOs to take over legislative, executive, and juridical roles simultaneously.

A second conclusion deals with the paradox of Northern commitment and Southern empowerment. Although actors from the Global North adopted most supply chain regulations to effectively bypass Southern governments' opposition to international or bilateral agreements, the regulation mainly targets circumstances of production in countries of the Global South. New regulative approaches weaken specific actors: not only rebels benefitting from the trade in conflict minerals, for example, but also large corporations buying from them at "discounted prices" (Swilling and Annecke 2012, 188; see chapter 4). Another example of weakened actors is found in conventional cotton producers who increasingly compete with organic and fair-trade-certified farmers and manufacturers for outreach into higher-priced export markets (see chapter 3). In consequence, marginalized actors—in particular, certified producers with NGO support—gain new *power to* develop sustainably. Nevertheless, while new regulative approaches address issues of burden shifting between actors in consuming countries of the Global North and actors in producing countries of the Global South, they fail to overcome respective asymmetries.

The third conclusion provides a new insight on world trade. We observe that governments of both importing and exporting countries simultaneously and increasingly exercise *power with* TNCs and NGOs to address social and environmental problems in global supply chains. The free-trade paradigm is fading, but blood consumption (Swilling and Annecke 2012, chapter 7) is still the rule, rather than an exception. There are substantial differences among sectors and countries. Diverse sectors provide illustrative examples of successful but selective and limited approaches. This book deals with these approaches, arguing that we can learn from such first steps to change our system more fundamentally and to prevent environmental and social problems resulting from economic globalization. In the end of the book, I formulate central topics for further research, as well as ideas for cross-sectoral policy learning. A fundamental reform of the world trade system is critical if we want to prevent other disasters like Rana Plaza. The good news is that there are alternatives available: pioneers have trialed and developed viable approaches that allow for greater social justice and environmental sustainability.

2 Three Central Perspectives on Power in Global Supply Chains

This chapter lays the theoretical and empirical foundation of the book. It outlines the major research debates on globalization and governance. Based on a literature review, I derive three perspectives on power in global supply chains. Each perspective is outlined in two parts: first, a more descriptive part reflecting the state of research debates, and second, a part that defines a research task. The three perspectives deal with ongoing power dynamics in world trade and IR. As I outline ahead, power in IR is usually understood as *power over* (coercion and manipulation; see Berenskoetter and Williams 2007; Nye 2011). This helps to explain gridlock with regard to environmental and social problems in global supply chains. However, to study change dynamics over time—for example, through alternative forms of governance—I argue that acknowledging *power to* (empowerment and resistance) and *power with* (cooperation and learning) is essential (see table 2.1; see Partzsch 2017b). Ahead, I identify respective tasks for the study of power in global supply chains regarding "power shifts" (Mathews 1997) between public and private actors (Dauvergne 2018b; Green 2013), asymmetries between the Global North and South (Azubuike 2018; Brooks 2015), and universal norms and ethical values (Manners 2015; Renckens, Skogstad, and Mondou 2017). The appendix provides an overview of the three state-of-the-art perspectives and questions for empirical analysis in chapters 3 to 5 in the second column.

2.1 Globalization and Governance

Although economic globalization is often portrayed as something skillfully arranged by TNCs for their own benefit, a political integration actually

Table 2.1

Types of power

Power over	
Visible power (first dimension)	"A has *power over* B to the extent that he can get B to do something that B would not otherwise do" (Dahl 1957, 201).
Hidden power (second dimension)	"Power is also exercised when A devotes his energies to creating or reinforcing social and political values and institutional practices that limit the scope of the political process to public consideration of only those issues which are comparatively innocuous to A. To the extent that A succeeds in doing this, B is prevented, for all practical purposes, from bringing to the fore any issues that might in their resolution be seriously detrimental to A's set of preferences" (Bachrach and Baratz 1962, 948).
Invisible power (third dimension)	"A may exercise power over B by getting him to do what he does not want to do, but he also exercises power over him by influencing, shaping, or determining his very wants" (Lukes 1974, 23).
Unconscious power (fourth dimension)	"Power postulates that subjectivity or individuality is not biologically given. Subjects are understood as social constructions, whose formation can be historically described" (Digeser 1992, 980).
Power to	"One man . . . may have power to do or accomplish something by himself, and that power is not relational at all; it may involve other people if what he has power to do is a social or political action, but it need not" (Pitkin 1972, 177).
Power with	"There are situations in which power is neither attributed solely to A nor to B, but to both. Power with refers to such processes of finding common ground among diverse interests, developing shared values and creating collective strength by organizing with each other" (Partzsch and Fuchs 2012, 360).

preceded the integration of markets and the formation of most TNCs. In fact, nation-state governments collectively adopted international trade rules that allow TNCs to invest globally and spall supply chains across jurisdictions (Strange 1997; Sassen 2009). In particular, the establishment of the World Trade Organization (WTO) in 1995 led to the deregulation of international trade. At the same time, WTO rules impede efforts of environmental and social regulation at the nation-state level (Kulovesi 2014; Ponte and Daugbjerg 2015). Thus, a first perspective that I elaborate in sections

2.1.1 and 2.1.2 is this: *Globalization and the withdrawal of the state led to a new private power over nation-states at the expense of environmental and social considerations.*

2.1.1   The Withdrawal of the Nation-State

The WTO is formally charged with international regulation of all export activities. It replaced the General Agreement on Tariffs and Trade, which had regulated global trade since 1947. The GATT provided a negotiation context in which any country could extend tariff concessions agreed upon bilaterally to third countries. Yet by the 1990s, with the increase in global trade after the end of the Cold War, it had become increasingly unsuited to the purpose for which it was designed. States considered the need to individually negotiate every third-country contract too burdensome (Goldstein and Steinberg 2009; Sifonios 2018).

The WTO is a member-driven organization with 164 member countries. The member governments make all decisions, and WTO rules are the outcome of negotiations among members. The countries with the largest advanced economies—the Group of Seven (G7)[1] and the Group of Twenty (G20)[2]—have more resources to back their positions, whereas the majority of the WTO members are developing countries, including the Group of 77 (G77;[3] see WTO 2019). For them, WTO membership is attractive because it signifies not only that specific trade rules are internalized, but also that a broader market-based mindset permeates the general approach to issues of macroeconomic management (Azubuike 2018). When China became a WTO member in 2001, this was a significant milestone and impacted many global supply chains, including cotton/textile, palm oil, and timber supply chains (Quark 2013; Cashore and Stone 2014; Schleifer and Sun 2018).

The structure of decision making at the WTO is based on the principle of "one country, one vote" (WTO 2019). In practice, however, these provisions are generally overridden by the requirement for members to agree to a package of reforms in its entirety for fear that if they do not, the ongoing round of multilateral trade talks will collapse (Azubuike 2018). There is no possibility of individual opt-out clauses. A package of reform is a single undertaking; that is, members can only decide whether they accept the whole package. As governments negotiate agreements at the international level, legislators (parliaments) at the national level are forced to make a single, take it or leave it judgement, like the several-thousand-page Uruguay Round that led to the creation of the WTO (Azubuike 2018; Green 2005).

International trade disciplines affect national-scale social and environmental efforts. Scharpf (1999) distinguishes between a *negative integration*, the dismantling of trade regulations in the course of globalization, and policies of *positive integration*, which establish new market-correcting regulations. While the WTO and regional trade organizations, such as the European Union (EU), pushed the *negative* integration of national markets for both traded goods and financial flows, they simultaneously impeded *positive* environmental and social regulations (Scharpf 1999). In consequence, large numbers of corporations began to spall supply chains across jurisdictions. Corporations are now participating in foreign markets, through trade, direct investment, and subcontractor relationships (Dauvergne 2018b). Examples include JP Morgan and Exxon Mobile, with annual revenues of USD 118.18 billion and USD 230.06 billion, respectively (in July 2018; see Murphy et al. 2019; see figure 2.1).

Although they usually prioritize economic benefit over environmental and social considerations, TNCs are able to decide whether they converge standards at a high or low level (Bloomfield 2017; Fuchs 2007). In this context, we also observe increasing power of individuals—for example, Mark Zuckerberg as CEO of Facebook (Partzsch 2017c). Facebook tended to apply data security standards at the lowest possible level. This ultimately led to Zuckerberg testifying to US lawmakers in April 2018, and appearing before European Parliament in May 2018, on his company's global influence and use of personal data following the Cambridge Analytica scandal. The scandal involved the collection of personally identifiable information that might have been used to attempt to influence voters' opinions in the 2017 US presidential elections (Osborne and Parkinson 2018).

In this vein, critics of globalization have argued that, in an ever more integrated global market, nation-states and subnational units increasingly compete with each other for the most mobile factor of production: financial capital (Altvater and Mahnkopf 1999; Sassen 2005; Eliasoph 2015). They warned that TNCs and "mobile capitalists" prefer lax regulation and less government intervention, leading to the so-called Delaware effect, named after the US state with the lowest corporate taxes. As all states follow this logic, there is a race to the bottom and a continuous lowering of protection standards (Scharpf 1999). Fuchs (2007) explains that TNCs do not even

(a)

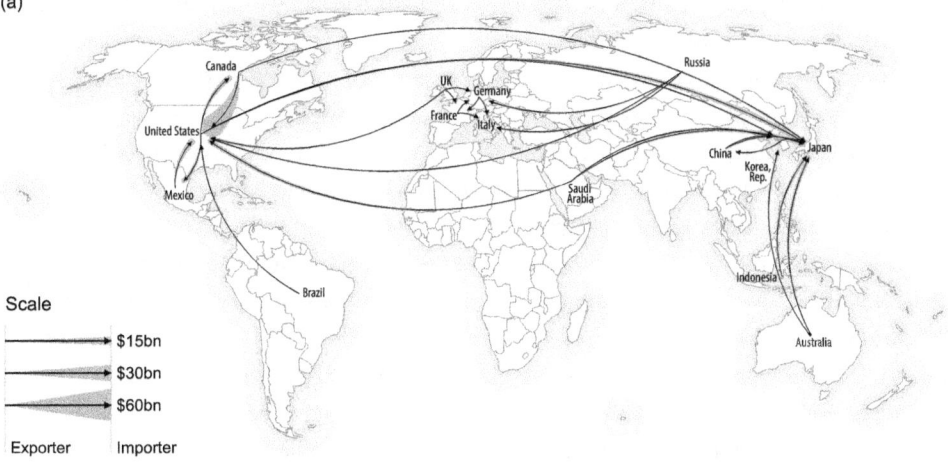

Scale

→ $15bn

→ $30bn

→ $60bn

Exporter   Importer

(b)

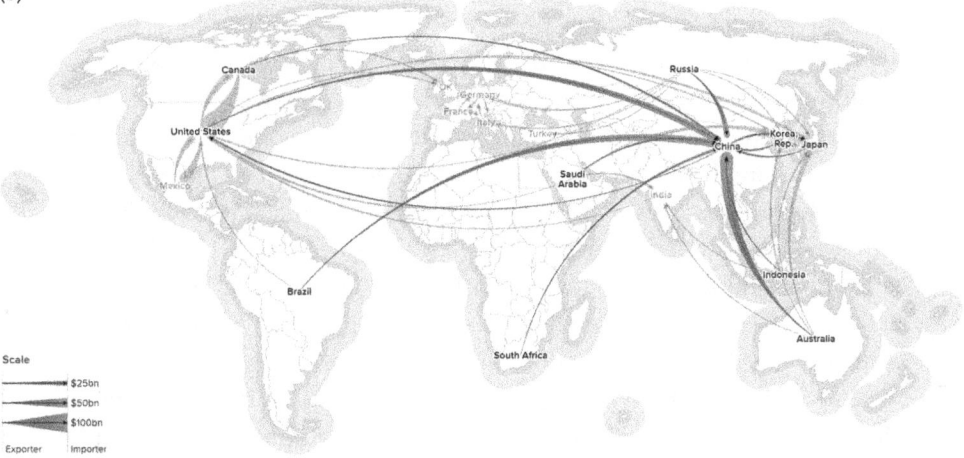

Scale

$25bn

$50bn

$100bn

Exporter   Importer

Figure 2.1
Global commodity trade flows in (a) 2000 and (b) 2016. *Source:* Chatham House 2019.

need to voice demands; only the implicit threat to shift investments abroad influences political decisions in their favor. Environmentalists and social justice activists therefore have argued that, in consequence, expanded trade leads to competitive pressure, which pushes down environmental and social standards (Altvater and Mahnkopf 1999; Green 2005; Sassen 2005). The fear of the 1970s that TNCs are an arm of foreign governments has been complemented by the general concern that TNCs and other nonstate actors are generally eroding nation-states' sovereignty and bypassing public regulation, even in their own countries of origin (Dauvergne 2018b; Lucier and Gareau 2015).

The alternative dynamic is the California effect, the name of which is inspired by the state of California's 1970 Clean Air Act (Vogel 1997). As California was by far the largest US market for new cars, the entire US automobile industry had to comply with the state's (higher) standards. Therefore, the state did not suffer competitive disadvantages from adopting stricter environmental regulations. To the contrary: as other states followed, the Californian industry benefitted from first-mover advantages. Jänicke (2005) emphasizes that new environmental regulation obliges domestic industries to an earlier implementation of standards that will be required elsewhere at a later date (see also Cashore and Stone 2014). In a similar vein, Bloomfield (2017) argues that firms in which leaders adapt early to activists' demands benefit from mitigating reputational risks (see also Mattli and Woods 2009, 8; Sarfaty 2015, 459). At the same time, these firms may push for (stricter) regulation in those countries in which they already operate and aim to expand their operations (Risse, Börzel, and Draude 2018; Vogel 1997). However, in terms of public regulation by the nation-state, this logic only applies to product standards (Green 2005; Kulovesi 2014).

The WTO allows states to adopt regulations defining what process requirements must be met to ensure that end products are safe to consume or use—for instance, rules on the environmental conditions in fuel-processing plants to prevent toxic emissions when refueling. These production process methods (PPMs) have an impact on the physical content of the product. Other production processes, referred to as non-product-related PPMs (npr-PPMs), do not leave traces that are materially evident in the end product but may nevertheless affect its perceived consumption value or its classification in relation to regulatory standards—for example, deforestation impacts. Npr-PPMs are not allowed under WTO rules (Sifonios 2018).

Furthermore, the WTO established a dispute settlement mechanism, which allows sanctioning nation-states in case of noncompliance (Azubuike 2018, 141–145; Widiatedja 2019).

The debate on PPMs originates from the product-process distinction applied in two US tuna-dolphin dispute settlement cases (Sifonios 2018, 2). The United States banned Mexican tuna imports because the Mexican fishing methods resulted in incidental dolphin deaths. In 1991, Mexico obtained a GATT panel decision declaring that the United States was in violation of its GATT obligations for imposing such a ban (the Tuna-Dolphin I case). The United States also enacted a secondary embargo applying to all third countries that did not prohibit imports of tuna from Mexico. The European Communities challenged this secondary embargo (the Tuna-Dolphin II case). In the latter case, the GATT panel rejected the possibility of justifying a PPM measure conditioning market access to the adoption of particular environmental policies by exporting members (Sifonios 2018, 2). The WTO has generally continued to prioritize free trade over environmental and social considerations. However, the product-process distinction, as expressed mainly in the US Tuna GATT Panel reports, has been largely undermined by different evolutions in case law (Sifonios 2018, 279). As such, we can observe a "juridical liberalization" at the WTO (Goldstein and Steinberg 2009, 213). The precedents of the Tuna-Dolphin II case have allowed for measures that influence free trade on the grounds of animal welfare or labor rights (Jakir 2013). In particular, the WTO has acknowledged in its rulings that member countries can implement "technical regulations," such as the Dolphin Safe label for tuna products, so long as they do not discriminate against products with a different country of origin or form an unnecessary obstacle to free trade (WTO 2015). Moreover, voluntary (private) standards are not subject to the WTO rules, which only apply to its member states, not directly to private bodies (Du 2018).

With the creation of the WTO, globalization first appeared to produce incentives for large-scale territorial governance and nation-states alike in institutions and policies at the supranational level. The "postsovereign" system of the EU, which includes "positive" integration efforts of environmental and social regulation, served some scholars as the prime example of large-scale territorial governance (Sachs and Santarius 2007; Piattoni 2009). They suggested establishing a World Environment Organization or, at least, strengthening United Nations (UN) institutions, such as the UN Framework

Convention on Climate Change (UNFCCC), in order to outbalance the WTO at the international level (Biermann and Bauer 2016; Biermann and Simonis 2000). There were also suggestions to establish control schemes that could prevent world prices of agricultural commodities, such as coffee and cocoa, falling below a level that causes misery and poverty in producing countries (Barratt Brown 2007). However, environmental and social regimes have remained comparatively weak, and environmental provisions are included and hence subordinated to trade agreement (Biermann and Bauer 2016; Morin and Jinnah 2018).

Instead of further centralization and the development of large-scale territorial governance, we have increasingly witnessed fragmentation and polycentrism in international politics over the last three decades (Jordan et al. 2015; Ostrom 2010; Zelli and van Asselt 2013). In addition to the distribution of authority between the national and international levels of state governance, we can also observe the rise of activities by subnational actors, such as regions and cities, in transnational governance (Bansard, Pattberg, and Widerberg 2017). For example, Bulkeley and Betsill (2004, 472) argue that "networks of local government" are a "significant phenomenon in environmental politics." The authors trace the emergence of subnational networks to the 1992 Rio Earth Summit, including the development of Local Agenda 21 suggesting that cities are "key sites in the production and management of energy use and waste production, through processes over which local authorities have a (varying) degree of influence" (Bulkeley and Betsill 2004, 477; see also Bulkeley and Betsill 2013; Kahler and Lake 2009). Likewise, Bansard, Pattberg, and Widerberg (2017) argue that transnational municipal networks (TMNs) are a viable substitute for ambitious international action under the UNFCCC. Some of the city networks, especially in the context of climate politics, have become incredibly large. The C40 network consists of ninety-six cities and 25 percent of global gross domestic product (GDP). The Global Covenant of Mayors engages over nine thousand cities, representing nearly eight hundred million people and 10 percent of the global population (Bansard, Pattberg, and Widerberg 2017).

In sum, nation-states are no longer the only actors in international politics. Many scholars therefore started to use the term *governance* rather than *government* (Czempiel and Rosenau 1992; Haufler 2010). Nation-state governments have been complemented by other state or public actors—that is, supranational organizations and subnational units—as well as nonstate or private actors—in particular, TNCs and NGOs. We increasingly see global governance arrangements complementing inter*governmental*, or inter-*national*, relations.

2.1.2   New Private *Power over* Nation-States

As supranational organizations and subnational units have only partially offset the withdrawal of nation-states, globalization has caused a tremendous "power shift" (Mathews 1997) toward markets and civil society (Ruggie 2013). In the wake of the WTO, individual states—in particular, states of the Global South—lost power over their own territories. On the other hand, the WTO gives private actors a new power over all nation-states. Scholars have developed different analytical frameworks on the power of nonstate vis-à-vis state actors at the global scale (Fuchs 2007; Holzscheiter 2005). These frameworks tend to be based on Weber's definition of *power* as the "probability that one actor within a social relationship will be in a position to carry out his own will, despite resistance, regardless of the basis on which this probability rests" (Weber [1922] 1978, 53). Even if power is not simply perceived as a zero-sum game, actors are usually conceived of as subordinate to powerful agents, structures, or discourses.

Without facing the increasing power of private actors, following this perspective, state actors would not have needed to transfer governance functions to supranational organizations or subnational units in order to *re*-regulate environmental and social issues (Biermann and Bauer 2016; Mattli and Woods 2009). In the following sections, I illustrate the new private power over nation-states in the age of globalization, further differentiating along the lines of the four dimensions or four "faces" of *power* (*over*) that are well known in political theory: visible, hidden, invisible, and unconscious power (Digeser 1992; Fuchs 2007). (The fourth dimension does not understand power as a zero-sum game and can also be added to *power to*, as discussed ahead).

The first dimension is agent-based. It refers to *visible power over* another. Studies based on this perspective assess which actors or groups of actors prevail in political decision-making processes. Dahl (1957, 201, emphasis added) defines it thus: "A has power over B to the extent that he can get B to do something that B would not otherwise do." Power can be measured in terms of votes in parliament (e.g., for and against environmental regulation). Following this understanding of power, scholars explore how nonstate actors influence decisions made by formal political decision-makers—for example, via lobbying and campaign financing (Betsill and Corell 2008; Lund 2013). These scholars agree that nonstate actors have gained power over state actors in recent years, and this holds true for both TNCs and NGOs (Fuchs 2007; Arts 2003).

NGOs are usually seen as representatives of civil society (for a critique, see Kaldor 2003) and a counterpart to TNCs (Betsill and Corell 2008; Eliasoph 2015). They have special interests, albeit not ones motivated by personal profit. For instance, while TNCs are considered responsible for climate change, Walk (2008) presents NGOs as "climate savers" (author's translation). Betsill (2006, 190–191) finds that without the presence of the Climate Action Network (CAN) in the Kyoto Protocol negotiations under the UNFCCC, Europeans might not have maintained the 15 percent reduction target and the Kyoto target may have been even lower. Thus, although NGOs have fewer resources than TNCs, they too are shown to have an impact on international negotiations. Although their political action is considered legitimate and urgently required—not only in climate politics but also in, for example, resisting nuclear power (Ho 2014) and genetically modified organisms (GMOs; see Andrée 2011)—these nonstate actors take over functions formerly performed by political parties and parliaments within nation-states. Hence, here there is again a zero-sum power shift away from state actors. At the same time, it is unclear whether NGOs can move corporate actors to improve their environmental and social performance.

Bachrach and Baratz (1962) speak of "two faces of power," emphasizing that some issues never even make it onto the political agenda and are dismissed before observable negotiations start. This is the case for many environmental and social problems in IR. For instance, forest and water policies receive far less attention than climate and biodiversity policies (Simonis 2006). Narain (2010) explains that in climate politics, negotiations about a temperature ceiling affect developing countries in a hidden way, although their emissions are officially not part of the political agenda: a global temperature ceiling leaves little leeway to developing countries for a carbon-rich course of development.

The traditional concept of structural *hidden power over* in the international arena addresses coercion resulting from the capital mobility of transnational corporations. Scholars argue, with respect to the Delaware effect, that threats to shift investments abroad do not even need to be voiced to influence institutional politics in corporations' favor. More recent studies point to the fact that business also exercises structural hidden *power over* through self-regulation and coregulating institutions that allow business actors to actively set rules (Green 2013). As discussed previously, the WTO sets structural limits for non-product-related PPMs. Against this backdrop, self- and coregulating institutions are seen as a symptom, rather than a solution, of the new power of private actors over nation-states (Ponte and Daugbjerg 2015).

The amount of private regulation in the forms of self-regulation and coregulating institutions and the degree of autonomy and influence of nonstate actors in these institutions have risen dramatically over the last two and a half decades. Nonstates have created, implemented, and enforced rules to address problems, such as human rights violations and environmental degradation, on a global scale (Fuchs 2007; Green 2013). Until recently, international organizations were institutions of, by, and for nation-states, such as the WTO. Now, these organizations are often founded by private actors, competing with intergovernmental constituencies for funding and direct connections to the peoples of the world (Partzsch 2014; Pattberg, Betsill, and Dellas 2011). An impressive example is the Bill and Melinda Gates Foundation (BMGF) with its annual budget of over USD 4 billion (BMGF 2018).

In this context, again, we observe an increasing power of not only nonstate collective actors, but also individual actors—for example, Bill and Melinda Gates as the CEOs of their foundation. Furthermore, some celebrities and social entrepreneurs matter as individuals in their own right (Richey 2016; Partzsch 2017c). However, state actors often promote private forms of regulation. Governments cooperate with Bill and Melinda Gates and follow their agendas in programs such as the Global Alliance for Improved Nutrition (GAIN) and the Global Fund to Fight AIDS, Tuberculosis, and Malaria (Partzsch 2014; Moravaridi 2012). Therefore, some scholars argue that while globalization has led to a delegation of authority to a greater range of entities, states still remain dominant actors and have the ability to revoke this authority at will. Bypassing domestic regulation is nearly impossible, at least at the stage of implementation (Bartley 2018). Delegation and transfer of authority can be observationally equivalent, and thus it is difficult to distinguish who has power and authority in complex supply chains. For instance, when states create international dispute-settlement procedures, they may delegate authority to the new entity, allowing it to act on their behalf. Given that private actors usually prioritize their economic benefit, most scholars have remained cautious about whether such delegation of authority favors social justice and environmental sustainability (Dauvergne 2018b; Fuchs 2007). Sneyd argues that although certification schemes may have more vigorous environmental or social standards with NGO involvement, they are still left at the mercy of large corporations. The "very real threat" associated with market approaches such as certification is that "lowest common denominator, lowest cost approaches will dominate" (Sneyd 2015, 57). Only a few scholars have considered the possibility of "privatizing up" (Cashore, Auld, and Newson 2004, 5) existing public rules, which would consist of co- and self-regulating institutions pioneering environmental and social regulations (Börzel and Risse 2005; Esty and Winston 2009; Ruggie 2013; see chapter 3).

When identifying asymmetries between state and nonstate actors, scholars are increasingly focusing on *power over* relations linked to latent conflicts of interest. In a third dimension, *invisible* power comes into play as a result of norms and ideas (Lukes 1974). Such research analyzes discourses, communication practices, cultural values, and institutions, all of which work to shape relevant thoughts and actions. These provide actors with social properties to define their interests and ideals and to virtually follow them (Barnett and Duvall 2005; Berenskoetter and Williams 2007). Following this understanding of power, a shift in discourse led to a new trust in nonstate actors and their ability to obtain desired results, as well as in their intentions (Levy and Newell 2004; Holzscheiter 2005). These scholars deny an agent-based antagonism between state and nonstate actors, or TNCs and NGOs. In particular, the simple differentiation between the WTO as a "blocker" of and UN organizations (or the suggested World Environment Organization; see Biermann and Bauer 2016) as "advocates" of environmental and social regulations is immediately rejected. Bedall (2011) shows, for example, how dominant NGOs, such as CAN, secure neoliberal hegemony within a heterogeneous civil society community. If we only measure the power (over) of civil society in terms of how successful CAN was in a specific negotiation process (first dimension of visible power), we may lose sight of how this NGO neglects issues beyond the agenda of inter-governmental negotiations (e.g., hidden emission targets for developing countries).

With reference to Foucault (1982) and Bourdieu (1987), we can capture links among knowledge, power, and politics in a fourth dimension of power (over; see Digeser 1992). Constructivist and poststructuralist approaches that deal with such *unconscious power* are increasingly prevalent in research on environmental politics and sustainability (Feindt and Oels 2005; Methmann, Rothe, and Stephan 2013). Through the production and reproduction of knowledge (seen in terms of shared understandings or dominant discourses reflecting categories like *climate change*), actors work mainly to reproduce systems and positions (Guzzini 2007). *Power over* in this fourth dimension means that subjectivity is only a social construct, and scholars aim to explain this construction genealogically (Digeser 1992; Guzzini 2007). In particular, scholars have shown that NGO participation relies on and produces particular forms of subjectivity. Although some forms of activist subjectivity are treated as normal, credible, and acceptable, others are constructed as undesirable and unacceptable (Tucker 2014). For example, Cheyns (2014) describes how the Roundtable on Sustainable Palm Oil (RSPO), a private certification scheme (see chapter 5), is based on a liberal format of participation. This format discredits voices of smallholders and local communities, who come with a desire to raise and solve critical issues of injustices and/or engage in the most familiar attachments of their daily lives, sometimes with strong emotions. Civil society groups that gain global attention for their causes often do so only by distorting their principles and alienating their constituencies for the sake of appealing to donors in the Global North (Bob 2005). In consequence, negative social and environmental on-the-ground consequences may not even be voiced, let alone regulated.

In sum, though economic globalization was effected by government decisions and enforced through the WTO, government decisions have (also) resulted from environmental and social problems not being present in the political agenda and from a neoliberal discourse that manipulated subordinate actors as much as the decision-makers themselves. In consequence, there has been a (zero-sum) power shift to a range of actors other than nation-states, which were long the dominant form of political organization in world politics. Governance of the new private actors often is not locatable only within the territory of one particular nation-state any longer; boundaries between international and external actors tend to blur (Lederer 2018). As much as supply chains have become more complex, so have governance structures. In consequence, it has become even more difficult for state actors to control private actors and enforce social and environmental rules. Initially, only a few scholars considered the possibility of environmentally and socially ambitious nonstate actors (Cashore, Auld, and Newsom 2004; O'Rourke 2003). More recent literature has elaborated on in which sectors and under which conditions nonstate actors adopt measures beyond the lowest denominator (Pattberg and Widerberg 2016; Schleifer, Fiorini, and Auld 2019). However, there is broad and persistent concern that the new private power comes at the expense of environmental and social considerations.

2.2   Asymmetries between Northern Consumers and Southern Producers

Although global market integration affects all countries, the emergence of globalization hot spots has been particularly prominent. Markets are centered on the most advanced industrialized countries, and poorer countries have fewer connections to these globalization hot spots (Sassen 2005). The European single market used to be the first destination of most goods and services (Damro 2012, 686). Meanwhile, China has overtaken the EU, but only in terms of total trade volume. The EU's share in commodity imports per capita is still twice as high as China's share. With 20 percent of the world population, China has a share of 20 percent in commodity imports, whereas the EU, with only 7 percent of world population, has a share of 14 percent (in 2016). The United States ranks similarly with 4.4 percent of world population and a share of 5.9 percent in commodity imports (see figure 2.1; Chatham House 2019).

Supply chains have become more complex and span over ever-longer physical distances. For example, the supply chain of an average t-shirt covers a distance of 50,000 km (Fairtrade 2017). Most scholars argue that, in consequence, asymmetries between actors in the upstream and downstream parts of supply chains are increasing, rather than decreasing, in the course of globalization (Hoskins 2014; Brooks 2015; Kalfagianni and Skordili 2019). *There are increasing asymmetries between actors in consuming countries of the Global North and actors in producing countries of the Global South.*

2.2.1 Divide between Consuming and Producing Countries

International trade still reflects the heritage of colonialism (Quark 2013). Colonial powers developed their manufacturing industry while they drew raw materials from the colonies in Africa and in America, and elsewhere in the Global South. The result was that countries in these regions could not develop their own industries (Barratt Brown 2007, 268; Brooks 2015, 116). In each colony, production of only two or three particular commodities was encouraged, with total dependence on the colonial power for manufactured goods and particularly for the equipment and financing necessary to achieve any kind of development. Still, the export sectors of many developing countries are oriented almost solely toward trade with either the EU or the United States (Barratt Brown 2007).

Emerging economies promise to change the rules of the game (Quark 2013). Countries with emerging economies have not yet reached a developed country's G7 status but have outpaced, in a macroeconomic sense, their developing counterparts among the G77. Brazil, Russia, India, China, and South Africa (BRICS) are outstanding in this sense (Azubuike 2018, 141; Lederer 2018, 193). For example, China, as the world's largest manufacturer of textiles and other products (West and Lansang 2018), has also become the largest importer of cotton from Africa (36 percent; see Brooks 2015; Quark 2013). However, new Chinese manufacturers put an additional burden on less developed countries—for instance, duties from 5 percent up to 40 percent on cotton imported outside of fixed annual import quotas related to WTO obligations (Brooks 2015, 116). If we understand power to be a zero-sum game, in which the "winners" take it all, the rise of emerging countries like China hence comes at the expense of weaker countries, such as those in Africa. It does not directly disadvantage or harm the EU and North America at the downstream end of global supply chains.

The supremacy of the EU and the United States is preserved in diverse ways, including their dominance in the WTO. The credibility of the WTO is wholly dependent on keeping the EU and the United States on board and engaged as active participants. This gives them significant hold over the policy output of the WTO and allows them to pursue trade policies that are deeply hypocritical (Azubuike 2018). The WTO is often described like a star chamber or black box in which insiders take advantage of their access to the levers of power (Baldwin 2016; Sneyd 2015). The exposure of developing countries to the EU and US agenda-setting power has led WTO critics to accuse it of inherent democratic deficit and to concertedly oppose its influence. The WTO Ministerial Conferences at Seattle in 1999 and Cancún in 2003 were subjected to massive protests from civil society groups. Utilizing dramatic tactics, activists forced the issue of corporate globalization into the news (Eliasoph 2015). While TNCs are seen as the main profiteers of economic globalization, these campaigns and related research finds smallholders and women in the Global South to be the major "losers" of the withdrawal of the state (Brooks 2015; Elder and Dauvergne 2014; Sachs and Santarius 2007).

In contrast to such civil society campaigns, however, Global South governments often interpret measures that require compliance with certain social and environmental standards, such as restrictions on fishing methods resulting in incidental dolphin deaths (discussed earlier), as forms of hidden protectionism (Biermann 2001; Ponte and Daugbjerg 2015). In this vein, some scholars argue that "dominant actors reconstruct rules to at once appease their challengers and protect their institutional privileges" (Quark 2013, 7). There are very few cases in which developing countries successfully turned against the EU or the United States in WTO dispute settlements (Biermann 2001; Sneyd 2015). While the WTO is resisting free trade in areas like intellectual property rights, in which developed countries benefit at developing countries' expense, the EU and the United States are blocking free trade in areas like agriculture, in which the roles would be reversed (Azubuike 2018). Volatile world prices of agricultural commodities—cocoa, cotton, palm oil, tea, sugar, tobacco, bananas—often force farmers in the Global South to sell their products under production costs, compounded with smallholders' lack of access to social infrastructure and services and, frequently, insecurity of land tenure (Barratt Brown 2007; Macdonald 2014).

As explained earlier, the WTO promotes and enforces the unlimited exchange of goods between countries, without controlling any adherence to human rights or environmental standards abroad. Due to this situation, TNCs may often be involved in harmful practices abroad with impunity in the producing and in the consuming countries (Dauvergne 2018b; Sachs and Santarius 2007). The case of Shell in Nigeria gained a lot of attention. The transnational oil and gas company, headquartered in the Netherlands and incorporated in the United Kingdom, was not held liable, although it was undoubtedly responsible, for human rights violations and the devastation of the Ogoni people's lands through massive oil spills in Nigeria

(Kohl 2014). Remarkably, TNCs do not only stem from North America and Europe. Underlining the trend of countries with emerging economies becoming more powerful, two Chinese companies are currently topping the Forbes annual list of the world's biggest companies: Industrial & Commercial Bank of China (ICBC) and China Construction Bank (ahead of JP Morgan, General Electric, and Exxon Mobile, as of July 2018; see Murphy et al. 2019).

Swilling and Annecke (2012, chapter 7) go as far as blaming China, the EU, and the United States for intentionally fueling armed conflicts to further access natural resources in Africa and elsewhere in the Global South. Hinting at *blood diamonds*—diamonds that are sold on the international market to finance wars—Swilling and Annecke invent the term *blood consumption*. This new term emphasizes the fact that not only the purchase of illegal diamonds, but also, more fundamentally, the resource-intense lifestyles of developed countries contribute to resource depletion and (armed) conflicts in other parts of the world. Swilling and Annecke (2012) locate affected people in Africa and other countries of the Global South, in which unsustainable patterns of production persist. However, local elites of the affected countries often benefit from and participate in blood consumption, and there is an increasing number of disadvantaged people also located in the Global North (Hoskins 2014).

Especially against the backdrop of the WTO Ministerial Conferences at Seattle in 1999, which made the negative environmental and social impacts of globalization widely known, the international Jubilee 2000 campaign gained a lot of attention (Eliasoph 2015), similar to the current Fridays for Future movement (Hagedorn et al. 2019). The Jubilee 2000 campaign consisted of a broad coalition of civil society activists from over forty countries who demanded the cancellation of all developing countries' debts by the year 2000, which, as well as the turn of the millennium, was also the year of the Catholic Church's Great Jubilee (Easterly 2002, 1677). In particular, Oxfam, an international NGO, has continued to advocate for trade justice, including the Make Trade Fair campaign underway since 2001. Many celebrities are committed to this issue, including Bono, who is arguably the epitome of a celebrity activist (Busby 2007; Partzsch 2015). With celebrities thinking beyond the possible and wanting to create better societies, their attempts have become pervasive in the age of "everyday humanitarianism," which accounts for the "expansion of the willingness of humans to incorporate the suffering and welfare of others into their everyday decisions" (Barnett 2010, 210). While the rhetoric and practice of humanitarianism and doing good becomes increasingly widespread in Western public life, it has not been without criticism, and scholars question its impact in the Global South (Huliaras and Tzifakis 2011; Richey 2016).

Most civil society campaigns and other voluntary institutions that address problems such as human rights violations and environmental degradation in the Global South are *proxy accountability* arrangements, in which NGOs and consumers in the Global North hold governments and TNCs accountable *on behalf* of affected communities (Koenig-Archibugi and Macdonald 2013). In a similar manner, scholars have characterized societies in the Global South as "areas of limited statehood" (although the same scholars admit that law and order is also not always guaranteed in the Global North—for example, in case of natural disasters; Risse, Börzel, and Draude 2018). However, contradicting these studies, Bartley (2018, 41) demonstrates that there is rarely a true "regulatory void." Developing countries are no "empty spaces" (Bartley 2018, 34). All countries tied into global supply chains have their own sets of laws about land, labor, and the rights of citizens (Bartley 2018; see also Malets 2015; Li 2014; Silva-Castaneda 2012).

In this context, studies have questioned the legitimacy of NGOs speaking on behalf of others as they were "not elected by anyone" (Gebauer 2001, author's translation). Only interested and well-organized groups, especially from Anglo-Saxon countries, have been shown to accomplish participation in intergovernmental meetings and self-regulating bodies (Macdonald 1994; Wijaya and Glasbergen 2016). Coincidentally, Global North–South proxy arrangements have been found to be prone to generating policy instrument choices deviating significantly from those actually preferred by affected communities (Koenig-Archibugi and Macdonald 2013). In consequence, campaigns such as Jubilee 2000 tend to stabilize existing asymmetries among civil society groups in the Global North and South (Gebauer 2001, 103; Dieter and Kumar 2008). For Jubilee 2000, the most contentious issue was the conditionality of debt cancellation. Groups from the South had more radical positions, considering the debts as unlawful. When their positions were not accepted, the campaign split into Jubilee 2000 and Jubilee South, and Jubilee South received considerably less public attention (Gebauer 2001, 109).

2.2.2   The Global South's Power to Develop Sustainably

Most scholars demonstrate how power asymmetries have continued and even intensified in the course of globalization. Civil society movements such as Jubilee 2000, which can counterbalance global business and at least potentially strengthen the voice of the Global South, are often excluded from political negotiations. However, we also find resistance and empowerment. For example, besides the dominance of CAN, Bedall (2011) also discusses the formation of a counterhegemonic project in the context of Never Trust a COP (NTAC). NTAC turned against any kind of market-oriented regulative approach, against "green" capitalism and all forms of political representation; instead, activists advocated direct forms of participation. The NTAC activists mobilized against the UNFCCC Conferences of the Parties (COPs) and organized demonstrations and street blockades (Bedall 2011, 78). More recently, the Extinction Rebellion and the Fridays for Future movements formed. Extinction Rebellion activists plaster the streets with posters and chain themselves onto government buildings (Brülls 2019). Fridays for Future activists resist compulsory education when regularly "striking for the climate" on Fridays (Hagedorn et al. 2019). They demonstrate their consciousness, the *power to* gather with each other and raise broader awareness. Although their resistance in the forms of street blockades and school strikes is illegal, many consider it legitimate as it serves the value of climate protection (Hagedorn et al. 2019).

Power to is a concept that refers to single actors and separate groups that take action; for example, producer groups in the Global South or activist groups in the Global North. Pitkin (1972, 177) emphasizes that "one man . . . may have power to do or accomplish something by himself, and that power is not relational at all; it may involve other people if what he has power to do is a social or political action, but it need not." Based on this understanding of power, poorer countries can simply start a more sustainable development by, for example, prioritizing organic agriculture or conserving natural forests, without any permission or interference from others. Bhutan announced in 2012 that it would be the first country to fully convert to organic agriculture by 2020 (Neuhoff et al. 2014). Norway, in 2016, was the first country to commit to zero deforestation (Wanshel 2016).

Pitkin's understanding of *power to* assumes that actors are self-determined—that is, have the self-confidence and capabilities to pursue their decisions (Eyben, Harris, and Pettit 2006). The concept of *power to* is therefore linked to Parsons's definition of *power* as the ability "to get things done" (Parsons 1963, 232). Parsons highlights productive agency despite structural constraints, especially in cases in which actors' goals are opposed or resisted. Research on civil society movements and NGOs is often (not always) based on this perception of power. For example, when Greenpeace confronted Shell in its Brent Spar campaign in 1995, some scholars drew parallels to the story of David versus Goliath (Roth, Semle, and Pötter 2001), highlighting the agency of David, or Greenpeace and environmental movements. Scholars taking a perspective of *power to* are less interested in exploring the confrontation (i.e., in killing Goliath) than in understanding the possibility of alternative ideas and values (i.e., in transforming Goliath societies).

However, as outlined earlier (fourth dimension of *unconscious power over*), constructivist and poststructuralist research has demonstrated, and continues to demonstrate, that every actor or group is defined "against" others—that is, through socially constituted relations that at least indirectly shape the actions of individuals (Wendt 1992; Barnett and Duvall 2005; Guzzini 2007). This means that structures define who the agents are and what they are able to do. For example, in many societies the industrialization of agriculture stands for modernization and progress. Exports of timber and agricultural products from deforested land serve to stabilize the national currency. The neoliberal discourse is prevailing in international politics (Levy and Newell 2004).

While constructivists have mainly been busy explaining how subjectivity is socially constituted and and how NGOs, such as CAN and Greenpeace, are themselves effects of socialization to structures, many constructivists do acknowledge the (rare) possibility of agency (Wight 1999, 130). Mikhail Gorbachev, last leader of the Soviet Union, serves as an example of an agent who was crucial for system change. Wendt (1992, 419–422; see also Nye 2008, 8) explains how Gorbachev's new thinking about the nature of IR was the first stage of a process that flowed into a structural transformation, which was the end of the Cold War. There are situations in which both dominant and marginalized actors can initiate transformational change—by empowering and resisting structures and by not reproducing their own and others' positions and, hence, systems. This holds true for actors from both developed and developing countries in global supply chains.

Application-oriented development and environmental studies have already analyzed the self-determined aspect of subjectivity—the real agency—to better understand and promote phenomena of sustainability transitions (Roth, Semle, and Pötter 2001; Eyben, Harris, and Pettit 2006). In this vein, we may study not only if asymmetries in global supply chains increase but also whether new forms of global supply chain regulation allow the Global South's *power to* develop sustainably and allow it to partcipate in IR on an equal basis with the Global North.

2.3   Universal Norms and Ethical Values

Globalization reveals diverse power dynamics, especially with regard to the withdrawal of the state and asymmetries between the Global North and South. While individuals' origins still define their legal (citizenship) rights and financial capabilities to participate in the global economy, their relative attachment to a particular nation-state is dissolving (Ruggie 2013). Nation-states may give priority to free markets, but there are diverse transnational movements that prioritize and pursue universal norms and ethical values others than the free-trade paradigm (Bartley 2007; Bloomfield 2017).

Acknowledging that ethical considerations sometimes become an end in themselves, rather than only serving as a means to increase the material interests of the home state, confirms the phenomenon of globalization (Manners 2002, 2015; Partzsch and Fuchs 2012). This acknowledgement, however, conflicts with the first power perspective formulated earlier, which says that the withdrawal of the state led to a dominance of private business at the expense of environmental and social—and, hence, ethical—considerations. Furthermore, as actors from the Global North are assumed to take not only selfish actions, this acknowledgment also contradicts the second thesis of increasing asymmetries between the Global North and South. *Power with* is a term that implies learning processes that allow actors to question self-perceptions and to actively build up a new awareness of individuals or groups (Eyben, Harris, and Pettit 2006; Allen 1998). Following this perspective, actors with a transformational orientation have substantial agency, if they act in concert, possibly across nation-states' borders. In this vein, a third perspective regarding power dynamics in a globalized world is thus: *State and nonstate actors are not continuously selfish but exercise power with others to pursue collective norms of environmental sustainability and social justice.*

2.3.1 Environmental Sustainability and Social Justice

An increasing number of scholars assume that the spread of particular norms can be a principal foreign policy goal (Niesen and Herborth 2007; Partzsch 2017b; Janusch 2016). Manners (2002) invented the term *normative power Europe* (NPE) in contradistinction to other powers. He argues that the EU's specific history "pre-disposes it to act in a normative way" (Manners 2002, 242) with its "ability to shape conceptions of 'normal' in international relations" (Manners 2002, 239) based on norms such as democracy, rule of law, social justice, and respect for human rights. Empirical studies on normative or ethical power often put such universal norms in opposition to economic market interests (e.g., Afionis and Stringer 2012; Lightfoot and Burchell 2005). The concept therefore frequently has been criticized as reproducing Eurocentrism and hegemony (Diez 2013).

Poststructuralists emphasize that when putting specific "good" norms, such as democracy and sustainability, and interests based on supposedly inferior norms, such as free trade and national sovereignty, in opposition to one another, scholars themselves are "writing norms" (Engelkamp and Glaab 2015). When NPE scholars define an "ethical ideal-type of cosmopolitan normative power" (De Zutter 2010, 1106) and "spell out what kinds of norms are meant by 'the normative'" (Forsberg 2011, 1184), they participate in defining how Europe and other actors ought to act. Scholars take a normative stance themselves, at least implicitly. For example, using the NPE concept, Lightfoot and Burchell (2005) examine the claim that the EU played a leadership role at the 2002 World Summit on Sustainable Development. Afionis and Stringer (2012) also study whether the EU is really pursuing sustainability with the Renewable Energy Directive (RED). By doing so, the scholars themselves prioritize sustainability over trade competitiveness and economic growth, to which both studies find the EU is giving precedence (Afionis and Stringer 2012; Lightfoot and Burchell 2005).

From a neo-Gramscian perspective, the EU takes rhetorical action to pursue cultural domination based on its material capabilities and constitutive norms (Diez 2013). Scholars argue that normative power hardly differs from soft power *over* others. Nye (2011) differentiates between hard power and soft power. *Hard power* (*over*) describes the capacity of a nation-state to make use of material resources (military or militarily usable resources, finance) to get another nation-state to do something that it would not otherwise do.

Soft power (*over*) stands for the co-optation of others based on nonmaterial incentives or threats. The combination of hard and soft power is what Nye calls *smart power*.

To this effect, Damro (2012) argues that we should understand the EU as a "market power," which, due to its large common market and institutional features (regulatory expertise, regulatory coherence, and sanctioning authority) is able to pursue all kinds of norms and interests in international relations. In this vein, Swilling and Annecke (2012, 191) reject activist campaigns, such as fair-trade initiatives for higher and more stable resource prices to producers of developing countries, as "minor adjustments." They stick to understandings of *power over* as a zero-sum game when they assume that Western governments (and China) simply secure their access to natural resources even at the price of military violence.

The relation between Europe's normative and market power is controversial. Manners (2015, 307) himself clarifies that NPE is not "simply the absence of force [and material incentives]" and hence does not stand in contrast to the EU's market power. Market power often allows the EU to be a potential norm leader as third (nonmember) states may comply with EU requirements to obtain access to the European market (Holzinger 2007). Foreign firms may even lobby their home governments to adjust policies upward to the EU level and impose the same regulatory standards on their domestic competitors that do not export to the EU, for which Vogel (1997) has coined the term *trading up* (see earlier discussion of the California effect). In addition, international demonstration effects and contagion among states may become more important than domestic dynamics that prioritize specific norms. Empirical studies suggest that one-third of total states in the system must accept a norm in order to "tip" a process of norm change (Finnemore and Sikkink 1998). The major difference between coercive market power, on the one hand, and NPE based on market means, on the other hand, is the orientation of the state in action. Limiting market access may serve protectionism and collective norms; however, soft and smart power are distinct from normative and ethical power, in which norms are not a means but rather an end in themselves (Diez and Manners 2007). At the same time, this means that finding evidence of market asymmetries and of trading up does not falsify the priority of social and environmental over free-trade norms.

2.3.2 *Power with* in International Relations

In contrast to findings of a unidirectional exercise of power, a small number of studies demonstrate that persuasion and learning do exist in IR (Prittwitz 1996; Niesen and Herborth 2007). For example, Deitelhoff (2009) identifies "islands of persuasion" in the formation process of the International Criminal Court (ICC). She emphasizes the role of NGOs and other nonstate actors in this process. New transnational actors often have preferences over governance that are difficult to explain using a simple political economy logic—and preferences can change over time (Kemper and Partzsch 2018). Furthermore, modern media can make people suffer from a distance and engage them in ways that are different from those employed in the past (Boltanski 1999).

Manners's concept of normative power is based on the assumption that persuasion and learning is possible in IR (see also Janusch 2016). The original NPE concept broke with an understanding of power as based on asymmetric relations. Manners defined the concept of a different kind of power, one that is constituted by nonhierarchical relationships among EU member states, as well as third countries (Manners 2002). Transnational human rights movements exemplify such joint processes of norm creation. In this vein, Arendt (1970, 44) defines power as corresponding to "the human ability not just to act but to act in concert."

Habermas's (1998) concept of communicative action builds on Arendt's concept of power. Another concept linked to Arendt's definition is the concept of *power with* (Partzsch and Fuchs 2012). *Power with* is a term that does not necessarily refer to the diffusion of already existing (predefined) norms. It does not mean the diffusion of but instead the generation of commonly shared (universal) norms. *Power with* implies learning processes that allow actors, including the EU, to question self-perceptions and to actively build up new awareness (Eyben, Harris, and Pettit 2006; Gaard 2010). It refers to "processes of finding common ground among diverse interests, developing shared values and creating collective strength by organizing with each other" (Partzsch and Fuchs 2012, 363). This implies processes of mutual learning that allow actors to actively build a new understanding of what is just and what is unjust. In this sense, for example, there is a need to commonly define organic/sustainable agriculture and fair trade, rather than promoting predefined concepts. Scholars of ethical and normative power Europe assume that such joint action is possible.

Power with deals with collective empowerment, whereas *power to* stresses the agency of individuals or separate groups to develop alternatives (Partzsch 2017b). From the perspective of *power to*, initially there is a clear opponent—for example, organic farmers opposing industrial agriculture. "Pioneers of change" or "agents of transformation" (WBGU 2011, 241, 287) are—at least for the time being—exceptional actors, such as NGOs as "climate savers" and countries such as Bhutan pursuing organic agriculture. However, in contrast to *power over*, from this perspective, an imperative for action does not follow from self-interest and competition; rather, it is based on values of a higher normative order. Actions and also specific discourses and structures are (first of all) not directed *against* others but stand *for* specific values and developments. When exercising *power with*, norms and values are commonly generated and shared.

However, as Partzsch and Fuchs (2012) argue, processes of *power with* are not independent from existing asymmetries—that is, the more capable actors' coercion and manipulation of others in finding only supposedly common ground. Arendt's (1970) definition of power is characterized by her understanding of the polity and should not be considered independently (Pitkin 1981; Göhler 2009). She refers to Aristotle and the ancient polis when she describes politics as a relation among equals who govern themselves. However, only citizens, those who presided over the household in the ancient world, had access to the public sphere of the polis. This means that Arendt's power conceptualization is based on the exclusion and displacement of noncitizens such as women and slaves into the private sphere of the household, including in regard to supposedly nonpolitical issues such as economics and bodily health (Pitkin 1981). Today, similar forms of exclusion take place—for example, in WTO negotiations when the G7 or G20 dominate decision making due to their material predominance (Azubuike 2018). As Arendt simply assumes that people have basic capabilities at their disposal to act upon in the public sphere, her conception of power is often said to be based on a utopian or elite version of polity (Canovan 1978). In a similar vein, Brunnengräber (2017) calls *power with* a normative concept that neglects material asymmetries, and Altmann (2017) warns that this neglect may further marginalize actors in the Global South.

As outlined earlier, China, the EU, and the United States alone import 40 percent of the world's commodities, making those states significant commercial powers in the world (Damro 2012). When exercising *power with* other countries, respective businesses, and NGOs, neither the EU nor the United States are operating from an equal position as their ethical actions are based upon their material capabilities, their "consumer power." Although the EU and the United States may pursue universal norms, such as human rights and sustainability, their privileged material capacity creates an unequal relation to most partners (Damro 2012).

2.4 Summary

Links between globalization and governance are more complex and contingent than many observers claim. Although there obviously is a power shift from state to nonstate actors—including the emergence of new types of actors, which for the most part originate from the Global North—power dynamics are multifarious. By giving priority to economic liberalization, China, the EU, and the United States (and all other states) have generally accepted harmful practices of business actors outside their own borders over the last decades (or even longer), especially in the Global South. However, this "triad of omnivores" (Sachs and Santarius 2007, 36)[4] is no uniform actor that is intentionally fueling armed conflicts in Africa and elsewhere to further access resources at "discounted prices" (Swilling and Annecke 2012, 188). There are many movements and NGOs that are advocating for political change (Bedall 2011; Betsill and Corell 2008; Kemper and Partzsch 2018).

If we hold on to assumptions of power as being zero-sum, the ever-growing power of TNCs and the increase of Global North–South asymmetries become a self-fulfilling prophecy. The free-trade paradigm will dominate more and more areas of life. Moreover, from this perspective, by committing to ethical values, the EU risks its powerful position in IR, and "it will indulge in quixotic moral crusades—with the attendant risk of hubris leading to nemesis" (Hyde-Price 2008). Instead, we can decide to seriously challenge those assumptions about power dynamics currently made in the literature. New forms of supply chain regulation invite us to do so.

When studying new forms of global supply chain regulation in the following chapters, challenging the first perspective outlined earlier, I will analyze whether their emergence does or does not support the new private *power over* nation-states. If yes, we should scrutinize whether the power shift is indeed discouraging environmental and social regulations. As outlined earlier, most scholars have shown that a neoliberal agenda contradicts environmental and social objectives (Altvater and Mahnkopf 1999; Strange 1997). However, a few scholars have considered the possibility of global market integration trading up (Vogel 1997; Jänicke 2008) or privatizing up (Cashore, Auld, and Newsom 2004, 5; Ruggie 2013) existing public policy rules—that is, private actors pioneering change with regard to environmental and social issues. Complementing these studies, a research task is hence to study whether globalization and the withdrawal of the state led to a new private power over nation-states at the expense of environmental and social considerations.

The second perspective on power derived in this chapter concerns Global North–South asymmetries. Most scholars agree that asymmetries between the Global North and South have increased with economic globalization. It is uncontroversial that this comes at the expense of environmental and social regulations, especially in the Global South (Brooks 2015; Quark 2013). A research task is thus to better understand how actors in the Global South can empower themselves from an unfair-trade system and exercise *power to* develop sustainably. When studying new approaches to regulate global supply chains, I will thus analyze whether these approaches are decreasing or increasing asymmetries between actors of consuming countries in the Global North and actors of producing countries in the Global South.

The third power perspective deals with universal norms and ethical values in IR. An increasing number of scholars acknowledge that norms of environmental sustainability and social justice matter in global supply chains (Manners 2002, 2015; Janusch 2016; Aggestam 2008). A research task is hence to analyze whether state and nonstate actors are not continuously selfish but exercise power with others to pursue collective norms of environmental sustainability and social justice.

In the following chapters, I use these three perspectives on power to discuss the effects of new forms of private regulation (chapter 3), public supply-chain-related laws (chapter 4), and transnational hybrid governance (chapter 5). Each of these chapters includes a case study: voluntary cotton certification in Ethiopia, conflict minerals and timber supply chain laws in the Democratic Republic of the Congo (DRC), and transnational hybrid governance of palm oil in Indonesia. Each chapter will elaborate that global economic integration is producing a new fabric of global governance that displays many variations and shadings of power in IR.

3   Private Regulation in Global Supply Chains

Social and environmental aspects have generally fallen behind economic ambitions in globalization processes (Sachs and Santarius 2007). Private regulation has emerged as a solution to perceived shortcomings. It varies widely in the forms it takes, ranging from individual codes of conduct and reporting standards to international certification programs (Ruggie 2013; Schleifer, Fiorini, and Auld 2019). Voluntary certification programs—organized and coordinated by nonstate actors—are the most substantial private regulation effort. The assumption is that if suppliers disclose information and certifiers guarantee compliance to specific standards, buyers are willing to pay a higher price for their products. In turn, if buyers refrain from purchasing (non)certified products, they may endanger the financial viability of the supplier—and of the certifier as well (Haufler 2010; Koenig-Archibugi and Macdonald 2013).

This chapter discusses power dynamics resulting from private regulation, especially voluntary certification in the field of cotton/textiles using Ethiopia as a case study. The Rana Plaza tragedy in 2013 made many consumers aware of serious social and ethical problems in textile supply chains. Deep cracks had appeared in the eight-story building outside Dhaka the day before the tragedy happened. Workers, who had been producing clothes sourced by major international brands, were sent inside the building despite safety concerns. When the building collapsed, over one thousand garment workers were killed and more than twice as many were seriously injured (Jacobs and Singhal 2017). In response to the dismay among consumers, Western consumers in particular, the garment industry started a campaign that calls upon consumers to join a "fashion revolution" by buying certified textiles (Armedangels 2016). In the first part of this chapter, I introduce the background of voluntary certification, including its origins, the state of the research on private standards in global markets, and, in particular, debates on its impact in the Global South. This part of the chapter is based on document analysis and literature review.

In a second part, I present the case of cotton certification and Ethiopia. If the fashion revolution campaign is successful, voluntary certification may prevent the (most) negative consequences in this country. At the same time, while the Ethiopian government strives for textile market growth, there are also plans for the country to become the fifth-largest cotton-producing country in the world (Aga and Woldu 2014).[1] For most certified textiles, the certification affects only the very first stage of the supply chain because the Better Cotton Initiative (BCI), the certification program with the highest outreach (20 percent of the global market), focuses on cotton production (BCI 2018). In Ethiopia, there are currently two initiatives that certify cotton: the Global Organic Textile Standard (GOTS) and a local partner of BCI, Cotton made in Africa (CmiA; see Textile Exchange 2017).

The case study is based on documents (homepages, self-portrayals, etc.); transcripts from fifteen semi-structured interviews conducted with farmers, certifiers, retailers (merchants, manufacturers, etc.), government officials, and nongovernmental organizations (NGOs); and notes from three group discussions with the stakeholders in Ethiopia. I also used notes from participatory observations at a Fairtrade Fair in Germany in May 2017, and I visited certified cotton farms close to Arba Minch, Ethiopia, in September 2017.

Based on the background and the case study results, in a third part, I discuss voluntary certification against the backdrop of power dynamics as outlined in chapter 2—that is, the withdrawal of the state in the era of globalization, asymmetries between Northern consumers and Southern producers, and normative or ethical power in IR. We will see that there are some very ambitious private actors, as well as individual governments, that use voluntary certification to compensate for a lack of environmental regulation in global supply chains. However, there are Global North–South discrepancies regarding international NGOs that speak on behalf of people in the Global South: typically, these NGOs are accountable to donors in the Global North, not to those people affected on the ground. Moreover, although certification is voluntary and pursues collective norms of environmental protection and greater fairness in world trade, it has been shown to effectively limit Southern producers' access to global markets, and certification tends to depoliticize continuing resource flows from the Global South to the North.

3.1 Background: Voluntary Certification

Certification initiatives not only define *product* standards, but also an array of *process* standards related to the conditions under which items are produced or traded (Gupta 2008; Koenig-Archibugi and Macdonald 2013). The World Trade Organization (WTO) agrees to the latter only so long as the standards are voluntary and do not discriminate against products based upon country of origin or form an unnecessary obstacle to free trade (Ponte and Daugbjerg 2015, 105–106). However, certification emerged long before the creation of the WTO. As early as 1928, the anthroposophy movement introduced the Demeter certificate, which labels foodstuffs produced in accordance with Rudolf Steiner's doctrine of organic agriculture (and the Christian Community's belief system; Demeter 2018). The concept of *fair trade* dates back to the 1960s (Barratt Brown 2007). Both early organic and fair-trade movements formed in clear opposition to the conventional economic system. While organic movements used voluntary certification to resist the industrial expansion of agriculture (IFOAM 2012; Paull 2010), fair-trade movements aimed to overcome the colonial division of labor between producers in the Global South and consumers in the Global North (Barratt Brown 2007).

Since the 1990s, private regulation won recognition and voluntary certification became an increasingly integrated part of conventional markets (Ruggie 2013). Founded in 1993, the Forest Stewardship Council (FSC) was the first overarching certification body with an international seal, labeling timber from sustainably managed forests (Cashore, Auld, and Newsom 2004; Green 2013). Demeter International was founded in 1997 (Demeter 2018), and with the establishment of the Fairtrade Labelling Organizations International (FLO) in the same year, a fair-trade international certificate was created that caused fair-trade movements to leave their alternative niche markets and include products in the conventional trade system (Barratt Brown 2007).

Most scholars have shown that since the 1990s, voluntary certification emerged from a neoliberal agenda (Levy and Newell 2004). Scholars have

warned against "the retreat of the state" (Strange 1997) and "the privatiza-
tion of world politics" (Brühl et al. 2001, author's translation). Moreover,
standards are often seen as "hidden protectionism" and "trade weapons"
that Western firms and states use to retain their dominance in global markets (Du 2018). Scholars have remained generally cautious about whether
certification benefits poor producers in the Global South (Hilson 2014;
McDermott, Irland, and Pacheco 2015; Sneyd 2015). Levidow (2013, 211)
claims the EU uses sustainability certification as a means to depoliticize
global resource flows in order to continue its "global plunder of resources"
(see similar discourse in, e.g., Dauvergne and Lister 2013). Only a few scholars have considered the possibility of voluntary certification *privatizing up*
(Cashore, Auld, and Newsom 2004, 5) existing public policy rules—that is,
pioneering change with regard to environmental and social issues (see similar discourse in, e.g., Risse, Börzel, and Draude 2018; Ruggie 2013). Whether
we consider private regulation as a means to improve social and environmental conditions in global supply chains or as a mechanism that only
reaffirms Global North–South asymmetries very much depends on whether
or not we assume ethical or normative power to be possible in international
relations (Manners 2002).

3.1.1   Origins of Voluntary Certification

Organic movements started certifying foodstuffs produced in an ecologi-
cally sustainable way almost a century ago (Demeter 2018; Paull 2010).
In parallel to anthroposophical groups associated with Rudolf Steiner, in
countries such as Germany, the life reform movement campaigned for a
more "natural" way of life. Movement members established a retail network that provided health-conscious consumers with natural (whole-grain)
foods, including Demeter-certified foodstuffs, and other products such as
reform shoes and porous or breathable underwear (Fritzen 2010). In 1972,
alternative farmer and consumer associations established the International
Federation of Organic Agriculture Movements (IFOAM), an international
umbrella organization, in Versailles, France (IFOAM 2012). In his invitation
letter to Versailles, Roland Chevriot, then president of Nature et Progrès,
a French farmer organization, explained that "at the time when industrial expansion is questioned and notions of 'Quality' and 'Survival' are
raised, it seems necessary to me that organic agriculture movements make
themselves known and coordinate their actions. . . . The food quality and

ecology crisis is no longer a national problem, but an actual international concern to [which] we must rapidly bring our solutions" (Chevriot 1972).

Besides Chevriot, there were four further founding members representing different organizations: Lady Eve Balfour from the Soil Association (UK), Kjell Arman from the Swedish Biodynamic Association, Pauline Raphaely from the Soil Association of South Africa, and Jerome Goldstein from Rodale Press of the United States (IFOAM 2012). Today, IFOAM has eight hundred member organizations in over one hundred countries. All members have the opportunity to participate in revising IFOAM standard requirements. Recent General Assemblies have all taken place in the Global South (e.g., India in 2017), and electronic voting allows members to vote without being physically present (IFOAM 2019). This makes IFOAM a very democratic organization (at least among producer member organizations; consumers are only addressees at the receiving end). The reform movement and IFOAM consider themselves to be "pioneers" (IFOAM 2019; Fritzen 2010). Not only did they develop organic farming methods, but they also created supply systems that are, to a great extent, independent from conventional supply chains, including *Reformhäuser* (reform houses), organic shops, drugstores, and even alternative supermarkets. However, their actions were and have continued to be primarily politically motivated. One interviewee explained his organic organization's choice of a market approach as follows: "Our [corporate] members are catalysts for change. So, part of what [we] wanted to do is to create a market-driven solution, which means we get market leaders, sometimes that's brands, sometimes that's government, sometimes that's harmonization of standards, sometimes it can take different forms, but we work to identify barriers to growth and address them collectively, so it's that individual action that different members take. . . . I wouldn't say our advocacy is more important than the standards. . . . We promote these [organic] standards as a solution to drive change" (LRP, October 30, 2017).

In a similar vein, fair-trade movements first aimed to establish a system of direct exchanges of trade and technology in clear opposition to and independent from the (post)colonial trade system (Barratt Brown 2007; Raynolds, Murray, and Heller 2007). In the early 1960s, Oxfam shops started selling handicrafts and Christmas cards made in developing countries, giving small-scale producers fair prices, training, advice, and funding (Oxfam 2018). Parallel initiatives were taking place in other European countries. So-called Worldshops (or Third-World or Fair-Trade Shops) started to sell fair-trade commodities such as coffee and tea. Many of the shops were, and are still, located in churches, which indicates the Christian background of the fair-trade movement. Not only are the shops points of sale, but they also serve for awareness-raising and political campaigning (GEPA 2017; Oxfam 2018). In many countries in Africa, Asia, and Latin America, NGOs and socially motivated individuals established fair marketing organizations that provide advice, assistance, and support to Southern producers. These Southern fair-trade organizations established links to the new organizations in the north. The ultimate goal was greater equity in international trade relations (Barratt Brown 2007; Macdonald 2007).

As committed people in the Global North could not absorb the large quantities of commodities for which the cooperatives in the Global South wanted to find markets, the original concept of producers from the Global South selling their products directly through Worldshops failed to substitute for conventional trade chains. Moreover, activists did not have the technology that cooperatives in the Global South needed (Barratt Brown 2007).

Most research on fair trade has been conducted on coffee (Auld 2015; Dietz et al. 2018). In the Netherlands, where the first fair-trade coffee was sold in 1973, the Dutch organization Max Havelaar also launched the world's first fair-trade certification label in 1988 (Barratt Brown 2007, 270). Previously, the Worldshops had guaranteed compliance to fair-trade standards. Behind Max Havelaar was Solidaridad, a Dutch NGO that Catholic bishops founded in 1969 to provide development aid to Latin America (Solidaridad 2017). In the UK, Oxfam, Traidcraft, and Equal Exchange established a brand called Cafédirect in 1991 (as a response to the 1989 global collapse in coffee prices) that was sold in supermarkets (Barratt Brown 2007, 270). In Germany, GEPA imported the first fair-trade coffee (Café Orgánico) from the smallholder cooperative UCIRI (Union of Indigenous Communities of the Isthmus Region) in Mexico in 1986 (GEPA 2017). Three years later, in 1989, GEPA decided to use its brand name to expand sales opportunities to supermarkets (in parallel, however, the number of independent Worldshops grew from two hundred shops in 1985 to six hundred shops in 1992 in Germany alone; see GEPA 2017).

Fair-trade products started being sold in supermarkets in parallel to the Worldshops; however, it was still only brand names that sold fair-trade products in the 1980s and early 1990s—Max Havelaar, Cafédirect, and

GEPA. Getting a brand onto the supermarket shelves is a costly business. It is not unusual to have to spend a million euros annually to promote and advertise a brand product to get and keep it on the shelves (Barratt Brown 2007). For instance, Cafédirect was launched with large posters in railway stations with pictures of an African child and this slogan: "He gets inoculations and you get excellent coffee" (Barratt Brown 2007, 272). Due to an increasing number of fair-trade products and organizations, consumers lost sight of the variety of brands. Having an internationally unified labeling system was, at that time, seen as a precondition for establishing a functioning market, reducing transaction costs, and overcoming information asymmetries (Macdonald 2007). Therefore, in 1989, more than three hundred organizations in over seventy countries founded the World Fair Trade Organization (WFTO), formerly the International Federation of Alternative Traders (IFAT), for these main purposes (WFTO 2017). However, it still took eight years before the participating organizations agreed upon FLO certification in 1997.[2] In the meantime, conventional retailers created their own certificates, which competed in supermarkets with the "alternative" brands (Barratt Brown 2007).

3.1.2 Private Standards in Global Markets

It was after the United Nations Conference on Environment and Development (UNCED) in Rio in 1992 that private certification won recognition and became an increasingly integrated part of conventional markets. At the time, the forestry sector was pioneering private standards on a global scale, potentially because the adoption of an international forests agreement had failed in Rio (Haufler 2003). However, in the late 1980s, the World Wide Fund for Nature (WWF) had already taken the lead in setting up a voluntary forest certification scheme. After UNCED, two international NGOs, WWF and Greenpeace, joined forces. Complementing and partly replacing strategies of naming and shaming, the NGOs began to participate in the formulation of voluntary certification to support businesses in "getting the process right" (Cashore, Auld, and Newsom 2004, x). This meant that Greenpeace[3] in particular fundamentally changed its strategy to accomplish stricter environmental standards in global supply chains (Bartley 2007).

WWF and Greenpeace brought together representatives from governments, the timber industry, foresters, indigenous people, community forestry, wood product manufacturers, and certification companies from twenty-five countries and created a new multistakeholder organization, the Forest Stewardship Council (FSC; see Bartley 2007; Haufler 2003, 246). A group of charitable foundations, including the Ford Foundation, the Rockefeller Brothers Fund, and Pew Charitable Trusts, formed the Sustainable Forestry Funders Network to allocate USD 40 million in funds collectively to the FSC, its certifiers, and supporting groups and to spur increased demand for certified wood from 1993 to 2001 (Bartley 2007, 322). In parallel, NGOs and environmental activists created buyers' groups (while more radical groups continued to pressure retailers through protests; Bartley 2007, 324). Moreover, several governments actively supported the implementation of the FSC in addition to other voluntary programs, in particular through public procurement policies that requested that state agencies and/or state-owned companies purchase only certified timber products (up to 20 percent of total timber consumption; Gulbrandsen 2014, 82). Bartley (2007, 322) highlights that the FSC did not emerge as a market response to consumer demands. Consumer demand was not even a particularly important factor; rather, companies anticipated demands of consumers. Charitable foundations funded the expansion of forest certification and worked to "make the market" for certified wood (Bartley 2007, 321; Lauber 1997, 106). In this vein, activism can create market opportunities that allow for corporate engagement in global governance (Bloomfield 2017, 27)

Although certification initiatives already existed before the WTO, its creation might have given them a new impetus. The Austrian government's support for the FSC illustrates this: When the UNCED failed to generate a binding international forest convention, the Austrian parliament adopted a national law in 1992 to restrict the import of tropical timber unless it could be shown to be sustainably produced. However, timber-exporting countries claimed that this constituted a protectionist nontariff barrier to trade under GATT. The Austrian government rescinded the law in 1993 but took the USD 1.2 million earlier allocated for the implementation and funneled the money into the emerging FSC (Bartley 2007, 321; Lauber 1997, 106).

In the neoliberal climate of the 1990s, voluntary certification became a steadily more accepted means of private (re-)regulation in an increasingly globalized trade system. The introduction of a unified label by FLO, independent from brands such as Max Havelaar, Cafédirect, and GEPA, paved the way for conventional companies such as Coop, Nestlé, and Starbucks to purchase some products produced in fair-trade conditions and to introduce fair-trade segments into their conventional supply chains (Barratt Brown 2007, 272; Macdonald 2007). At first, certification schemes were clearly politically motivated and used Worldshops as a means to resist the "unfair" trade system, but these conventional corporations have been inclined since then to participate for the sake of market gains (Haufler 2003; Barratt Brown 2007).

Haufler explains that the commitment of conventional businesses to certification comes as a result of "the twin threats" (Haufler 2003, 248; similar discourse in Bartley 2007, 2018): First, environmental activism targets the public reputation of specific firms and industry sectors as a whole; and second, there is a "shadow of hierarchy" or continuous negotiations among governments on command and control types of regulation. As a response to these threats, business actors, particularly transnational corporations (TNCs), care about and even export human rights and environmental norms by adopting relevant labeling and certification schemes. In many countries, if companies finance their activities in the schemes through a fund or foundation, they receive tax exemptions, and certification becomes a zero-sum game: "The textile companies don't want to reduce the margin or to increase their prices, because this will decrease their profit, and, on the other hand, they don't have any problem giving millions into a fund to support sustainable cotton production. . . . The one will be taxed, and the other one will reduce the tax. Because if I give money into a fund and say, 'oh, look, we do something great and supportive,' then it's tax free" (WB, November 13, 2017).

As a result of these threats and incentive structures, certification has become an essential element of branded marketing (Bloomfield 2017; Jacobs and Singhal 2017). Since expanding from their specialized shops and capturing conventional supermarkets in the 1990s, fair-trade and organic-certified suppliers have hence faced increasing competition for lower costs and prices and higher quality (Barratt Brown 2007).

In the agrifood sector, in which Demeter is still one of the most applied and strictest private standards, a multitude of international food labels has emerged since the 1990s. Kalfagianni (2015, 174) demonstrates that certification of foodstuffs has become a "normative obligation." However, few standards are as ambitious as Demeter. Growing unclarity about what *organic* meant caused the US government to introduce a unified label, United States Department of Agriculture (USDA) Organic, in 2000. To use this label, businesses must comply with the US National Organic Program (NOP). The EU Organic Regulation (EC 834/2007) is the equivalent in the EU and was adopted in 2007. If companies comply with the regulations, they are allowed to use official logos and qualify for public subsidies. While the US NOP applied to food and textile products from the very beginning, the EU Organic Regulation initially only addressed food products. However, in 2014, the European Commission also established an EU Ecolabel for textile products (2014/350/EU) based on the EU Organic Regulation. Both the United States and the EU now regulate how organic and ecological agricultural, food, and textile products in their markets have to be grown and processed. The regulations are based on the IFOAM guidelines, which require farmers to maintain and replenish soil fertility without the use of toxic, persistent pesticides and fertilizers. In addition, organic production relies on adequate animal husbandry and excludes the use of genetically modified organisms (GMOs; IFOAM 2019). Although certification continues to be voluntary, the IFOAM guidelines eventually took the form of public law, meaning that sovereign Westphalian authority is imposed on any farmer who wants to be organic certified (Cashore, Auld, and Newsom 2004, 22).

The legal clarification of what can be labeled organic and the introduction of unified labels, such as USDA Organic, aimed to bring greater clarity to consumers and prevent misinformation. However, they resulted in a greater variety of standards on a global scale. The IFOAM family encompasses forty-eight national and regional standards, including the US NOP and the EU Organic Regulation. The IFOAM standards also apply to smaller consumer markets, such as the East African Organic Products Standard, which defines criteria for labeling products as organic in Burundi, Kenya, Rwanda, Tanzania, and Uganda (if farmers produce organically for export, they need to comply with the standard of the destination market; IFOAM 2019). In addition to national and regional standards, we can observe a further sectoral differentiation. For example, as already mentioned, the EU created the organic textile label in addition to the organic food label (a green leaf) in 2014.

There is also a range of private standards that complements the public organic standards (see table 3.1). For textiles, Textile Exchange's Organic Content Standard (OCS) and the Global Organic Textile Standard (GOTS) are the most prevalent private organic labels used on a global scale. In the case of GOTS, the label emerged from cooperation among national textile

Table 3.1
Certification schemes for cotton from sub-Saharan Africa

Scheme	Stakeholder type	Initiator	Year founded	Certified products	Countries of production
Better Cotton Initiative (BCI)	Multistakeholder	WWF and International Finance Corporation (World Bank)	2010	Cotton	Australia, Brazil, China, CmiA countries (Burkina Faso, Ethiopia, Ivory Coast, Ghana, Mozambique, Tanzania, Uganda, Zambia, Zimbabwe), India, Israel, Mali, Pakistan, Senegal, Tajikistan, Turkey, USA
Cotton made in Africa (CmiA)	Multistakeholder	Aid by Trade Foundation (Michael Otto)	2005	Cotton	Burkina Faso, Cameroon, Ethiopia, Ivory Coast, Ghana, Malawi, Mozambique, Tanzania, Uganda, Zambia, Zimbabwe
Ecolabel for textile products (2014/350/ EU) based on Organic Regulation (EC 834/2007) (IFOAM family; GOTS)	Public	EU	2014	Organic textiles, including cotton	All
Fair for Life (FFL)	Business	Swiss Bio Foundation & IMO Group (ECOCERT)	2006	Various, including cotton	All
Fairtrade Labelling Organizations International (FLO)	Business	Solidaridad, among others	1997 (cotton since 2005)	Various, including cotton	All (for cotton: West and Central Africa, India, Pakistan, Central Asia)
USDA Organic based on National Organic Program (NOP)	Public	United States	2000	Various, including cotton	All

Source: Author's compilation based on information provided on the homepages of the certification schemes.

certifiers: the Organic Trade Association (OTA) from the United States, the International Association of Natural Textiles (IVN) from Germany, the Japan Overseas Cooperative Association (JOCA), and the Soil Association from the UK (GOTS 2018). An international working group started to develop an agreement on common license conditions in 2002, which were first published in 2009 and have regularly been revised since then (GOTS 2018). However, in addition to the GOTS label, for example, the OTA continues to use the USDA Organic label on textiles (OTA 2017), and IVN also continues to label textiles with its own earlier IVN Best brand (IVN 2018). Moreover, FLO started to certify cotton and textile products in 2005, with the option for smallholders to produce organically and receive a premium price (Fairtrade 2017). This means that the creation of a unified label for the international market did not lead to fewer but rather to more standards.

While earlier private standards such as IVN Best certify only textiles made of 100 percent natural and organically produced fibers (IVN 2018), GOTS compromised by providing the GOTS label grade organic to textiles containing a minimum of 95 percent certified organic fibers. Furthermore, GOTS has a second label grade, made with organic, for textiles that contain a minimum of 70 percent certified organic fibers (GOTS 2018). The Textile Exchange also offers two labels: the first, OCS 100, is similar to the first GOTS label and guarantees textile content of 95 to 100 percent organic fibers. The second Textile Exchange label indicates an organic blend of at least 5 percent of all cotton used for a textile (Textile Exchange 2017). Therefore, though there are legal requirements for what can be labeled as organic in each market, the example of organic textile certification illustrates that this does not always lead to greater clarity or the prevention of misinformation.

In contrast to organic branding, labeling of products as sustainable and fair trade is not restricted (only private brands and labels, such as Max Havelaar and FLO, are registered trademarks). Although FLO created its international label in 1997, for which businesses can receive licenses and which is recognized by consumers around the world, FLO member organizations, such as Cafédirect, Max Havelaar, and GEPA, have continued to use their own (original) labels on their products. In addition, a range of international labeling organizations emerged. For textiles, there are the Fair Wear Foundation (FWF) and the Fair Labor Association (FLA). The FWF certification scheme resulted from a European multistakeholder initiative in

1999. It aims to improve workplace conditions in the garment and textile industry (which is also covered by the general FLO standard; FWF 2017). In the United States, a range of TNCs and NGOs in cooperation with almost two hundred US universities and colleges founded the FLA as part of an initiative of US President Bill Clinton, also in 1999. The FLA is a business-to-business standard with no label on the final product (FLA 2017). Businesses often use it in combination with Social Accountability International (SAI), which owns the SA8000 Standard that guarantees compliance with UN conventions—in particular, the International Labor Organization (ILO) standards (Bartley 2007; SAI 2017).

In 2004, the WFTO, which cooperates with FLO and was founded by GEPA, among other fair-trade pioneers, launched a fair-trade-certification scheme to register fair-trade organizations worldwide (as opposed to label-ing products, in the case of FLO) and to guarantee that standards are being implemented regarding working conditions, wages, child labor, and the environment (WFTO 2017). Although there had been a general trend among organic and fair-trade pioneers to increasingly unify their national and regional labels since the 1990s, Fair Trade USA (FTUSA) announced res-ignation of its membership from FLO in 2011 (Fairtrade 2017). This allowed FTUSA to start certifying middle- and large-scale production sites, whereas FLO continues to work only with smallholder farmers (MK, interview Sep-tember 8, 2017).

In parallel to the emergence of pioneer schemes based on ambitious standards, in particular the guidelines of IFOAM and FLO (and FTUSA), a number of certification schemes emerged that were developed and are operated by conventional businesses. In the forest sector, after the FSC had already been established, members of timber (processing) industries started to create their own certification schemes, without participation of public actors or NGOs (Kleinschmit 2015). Such industry-driven "business-only" certification schemes were originally conceived to counter the influence of the more ambitious pioneer schemes (Dingwerth and Pattberg 2009). For example, the American Forest and Paper Products Association devel-oped its own Sustainable Forest Initiative—which some activist groups, such as the Rainforest Action Network, criticized as "greenwash" (Haufler 2003, 247). In particular, the Programme for the Endorsement of Forest Certification (PEFC) is interpreted as an industry response to the environ-mental NGO-based FSC. The PEFC is an umbrella organization that gathers thirty-five independent national forest certification schemes (Gulbrandsen 2014, 79; McDermott, Irland, and Pacheco 2015, 135). As an NGO representative stated: "I don't know the specifics, but some of [the schemes] are really like greenwashing, and they are an attempt to dilute the best standard in organic. . . . They are confusing consumers a lot; because you know you are a normal consumer . . . you see some certification with green letter and lalala. . . . And you are going to think you are buying something that is very beneficial for the environment and it comes with a price premium, but . . . I wonder really what the real benefit for the environment and the farmers for some of these schemes is" (RT, interview November 3, 2017).

In the cotton and textile sector, conventional retailers set up two schemes: Cotton made in Africa (CmiA) in 2005 and the Better Cotton Initiative (BCI) in 2010 (see table 3.1 for an overview of schemes; see also Sneyd 2011, 2014). Michael Otto established the Aid for Trade Foundation in 2005, which owns CmiA (CmiA 2018). Otto is a German businessperson and owner of one of the world's largest e-commerce companies, which bears his family name (Otto; see Partzsch and Fuchs 2012). About thirty conventional textile retailers (e.g., Aldi, BAUR, H.I.S. Jeans), cotton producers and traders (e.g., Reinhart, SECO), and public donor institutions (e.g., KfW, the German government-owned development bank) participate in or support CmiA. Several NGOs, such as the German NABU, WWF, and Welthungerhilfe, contributed to formulating the CmiA standard (CmiA 2018). The standard is less ambitious compared to fair-trade and organic certification. Similarly to CmiA, BCI, which has become the most popular scheme and certifies 12 percent of the global market, focuses on "minimum requirements" (BCI 2018). According to BCI, "minimum requirements are just the first stage. At the same time, farmers are encouraged to develop further through improvement requirements" (BCI 2013, 2), and "there are no requirements for farmers to step-up through the different levels and they can choose to stay at pass level [meeting only the minimum requirements] if they wish" (BCI 2013, 12). However, in contrast to the PEFC in forestry, NGOs and public actors participated in the standard setting for BCI and CmiA—like PAN UK, for example (whose sister organization PAN Ethiopia helps smallholders to accomplish organic certification on the ground, discussed ahead; see BCI 2018; CmiA 2018).

As there are legally binding minimum requirements (besides those for organic labeling in the EU and the United States, for example), certification standards vary considerably not only in the cotton/textile sector, but in other sectors as well. For example, in the coffee sector, FLO gives small-holder farmers a guaranteed price, at least 10 percent above the world price. Moreover, farmers receive 50 to 60 percent of the price in advance when the bags of coffee beans are delivered to the cooperative where they are hulled, and then the remainder when the product is finally sold (Barratt Brown 2007, 271). In comparison, conventional corporations such as Starbucks are paying prices that are higher than average in the specialty industry as a whole, but in most cases these prices are still lower than those paid by FLO (Macdonald 2007, 812). Further, conventional corporations, such as Nestlé and Starbucks, often buy conventional and fair-trade coffee from the same cooperative—for example, in Ethiopia. In these cases, while the price of fair-trade coffee is determined by FLO (or a different certification scheme), the TNC can simultaneously negotiate a lower bargain price for its conventional share; that is, it can undermine FLO prices (while those retailers buying only fair-trade coffee cannot and are hence disadvantaged; FH, interview January 13, 2017).

In the case of Cafédirect, GEPA, and Max Havelaar, 100 percent of the certified coffee comes from fair-trade plantations (Barratt Brown 2007, 271). For coffee, FLO requires 100 percent to be fair trade, but to receive the license for other products, only 50 percent needs to be fair trade (Barratt Brown 2007, 272). Barratt Brown (2007, 273) argues that this leads to a situation in which companies are considered fair trade despite only a minor share of their products actually being fair trade. In line with this, he recalls the case of Nestlé announcing that it was offering fair-trade coffee supplied from Ethiopia, but this Ethiopian coffee only contributed 0.02 percent of Nestlé's global coffee sales (Barratt Brown 2007, 273).

Moreover, some certification schemes use a "mass balance" approach, which means that the certified product itself does not necessarily need to contain materials produced under stricter environmental and social conditions. Instead, a company's overall share of products carrying the label needs to be consistent with the share of the material from certified production (similar to "green" electricity that is fed into the grid system but does not necessarily reach the consumer paying more for a renewable energy supply). This allows companies to use the same processing machines and transport infrastructure for both certified and noncertified products (CK, personal communication, July 10, 2017). In this case, certified products are completely integrated in the conventional system of agriculture and trade (as opposed to the movements' pioneers who had developed an independent supply system based on alternative shops and the like). FLO refuses the principles of mass balance and attaches importance to the physical traceability of products (Fairtrade 2017). Likewise, organic labels, such as GOTS, insist on the *pull effect*: a company aiming for certification needs to convince all its suppliers and potential customers of the benefits of certification (see figure 3.1; LP, interview, January 22, 2018). (However, both GOTS and OCS have the additional option of Made with Organic labeling, and this allows a share of up to 30 percent or 95 percent of conventionally produced cotton in their products, respectively.)

Because today most certification is concerned with either environmental or fair-trade/social standards, many products carry several labels. For example, more than 70 percent of fair-trade-certified cotton farmers are also farming in accordance with the IFOAM standard and hence comply with the USDA Organic and EU Organic labels (Textile Exchange 2016, 67). GEPA uses nine different certification schemes, including FLO and the EU Organic label for food and textiles (GEPA 2017). The Swiss Bio Foundation created the international Fair for Life (FFL) scheme in 2006, which combines organic and fair-trade certification (FFL 2018). Several other schemes combine environmental and social standards at a less ambitious

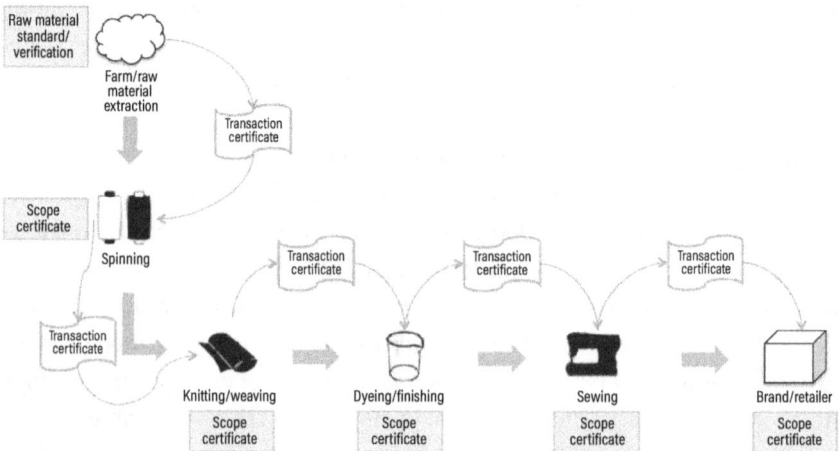

Figure 3.1
Pull effect in certified supply chains. *Source:* Textile Exchange 2016.

level. However, most schemes are only interested in particular production steps; for example, FLO concentrates on farming and manufacturing in the Global South (while, for example, wages of shop assistants in consumer countries are not addressed). Only a few schemes, such as FFL, certify the entire supply chain with regard to environmental and social criteria (FFL 2018).

3.1.3 Impact in the Global South

The volume of certified products is continuously growing as environmental and fair-trade/social certification is increasingly accepted in conventional supply chains. In particular, the organic sector is expanding. Since 1999, on a global scale, there has been a fourfold increase in organic agricultural land, from 11 million to 43.7 million hectares in 2014 (Textile Exchange 2016, 8). However, regarding the overall market share, uptake of voluntary schemes has remained limited, and alternative or ethical trade is far from substituting for industrial agriculture and the colonial division of labor between producers in the Global South and consumers in the Global North. Organic agriculture has a worldwide market share of only 1 percent (Rapunzel 2014, 3). Fair-trade and organic certified cotton together have a world market share of about 3 percent (FLO 2015, 24, 127; Textile Exchange 2016, 127, 5). Industry-driven certification initiatives have achieved a global market share of at least 12 percent (BCI 2018). In total, however, less than 20 percent of global cotton produced was grown under voluntarily stricter social and environmental conditions in 2016 (BCI 2018).

Most research on the impact of private regulation has been conducted on forest certification. Here, the vast majority of voluntarily certified area can be found "in the rather well-managed and commercially operated forests of temperate zones" (Pattberg 2007, 248). Although the FSC is one of the most successful voluntary schemes, accreditation rates range from 47.2 percent of total certified area in Europe and 36.3 percent in North America, to 6.8 percent in Latin America, 4.3 percent in Asia, 4 percent in Africa, and 1.3 percent in Oceania (data for May 2016, FSC 2019). In other words, if the FSC was meant as a response to the rapid destruction of tropical rainforests (Haufler 2003, 246), the numbers show that it failed to reach this objective; instead, forest certification failed to slow deforestation (Fishman and Obidzinski 2014, 258). Only 1 percent of Southern community forest groups have been able to obtain a certificate, and many of these groups are unable to pay the costs of certification without help from public development or NGO projects (Nygren 2015, 403–404).

When McDermott, Irland, and Pacheco (2015) systematically assessed the impact of voluntary forest certification in the Brazilian Amazon, they found that it did not accomplish the prevention of deforestation for three main reasons. First, higher prices for certified timber could not prevent the expansion of agriculture as the main driver of deforestation. Second, the costs of certification turned out to be too high for smallholders, excluding them from sustainable forest management, with additionally negative effects of market concentration. Third, the complexity of supply chains and products was higher for tropical timber export products than for European and North American timber products sold at domestic markets. In consequence, forest certification turned out to "favor large producers and concentrated supply chains destined for external markets . . . while extensive legal requirements inhibit local benefit-capture" (McDermott, Irland, and Pacheco 2015, 134). Private certification standards are animated by the idea of "pulling forests and factories out of their local contexts and up to global best practices" (Bartley 2018, 5). For global business, harmonized environmental standards have the same effect as a cartel: potentially harmful competition in voluntarily self-restricted markets is avoided (Du 2018). At the same time, they rest on the view of local sociopolitical contexts as "backwards, repressive, and incapable of effective regulation" (Bartley 2018, 5). In consequence, there is growing criticism regarding the effectiveness of the forest certification schemes, especially if timber originating from natural forests receives the FSC or PEFC seal. A lack of control, a divergence of national rules, and a dependence on the certifiers are the main points of criticism (Kleinschmit 2015, 85).

As certification initially focused on the environmental aspects of deforestation prevention, economic and social consequences, especially in the Global South, were often neglected (McDermott, Irland, and Pacheco 2015). Moreover, Nygren (2015) finds that certification builds upon images of Southern community producers as authentic and exotic "others." They are portrayed as people who cherish local traditions and toil for their living. Within this imagery, the Southern producer thus becomes a vehicle for selling cultural distinction as exoticism alongside tradition as beauty. The stories behind products are crucial to the sale of certified products, and the images of people are carefully selected. For example, people sawing timber barefoot or carrying planks on their shoulders on muddy slopes are not chosen. There is little consideration of the terms of Southern producers' participation in the global markets or the distribution of benefits and constraints among actors involved. Although certification schemes may increase transparency and shorten the distance between Northern consumers and Southern producers, they do not change asymmetrical trade relations (Nygren 2015). Studies on certification in diverse sectors found that pro-poor aspects of certification are generated through donations and not through the market (Hilson, Hilson, and McQuilken 2016; Hilson 2014; Sneyd 2011, 130; 2015).

In this vein, Koenig-Archibugi and Macdonald (2013) differentiate between, on the one hand, environmental certification that is aimed at producing benefits that are widely spread across the world's population and, on the other, fair-trade/social schemes that are directed toward specific groups of beneficiaries. These groups—normally producer groups in the Global South—are separate from "givers"—consumers in the Global North who voluntarily pay more for certified products (Koenig-Archibugi and Macdonald 2013). Cotton and textile certification is an exception to which this differentiation does not apply. Conventional cotton cultivation raises many environmental concerns, even though it is a cash crop with a fair-trade component.

Now that I have explained the concepts of environmental and fair-trade/social certification in general, I will analyze the case of cotton certification in Ethiopia in more concrete terms.

3.2 Country Study: Cotton and Ethiopia

Ethiopia, one of the least-developed countries with a nominal gross domestic product (GDP) per capita of USD 860.56 (in 2017), has a long tradition of producing and processing cotton (see figure 3.2). Newborns are traditionally wrapped in hand-woven cotton cloth, made with hand-spun yarn, and so are bodies of the deceased for burial (AM, group discussions, September 4–5, 2017). At the same time, cotton is a cash crop and its conventional cultivation causes major environmental and social challenges, including pollution and health risks due to (improper) use of pesticides and synthetic fertilizers (Brooks 2015; Partzsch, Zander, and Robinson 2019). When the cotton price went down in the 1990s, hardly any cotton was still produced

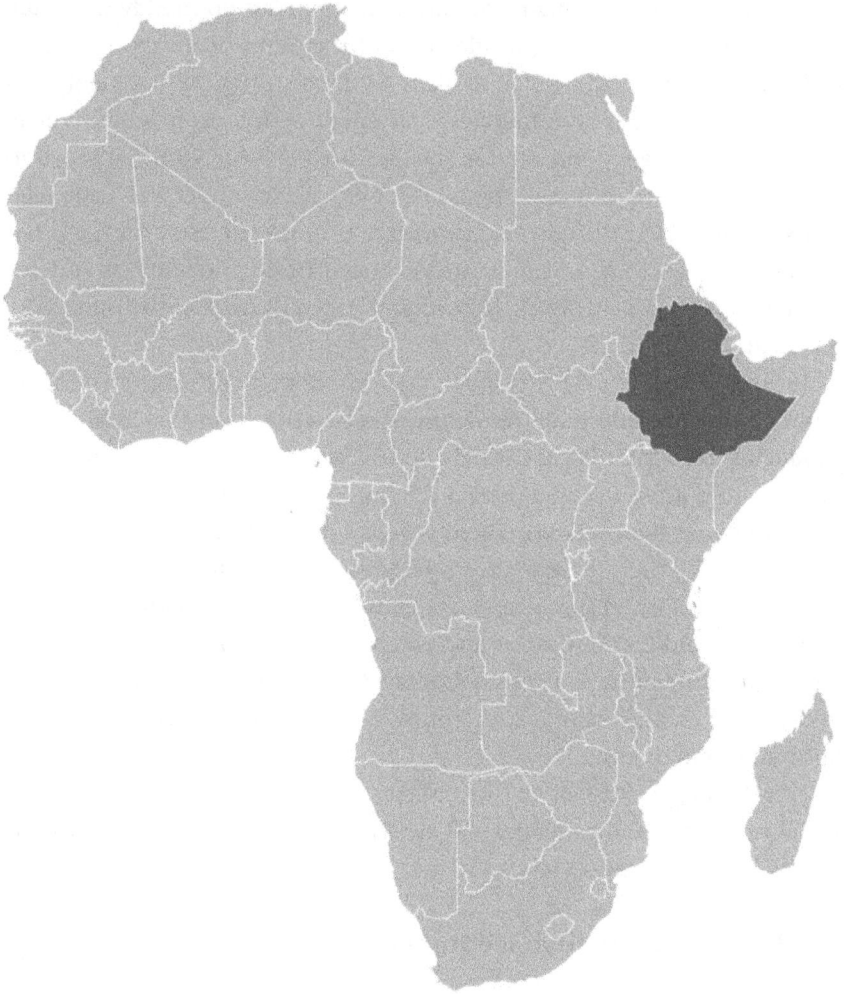

Figure 3.2
Ethiopia on map of Africa

in the country. Only with the recent price recovery have large corporate farms and smallholders restarted cotton production (BW, personal communication, June 27, 2017; AM, group discussions, September 4–5, 2017), with fifty-four thousand hectares of land designated for the cultivation of cotton (EIA 2012). In addition, between 2012 and 2017, the Ethiopian textile industry has grown at an average rate of 51 percent per year. More than sixty-five international textile investment projects have been licensed for foreign investors during this period (Alliance Experts 2017).

The Ethiopian government hopes that cotton and textile exports will increase foreign exchange earnings to stabilize the country's currency, generate fiscal revenue, and provide inputs for import-substituting industries (AT, interview, September 7, 2017). There are plans for the country to become the fifth-largest cotton-producing country in the world (Aga and Woldu 2014).[4] Voluntary certification programs promise to ensure the sustainability of this development (Textile Exchange 2017). Currently, two programs are active in Ethiopia: the Global Organic Textile Standard (GOTS) and Cotton made in Africa (CmiA). CmiA is the local partner of the Better Cotton Initiative (BCI), and the Fairtrade Labelling Organizations International (FLO) also works in the country but does not have any cotton projects at the current time (Fairtrade 2017; see table 3.1). The Ethiopian government generally supports the certification schemes as a means to adapt to global markets (Lefort 2012). This was supported by one interviewed representative: "We need to have [certification] at least for these big companies that work in this textile sector. Most of them are established here to 'interim' to the global market. And the global market needs this certification. . . . As a matter of fact, the market *dictates* it to them" (AT, interview, September 8, 2017, emphasis added).

3.2.1 Cotton in Ethiopia: Environmental and Social Challenges

Following limited success with agricultural policies since the 1990s, which placed a strong emphasis on smallholder productivity and domestic linkages, the Ethiopian government is now increasingly focusing on more trade-oriented, large-scale commercial agriculture as the impetus for agricultural industrialization. Against this backdrop, cotton agriculture is an example of the developmental state in Ethiopia (Lefort 2012; Raynolds, Murray, and Heller 2007). In its 2015 five-year Growth and Transformation

Plan (GTP II), the Ethiopian government made the promotion of large-scale commercial agriculture one of its core objectives (NPC 2016). It is building on earlier commitments made under its predecessors, the first 2010 Growth and Transformation Plan (GTP) and the 2005 Plan for the Acceleration and Sustained Development to End Poverty (PASDEP; see Schoneveld and Shete 2014, 18).

Between 1992 and 2010, up to 2.71 million hectares of land have been transferred to investors. This is equivalent to 58.2 percent of the total area suitable and available for agricultural production (Schoneveld and Shete 2014, 19). Land in Ethiopia is exclusively owned by the state. When allocating land for agricultural expansion, foreign investment contracts are based on the Agricultural Investment and Land Lease Directive and other pertinent legislation, such as the Labor Proclamation (no. 337/2003), the Water Resource Management Regulation (no. 115/2005), and the Environmental Pollution Control Proclamation (no. 300/2002). These encompass environmental requirements, such as planting trees that are good for the soil and the responsible use of pesticides. However, as these requirements are vaguely formulated, they leave significant latitude for interpretation. Socioeconomic considerations dominate environmental considerations in land allocation (Schoneveld and Shete 2014, 29).

For the most part, cotton is still grown by smallholders with one to three hectares of land, along with other crops, such as maize and sesame (Bassett 2010; EIA 2012), but there are now some of the first large-scale commercial cotton farms in Ethiopia (BW, personal communication, June 27, 2017). In consequence, however, Ethiopian farmers face increasing competition. Although middlemen lose significance at the local level (AM, group discussion, September 4, 2017), the cotton trade is increasingly concentrated on a few traders at the global scale (Quark 2013). As a raw material, cotton is a low-value good that is strongly affected by fluctuating world market prices (Brooks 2015, 116). The phaseout of the Multi Fibre Arrangement (MFA) from 1995 to 2005 liberalized trade in apparel and, paired with the accession of China to the WTO in 2001, shifted the geography of textile production. Since 2005, the textile trade has been subject to the normal WTO rules (Quark 2013, 26). Transnational merchants and retailers now play the leading role in setting up production networks. Only a handful of them link geographically dispersed cotton producers and geographically dispersed and relatively small-scale textile manufacturers who shifted from

Western Europe to Asia—and now continue to shift to poorer countries, including Ethiopia (Quark 2013, 26).

Observers remark that patterns of trade that were established in the colonial period prevail, although the companies and nations involved have changed (Brooks 2015, 105). Value is added in downstream industrial and service sectors outside Africa, and African labor for cotton production continues to receive only a tiny proportion of the final sale price (Brooks 2015, 106). Cotton field workers receive as little as USD 0.60 per day, and almost 90 percent are casually employed as day laborers, which generally provides between three and four months of full-time employment per year. Children and young adults are also commonly employed to gain supplementary family income (Schoneveld and Shete 2014, 31).

Today, China is the primary destination for African cotton, accounting for 36 percent of the world's cotton imports (followed by Bangladesh, Turkey, Indonesia, and Vietnam), whereas textiles manufactured in China continue to be sold to Europe and the United States (Hoskins 2014; Brooks 2015, 116). In the past, the WTO has twice judged US subsidies that enable American farmers to maintain their strong position as cotton exporters to be illegal, but the US government has failed to act, and world market prices are reduced by an estimated 10 percent due to the effect of US subsidies (Azubuike 2018, 141; Brooks 2015, 116). In 2009 to 2010, however, China even overtook the United States as the largest dispenser of cotton subsidies. In addition, China imposes import duties from 5 percent up to 40 percent on cotton imported outside of the annual 894,000 outside of the annual import quota related to WTO obligations, and this further disadvantages African farmers (Brooks 2015, 116; Quark 2013, 3). Furthermore, Sneyd (2015, 63) explains that when Brazil agreed to end its dispute on cotton subsidies with the United States, this deal was made at the expense of African farmers too. Brazil received a one-off USD 300 million payment, which directly funded the development of Brazil's capacity to export cotton. While its African competitors came away empty-handed, Brazil could develop a capital-intense, high-tech cotton-production industry.

Alongside (distorted) supply and demand, factors influencing the cotton market include weather and agricultural shocks (droughts, floods, pest attacks), fiber quality, the amount of cotton stock stored in reserve, and competition from other commodity crops (Textile Exchange 2016, 33). Fiber quality in particular has become a highly controversial issue (Quark

2013, 85–118). African farmers are generally considered to produce some of the highest quality cotton (CK, personal communication, July 10, 2017; Quark 2013, 26). However, the United States wants to form a single set of fiber-quality standards and a common instrument for measuring fiber quality based on its domestic system, and African countries accuse this system of being biased toward US cotton. Moreover, they are concerned that the capital-intense measurement instruments are inappropriate for poorer farmers in the Global South (Quark 2013, 2–3). At the same time, China has started to demand quality inspections based on its own criteria (Quark 2013, 3).

Besides such fair-trade issues, the production of cotton raises major environmental concerns. Cotton is one of the thirstiest agricultural crops, and irrigation allows for higher cotton yields and fiber quality. Most cotton crops in Ethiopia are irrigated (FAO and IFC 2015), which can deplete water resources, increase soil salinity, and exacerbate chemical runoff from farms (Williamson 2011). Although chemical inputs such as pesticides and fertilizers do not have a long history in Ethiopia, over 90 percent of farmers now rely on them. Pesticide application has adverse effects for human health and the environment, which are aggravated by a lack of knowledge on the part of cotton farmers and no access to alternatives (Amera and Abate 2008; Mekonnen and Agonafir 2002). Application of chemical inputs also can cause biodiversity loss; contaminate water, soil, and air; poison livestock and wildlif;e and compromise ecosystem services (FAO and ICAC 2015, 15). Twenty-eight percent of all African reservoirs and lakes have been found to be in a eutrophic state (IUCN 2018). At the same time, a large share of the population relies on untreated surface water—for example, 44 percent of the population in the highest region of Ethiopia, where 80 percent also rely on open defecation (WHO and UNICEF 2017, 96–103).

Against this backdrop, mega dam building and the introduction of genetically modified (GM, transgenic) organisms have been highly controversial issues in Ethiopia (BW, interview, September 2, 2017). Both demonstrate the Ethiopian path to further industrialize agriculture. Several scholars have outlined how dam building, such as the Gibe-3 dam venture on the Omo River, has taken away large tracts of land from pastoral and agrarian peoples for the sake of development and central state control (Lefort 2012; Beyene and Sandström 2016). Since 2015, the Oromo have been staging mass protests to decry, among other things, land grabs from farmers for textile factories (Donahue 2018). While the government insists on the damming to serve hydropower purposes, the expansion of irrigation is only the next logical step in enhancing large-scale cotton farming (FAO and IFC 2015; Schoneveld and Shete 2014). To this effect, the approval of genetically modified cotton in June 2018, only two months after Abiy Ahmed became prime minister, underlines the fact that the current Ethiopian government has continued to follow its chosen path of the developmental state since 2005 (Fikade 2018; Abbink 2011).

3.2.2 Organic Cotton Certification in Ethiopia

Voluntary certification programs are the most substantial private regulatory effort to address social and environmental challenges neglected or deferred by governments (Sneyd 2011; Raynolds, Murray, and Heller 2007). The International Federation of Organic Agriculture Movements (IFOAM) has two members in Ethiopia: Kihedam Trading PLC, a family company with one thousand hectares of farm land, and the Institute for Sustainable Development (ISD), a registered Ethiopian NGO that was founded by Sue Edwards and her husband and former director general of the Environmental Protection Authority Tewolde Berhan (IFOAM 2019). The ISD collaborates with the Pesticide Action Nexus Association (PAN) Ethiopia and Solidaridad (which established Max Havelaar, the first fair-trade label, in 1988). With funding from the Food and Agriculture Organization (FAO) and from UK charities Textile Reuse and International Development (TRAID) and the Sainsbury Family Charitable Trusts, PAN worked with two thousand cotton smallholders close to Arba Minch and helped them obtain EU Organic certification (Amera 2016, 2018; PAN UK 2017). Their cotton hence qualifies for GOTS.

There was a second organic cotton project in Ethiopia's Omo Valley, managed by the Turkish textile company Else Addis, on 880 hectares of land (1.6 percent of the country's land cultivated with cotton; Textile Exchange 2016, 39). However, the project stopped producing organic cotton in 2015–2016 due to critical social unrest in the region (LE, personal communication, October 31, 2017). Civil society groups accused the company of land grabbing and deforestation in a conservation area (Dove 2014). The Else Addis Industrial Development PLC, one of two companies certified by GOTS in Ethiopia (besides Ayka Addis Textile & Investment Group; see GOTS 2018), then imported certified organic cotton from India

(AT, interview, September 7, 2017), before it went completely bankrupt and disappeared from the GOTS website (GOTS 2018).

I met with both Ethiopian IFOAM members in Addis and visited the Arba Minch organic cotton project in September 2017. In the presence of a PAN Ethiopia representative, on September 4, 2017, I conducted a group discussion with farmers who did not participate in the certification process, but who PAN Ethiopia had trained in farming without pesticides. A second group discussion, on September 5, 2017, included the two heads of the cooperative that the farmers formed in order to apply for the EU Organic certificate. The farmers celebrated an annual agricultural day on September 5, with two stalls, several talks, a theater play, and field visits, to which I was invited. Again, I was able to conduct two semi-structured interviews before and after the event. I also conducted several semi-structured interviews in Addis with people involved in the textile industry and/or certification, including those who opposed organic farming as an alternative development path for Ethiopia. Moreover, I conducted several interviews and exchanged emails with organic companies in the downstream part of the supply chain in order to verify or discuss the information received in Ethiopia. All interviews and the discussions lasted between thirty minutes and three hours. The interviewees insisted on anonymity as they revealed sensitive economic and political information.

In line with the Ethiopian government's agenda, all interviewees voiced the aim of increasing the country's cotton export volumes and of receiving reasonable prices. However, whether this can be achieved by means of organic farming and certification was controversial. A general misunderstanding tended to be that as soon as the EU Organic regulation was fulfilled, European buyers would purchase the cotton at a higher price (AM, group discussion, September 5, 2017). In contrast to this assumption, finding trade outlets and marketing organically produced cotton turned out to be an insurmountable challenge. At the same time, to fulfill the requirements of the EU Organic standard, the farmers had to use organic seeds, and PAN imported those seeds from India (AM, group discussion, September 5, 2017). Therefore, although the Arba Minch project refrained from using imported pesticides and fertilizers, it still required imported inputs.

Furthermore, organic cotton currently does not achieve higher prices compared to conventional produce (Textile Exchange 2017, 34). Due to a lack of transport capacities, the Arba Minch farmers were forced to sell to the next ginning plant, which was not willing to acquire organic certification (AM, group discussion, September 5, 2017). Organic-certified plants existed only in Addis (GOTS 2018). In addition, as the smallholders had hardly any storage capacities (and no financial reserves), they were forced to sell their cotton right after harvest at a low price (AM, group discussions, September 4 and 5, 2017; BW, interview, September 2, 2017). In general, farmers have to follow the market, and most smallholders do not have the funds to hold on to their cotton and wait until they find the best buyer: it can be a very unequal transaction (Textile Exchange 2016, 34).

When I met with the Arba Minch farmers, they were still in the process of being certified. After receiving training from PAN Ethiopia on integrated pest management (IPM) and organic farming practices, they were already able to triple their harvest (AM, group discussions, September 4 and 5, 2017). PAN Ethiopia conducted a baseline survey on conventional cotton producers in January 2013 before the project started. The yield per hectare of seed cotton for conventional growers was 8–10 quintals per hectare. After one year of intervention, the yield of the involved farmers was 18–23 quintals per hectare for the 2013 crop, while the seed cotton yield for the 2014 production season for the farmers was 30–36 quintals per hectare, more than triple that of the baseline.[5] Moreover, the local cotton price was ETB 10 (around EUR 0.38) per kilogram in 2013 when the project started, but it increased to ETB 16 (around EUR 0.61) per kilogram in 2014. PAN Ethiopia attributes this price increase to the establishment of a farmer cooperative in which the farmers coordinated to avoid the interference of middlemen (Amera 2016). However, this price is still well below the world market cotton price (Cotlook A index[6]), which ranged between USD 1.5 and 2 (around EUR 1.68 and 2.25) per kilogram in 2014 (USD 1.9/kg in June 2017). Further, it does not include the third-party auditing costs for certification (around EUR 4,000 in the Arba Minch case; AM, group discussion, September 5, 2017; LB, September 4, 2017).

PAN Ethiopia received international donor funding to assist the smallholders in Arba Minch accomplish organic certification following the EU Organic Regulation (which is recognized by IFOAM; PAN UK 2017). Control Union Certifications Ethiopia performed the certification process. This group is a local branch of an international private company that was founded in the Netherlands in 2002 and offers auditing services for certification in more than seventy countries today (Certification Control Union

2017). In Ethiopia, there are in total only three employees who testify and check compliance with any certification standard for a range of products, including cotton production compliance with the EU Organic Regulation (LB, September 4, 2017). Although the three employees are from Ethiopia, the Control Union is perceived as a Western company controlling African farmers and processors. Certification schemes insist on international companies, such as the Control Union, as they do not trust Ethiopians (MK, September 8, 2017). The auditor in Arba Minch told me that he must avoid certifying projects in which his relatives are involved (LB, September 4, 2017). However, he often faced personal conflicts when examining the farmers. He explained that smallholders are lacking awareness and that they need assistance from NGOs. But PAN Ethiopia only visited the farmers every three to four months in the project phase, and the auditor did not consider this enough, as most of the smallholders were illiterate and overstrained with the formalities of certification (LB, September 4, 2017).

Because the primary interest of farmers is to receive higher prices for their yield, fair-trade certification would have been the better choice for the Arba Minch project. In 2016, FLO invented a special cotton program with a guaranteed minimum price that is supposed to cover the farmers' expenses in the long term (however, there are not any projects in Ethiopia yet). If the local cotton price is higher than the fair-trade minimum price, retailers have to pay the higher price. In the FLO program, buyers also need to pay more for organic cotton. In addition to the fair-trade minimum price, there is an organic premium of EUR 0.05 (ETB 1.6) per kilogram of cotton for community purposes, such as schools and health and infrastructure projects (Fairtrade 2017); that is, the Arba Minch farmers would receive higher prices through FLO compared to the EU Organic certification. However, PAN Ethiopia helped the Arba Minch farmers to achieve certification according to the EU Organic Regulation. Alternatively, farmers were only considering compliance to the US NOP (which was not possible because US NOP only issues organic certificates for combined cotton cultivation and ginning, and the farmers knew that they had no access to an organic certified ginning plant). They were not aware of other certification options besides the IFOAM family standards (AM, group discussion, September 4 and 5, 2017). Their choice of the EU Organic Regulation reflects their (false) expectation to be able to export their harvest at a high price to Europe.

3.2.3 Cotton Certification with the Conventional Industry in Ethiopia

By being certified, the organic farmers in Arba Minch joined the movements that originally aimed to oppose industrial agriculture and to develop valid alternatives to the conventional trade system. In addition to this type of certification, we can observe an even greater interest of the conventional cotton and textile industry in voluntary certification schemes, such as Cotton made in Africa (CmiA) and the Better Cotton Initiative (BCI; Sneyd 2011, 2014). In Ethiopia, the CmiA initiative is the local partner of BCI, and farmers who qualify for the CmiA certification are able to market their cotton as both BCI and CmiA (BCI 2018; Sneyd 2014). CmiA has three partners in the country: the Ethiopian Cotton Producers, Ginners, and Exporters Association (ECPGEA); Metema Union, a cooperative with ten thousand members in the northeastern portion of the country; and Kanoria Africa Textiles PLC Ethiopia, a subsidiary of an Indian chemical company. Their project sites are in Metema, Quara, Tach Armachiho, and Tegede woredas (BW, interview, September 2, 2017). Whereas NGOs were involved in the CmiA standard setting, they do not play a major role on the ground. Only WWF is involved in implementation (BW, interview, October 29, 2017; WB, interview, November 13, 2017).

While the GOTS label ensures certification of the entire supply chain from seed to sale (GOTS 2018), CmiA focuses on cotton cultivation and ginning (BCI 2018; CmiA 2018). CmiA only certifies smallholders with one to three hectares of land, rather than medium or large-scale farmers (CmiA 2018). CmiA emphasizes that certification does not depend on donor funding, in contrast to NGO-initiated projects, such as the externally funded PAN project in Arba Minch. Fifty million textiles were marked with the CmiA label in 2016. License revenues for the CmiA label reached almost EUR 1.5 million (CmiA 2018). The money raised is mainly used to provide trainings for smallholders on cultivation methods and business practices in order for them to be able to produce cotton in a less harmful and more efficient way (CmiA 2018). CmiA partners also guarantee the purchase of the smallholders' harvest as an incentive for them to participate (BW, interview, September 2, 2017). In 2014, the smallholders received ETB 14 (around EUR 0.50) per kilogram of cotton (BW, interview, September 2, 2017, while the Arba Minch farmers received ETB 16 per kilogram in the same year, and FLO would even pay a premium on top (AM, group discussions, September 4 and 5, 2017).

The CmiA standard includes ecological and social criteria but does not comply with the IFOAM guidelines of organic farming. Instead of prohibiting toxic pesticides and fertilizers, CmiA aims to progressively reduce their use. Only the use of illegal pesticides is not tolerated, and vulnerable people, such as pregnant women and nursing mothers, are kept from working with pesticides on CmiA farms. People working with CmiA (and BCI) generally denied problems resulting from the use of pesticides and synthetic fertilizers in Ethiopia, or they traced them back to their inadequate use by smallholders. One interviewee stated that "in Ethiopia, specifically [in] CmiA regions, pesticides application is very, very limited and minimal. So, I don't think we have . . . detrimental effects on the environment through the application of any form of pesticides, I mean, [of] herbicides or insecticides. . . . CmiA does not have a strong stance on pesticides" (BW, interview, October 29, 2018). In a similar vein, another said: "You know farmers are not happy. . . . Most of their money and effort are going with pesticides and fertilizers, *because they are indiscriminately using them too much.* So many problems are there, health problem[s], environmental problem[s], without any systematic study, if you want to have cotton production" (SVR, interview, November 2, 2017, emphasis added; similar in CK, personal communication, July 10, 2017).

Furthermore, CmiA does not allow farmers to use any artificial irrigation and prohibits deforestation of primary forests, as well as encroaching upon nature reserves. This can be considered more ambitious than the IFOAM guidelines, especially regarding the controversy about dam construction and the expansion of irrigation infrastructure in Ethiopia. In addition, CmiA restricts GMOs (while BCI allows growing Bt cotton). Again, however, CmiA does not necessarily exclude Bt cotton due to a political bias against GM techniques, but because the initiative assumes an inadequate use by smallholders in Ethiopia: "In Australia, 1,200 farmers are growing cotton and they are growing GMO cotton. It's easy to train 1,200 highly educated farmers on the proper use of GMO, but it's very difficult to train 500 African small-scale farmers, most of them illiterate on the proper use of GMO. That's the difference. It's like if you have a Porsche, but you don't have a federal highway" (WB, interview, November 13, 2017).

CmiA also commits to some articles of the ILO standards, including prohibition of forced and child labor, discrimination, commitment to equal remuneration for men and women, and free association. For other criteria, such as compliance to national minimum wages and fair pay on time, lower requirements are set, but improvements must be demonstrated (CmiA 2018). As smallholders certified under CmiA usually work on their own farms, they work at their own expense, without wages (BW, interview, September 2, 2017). To conduct the certification audits, the Aid by Trade Foundation signed the Control Union (which also certified the Arba Minch project) in addition to EcoCert and AfriCert, with a total of twelve African auditors under contract (CmiA 2018).

CmiA uses a mass balance approach that allows CmiA cotton to be processed together with conventional cotton (CK, personal communication, July 10, 2017). This means that consumers buying certified clothes are unlikely to hold a product in their hands that was made out of certified cotton. At the same time, CmiA products are completely integrated into the conventional textile supply system. They are not distributed through alternative organic shops, but rather expand the product range of conventional companies within established supply and market systems. This allows for modest prices on labeled products. For example, Otto Shopping (2018) offers three t-shirts carrying the CmiA label for EUR 24.99, compared to only one plain white t-shirt carrying the GOTS label for EUR 19.99 from the German organic retailer Armedangels (2018).

While CmiA partners present themselves as do-gooders within the conventional market, they continue to process conventional cotton in parallel to certified cotton, with growing volumes of both certified and noncertified cotton (CmiA 2018). Whereas partners refrain from GM technology and irrigation in certification schemes and guarantee the purchase of harvests from certified farmers, businesses participating in the initiative are simultaneously accelerating inverse dynamics. They are advocating for the use of Bt cotton and the expansion of large-scale irrigation agriculture, which increase the economic pressure faced by smallholders in Ethiopia (BW, interview, September 2, 2017). Conventional businesses have been discussing a second certification scheme, Sustainable Cotton Initiative Ethiopia (SCIE), which aims to certify large-scale and irrigated cotton farms close to Dansha and Humera in the Tigray Region and probably to the Afar Region (Awash Valley; BW, interview, September 2, 2017; PAN, group discussion, September 2, 2017).

3.2.4   Summary of Case Study Results

The certification of cotton is a form of private (re-)regulation aiming to address environmental and social shortcomings in cotton/textile supply chains. Confirming earlier studies (Bartley 2018; Sneyd 2015; van der Ven 2019b), the case of certified cotton from Ethiopia illustrates well that certification is not necessarily driven by the needs of the local people. Although IFOAM has two local members in Ethiopia, PAN Ethiopia as a sister organization of PAN UK and Solidaridad as another international NGO initiated the organic project with cotton smallholders on the ground. In the case of CmiA, the whole certification process is completely driven by international partners from outside Ethiopia.

When buying certified cotton/textiles from Ethiopia, Western consumers face the choice of various textile labels—EU Organic, GOTS, OCS, CmiA, and BCI. However, and this is something research has not taken into account so far, farmers on the ground are not aware of this variety of certification options. The schemes are certifying farmers in different regions of Ethiopia (see figure 3.3). While the organic farms are situated in the South, CmiA is more present in the North/Northeast, and SCIE will develop further regions of certified cotton in the North/Northwest. Cotton farmers either consider certification to be an opportunity, in line with the Ethiopian government, or a new requirement to fulfill the demands of the global market and achieve better sales. However, this expectation is not fulfilled in reality. Organic farmers lack marketing opportunities for their certified cotton ,and, in the case of CmiA and SCIE, license revenues are used to finance the farmers' trainings. In the case of organic farming, in particular, farmers only benefit from less environmental pollution and fewer health risks.

Although the different certification schemes target the same share of more conscious consumers in the Global North and farmers on the ground do not recognize variances among them, it is impossible to ignore their different origins. Organic and fair-trade movements, to which IFOAM and Solidaridad belong, use certification as a tool to oppose the conventional system of "dirty fashion" (Soil Association 2017). The Arba Minch project serves political purposes of resisting industrial agriculture. Participants pioneer an alternative system of "ethical" fashion. Their certification serves as a means to promote political change. Therefore, receiving donor funding does not conflict with the aims of certification.

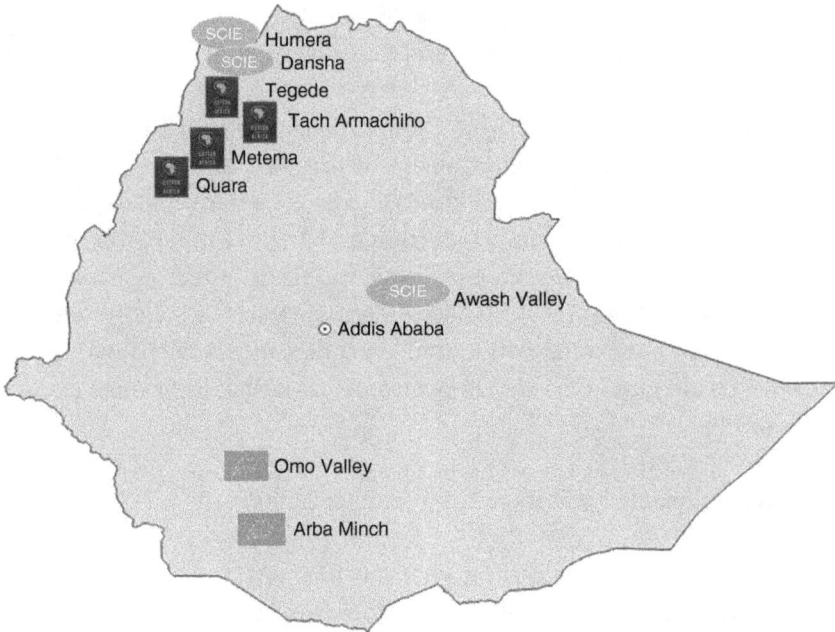

Figure 3.3
Cotton certification in Ethiopia

In contrast, schemes within the conventional industry, such as CmiA and SCIE, support the current system of agricultural production and trade. The above-cited analogy that compares GMOs to a Porsche and describes Ethiopia as a country without highways illustrates this perception (WB, interview, November 13, 2017). These industry-driven schemes offer certified products in response to consumers' growing demand. Following this logic, all expenses of certification are covered by license revenues. Further, the logic of the current market system includes buying cotton at the lowest possible price in order to offer certified products at a modest price to conscious consumers. These different attitudes explain why, although increasing smallholders' income is not a priority of IFOAM, the Arba Minch farmers already received a higher price for their cotton produce in 2014 (ETB 16) compared to the price paid by CmiA (ETB 14). This was before, and hence independent from, obtaining organic certification. Nevertheless, the certification initiative gave the farmers the impetus to organize among themselves and to get things done independently in order to overcome structural constraints.

In sum, less ambitious standards of initiatives in the conventional industry, such as those from CmiA and SCIE, are more appealing to cotton farmers at first sight as they are less demanding—for example, by allowing for mass balance. Farmers have an immediate benefit through training measures and purchase guarantees, for instance. In contrast, political pioneer schemes, such as IFOAM and FLO, aim for a transformation of the overall system of agricultural production and trade. Farmers will mainly benefit in the long run from a processing and retail system with environmental and social priorities. It is dependent on the NGOs and producers in the Global South, rather than the consumers in the Global North, to take this chance and to be able to overcome the lack of immediate market opportunities.

3.3   Discussion: Ethical Market Power and Its Limits

We have seen that movements and NGOs in the Global North were the main drivers behind the creation of private regulation, and NGOs play a crucial role in facilitating the implementation of private regulation in the Global South. However, so long as certification is completely voluntary, it does not face opposition from corporate actors or governments. To the contrary, conventional businesses have created their own schemes in order to respond to consumers' demands. In the following three sections, I discuss voluntary certification against the three perspectives on power formulated in chapter 2. First, confirming the current state of research, I also argue that private regulation has led to a further withdrawal of the state in favor of TNCs and NGOs. Second, regarding North–South asymmetries, again confirming dominant perspectives, I find that private alternatives to multilateralism are generally disadvantaging the Global South for various reasons (including auditing costs for certification, which are a de facto trade barrier for smaller producers). In addition, also complementing existing research, I emphasize that pioneer schemes enable people "to get things done" (Parsons 1963, 232), and Southern producers receive training to improve their situation. Third, private regulation proves on the one hand that actors are not continuously selfish, but rather exercise *power with* others to pursue environmental and social norms. Their ethical market power is, on the other hand, only practiced in niche segments of world trade and hence faces clear limits.

3.3.1   Further Withdrawal of the State

A central assumption made in the literature on private certification is that globalization and the withdrawal of the state led to a new private power over nation-states at the expense of environmental and social considerations. My findings only partly confirm this perspective. Globalization creates competition among producers around the world; for example, cotton producers in the EU and the United States compete with producers in poorer countries like Brazil and China, and even least-developed countries like Ethiopia. This global competition was initiated by state governments and, in particular, through the WTO. The case of Austria and the Forest Stewardship Council (FSC) illustrates well how governments' hands are collectively tied to the WTO and how voluntary certification remained the only option to re-regulate the supply of, in this case, tropical timber from the Global South. The Austrian government had to rescind its ban on tropical timber imports and instead supported the emerging FSC (Bartley 2007, 321; Lauber 1997, 106). In consequence, NGOs such as the WWF and Greenpeace, who initiated the FSC, gained power resources from state actors (while Greenpeace International did not renew its FSC membership in 2018 and returned to more confrontational strategies of campaigning, as discussed ahead).

We can see a similar development in the cotton sector—but only when textile trade became subject to the normal WTO rules in 2005 (Quark 2013, 26). Then, a few powerful, nonstate actors adopted private regulations (see the fourth column of table 3.1). Their private schemes compete with earlier organic and fair-trade schemes that accomplished the establishment of niche markets in the shade of international free-trade regulations (FLO started to systematically certify cotton and textiles in 2005). This growing competition among diverse schemes is reflected by the extension of the EU Organic Regulation to textiles in 2014. Obviously, there was a need for market clarification.

The concentrated power of the WTO faces an increasingly fragmented landscape of certification schemes across sectors and geographies. The schemes complement, rather than challenge, the WTO and the respective dominance of the free-trade paradigm in IR. Hence, we may argue that, although certification schemes set environmental and social standards, they contribute to an overall race to the bottom (Altvater and Mahnkopf 1999; Lucier and Gareau 2015) by offering an alternative to public policy regulations or intergovernmental regimes that might limit free trade more comprehensively. However, some schemes are very ambitious, such as IFOAM and FLO, and these are privatizing up (Cashore, Auld, and Newsom 2004, 5) existing public policy rules, at least in market niches. They also caused diverse states to adopt organic regulations, which are nevertheless voluntary in nature.

States only regulate the use of the term *organic* in their markets—for example, with the USDA Organic and the EU Ecolabel (green leaf and textile label). They do not restrict the labeling of products as Sustainable and Fair Trade (only the use of private trademarks such as the FLO label) and, hence, leave considerable leeway to private actors. For example, private actors normatively define standard contents—for example, what "sustainable forestry" (FSC and PEFC) and "better cotton" (CmiA and BCI) are supposed to be. Private regulation is hence moving authority into the hands of nonstate actors.

NGOs are usually seen as a counterpart to TNCs in multistakeholder schemes or as those actors that push for stricter standards in business-only schemes (Dingwerth and Pattberg 2009; Kemper and Partzsch 2018). By increasingly cooperating with business actors, the NGOs' strategic focus shifted from the political sphere to the market sphere (Cashore, Auld, and Newsom 2004, x). This shift reflects the growing dominance of the global market since the 1990s (when international certification became popular). At the same time, the nonstate (market) sphere allows NGOs to participate in private standard-setting processes, whereas before they could only influence decision-making processes of state actors. Thus, power has also shifted to the NGOs themselves, whereas many of them hardly have democratic structures; for example, Prince Philip, Duke of Edinburgh, was the first CEO of WWF, which initiated the FSC, and the WWF has never made transparent who its voting members are (WWF 2019). Hence, private regulation not only shifts power away from state actors but also increasingly concentrates power on only a very few nonstate individuals (Partzsch 2017c).

While private regulation leaves some special individuals with extraordinary power, the role of ordinary citizens is reduced to being "conscious" consumers. This shift in what is considered an appropriate field of political action becomes most obvious when considering that NGOs ask for donations in order to promote market approaches. Consumers can regulate the market by purchasing "ethical" products at the end of supply chains

(Jordan 2001, 4), and they are asked to make additional donations for people in the Global South who produce for a global market that clearly fails to accomplish environmental protection and social justice (see, e.g., Amera 2018). Ethically conscious consumerism "replaces" political activism (Barnett 2010). At the same time, as we have seen in the Ethiopian case of cotton certification, producers cannot select among a variety of certification standards, as different schemes are operating in different regions, and alternative retail systems are far from having a global reach. Moreover, if smallholder producers depend on external funding through NGOs in order to pay for third-party auditing, they also have to adapt to the donors' and/or NGOs' expectations. In sum, private regulation has therefore led to a further withdrawal of the state in favor of TNCs and NGOs that collaborate in standard-setting processes at the expense of state actors and ordinary citizens, including consumers—but especially producers in the Global South.

3.3.2 Reproducing North–South Asymmetries

The second dominant perspective regarding power dynamics in a globalized world is that there are increasing asymmetries between actors in consuming countries of the Global North and actors in producing countries of the Global South. Private regulation is meant to address environmental and social problems along global supply chains. Consumers in the Global North are supposed to pay more for the same final product to improve the well-being of actors further up the chain, especially in the Global South. Yet in some cases, the voluntary standards are unwanted by the supposed beneficiaries. Countries of the Global South interpret private certification as a form of hidden protectionism (Biermann 2001; Quark 2013, 5), and forestry studies have demonstrated that voluntary certification schemes indeed favor large-scale producers from the Global North (McDermott, Irland, and Pacheco 2015, 134).

In the case of tropical timber, there was a clear North–South divide among governments. The 1992 UNCED failed to generate a binding international forest convention, especially due to discrepancies of expectations and objectives between the Global North and South (Bartley 2007, 320; 2018, 31). Southern countries prevented a binding intergovernmental forest agreement (Fishman and Obidzinski 2014, 258). Their ideas of self-determination conflicted with the notion of treating forests—in particular, tropical forests—as global commons (Kleinschmit 2015, 83–84). Timber-exporting countries of the Global South charged that the Austrian ban on tropical timber amounted to a protectionist nontariff barrier to trade under GATT (Bartley 2007, 321). Environmentalists were divided over the legitimacy of tropical timber bans and boycotts too. Even the strongest supporters of boycotts admitted negative effects on Southern producers, and they sought voluntary certification as a more positive alternative (Bartley 2007, 319).

The Austrian government's move from import restrictions to the FSC demonstrates how private regulation allows consumer countries in the Global North to effectively bypass the opposition of the timber-exporting countries in intergovernmental negotiations (Haufler 2003, 251). At the same time, certification is in line with government policies in the Global South. For instance, the Ethiopian government considers certification to be a means to adapt to global markets and promote exports in line with the developmental state (Lefort 2012). To participate in the globalized economy and to increase their market share, Southern producers now increasingly have to readjust their production systems according to certification standards defined by actors in the Global North (AT, interview, September 7, 2017). Moreover, scholars point to a divergence of national rules and a lack of accountability—for example, in the forest sector (Kleinschmit 2015, 85). Haufler (2003, 251) notes that the increased degree to which citizens in developing countries now turn to the private sector for governance rather than to their own governments undermines the strength and health of those governments. Their self-determination is hence challenged twice, both by the foreign voluntary standards and by their own citizens' demand for private regulation. In this vein, the smallholders in Arba Minch were immediately willing to comply with EU regulation (as they expected to be able to export their cotton at a higher price to the EU afterward; AM, group discussion, September 5, 2017).

Because certification is voluntary and the FSC and similar schemes do not discriminate against products with a different country of origin, it does not conflict with GATT. However, the nondiscrimination principle of the WTO does not recognize North–South inequalities. As outlined earlier, when African cotton producers compete with those in the United States and China, for example, they do not compete as equals (Quark 2013, 26). While certification systems are widely used in North America and Europe, they are still only sparsely implemented in the Global South (Chan and Pattberg 2008). The attitude and perception of the International Control Union in Ethiopia gives a revealing insight: although the certification body suspects nepotism and demands employees decline to certify projects in which relatives are involved (LB, interview, September 5, 2018), the Ethiopian producers also perceive both the EU Organic standard and the Control Union to be foreign gatekeepers to international markets (MK, interview, September 8, 2018). The fact that only 1 percent of Southern community forest groups has been able to obtain a certificate (Nygren 2015, 403–404) indicates that it is more difficult and less beneficial for Southern producers to accomplish certification. In consequence, voluntary certification schemes indeed favor businesses from the Global North (McDermott, Irland, and Pacheco 2015, 134).

At the same time, producers continue to be dependent on actors further down the chain. Although the environment may benefit from standards such as the IFOAM principles, acquiring the certification and potential pro-poor benefits tend to only be possible with donor funding. Most producers in the Global South are unable to pay the auditing costs without development aid, philanthropy, or other forms of charity (Sneyd 2011, 130; Nygren 2015, 403–404). The Arba Minch case proves this finding. Besides the certification initiatives, such as IFOAM and FLO, and the auditors, such as the Control Union, NGOs are crucial gatekeepers. While they claim to represent the local people, they are often subsidiaries of international NGOs; for example, PAN Ethiopia is associated with PAN UK. What we see are *proxy accountability* arrangements, in which NGOs and consumers in the Global North hold governments and TNCs accountable "on behalf" of affected communities in the Global South (Koenig-Archibugi and Macdonald 2013).

Only well-organized groups are able to play a part in the certification business (Macdonald 1994; Tucker 2014), and we have seen in the case of certified cotton production in Ethiopia that they distribute the certification market geographically among themselves. The case of certified cotton from Ethiopia also indicates that the involvement of local NGOs relies on and produces particular forms of subjectivity. Smallholders are themselves unable to obtain donor funding, and they rely on NGOs as facilitators. NGOs, rather than smallholders, have the confidence of international donors, access to funding, and the know-how of implementation. Without the funding that PAN Ethiopia received from the FAO and the UK charities TRAID and the Sainsbury Family Charitable Trusts, the Arba Minch smallholders would not have been able to pay certification fees (AM, group discussion, September 5, 2018). Interviewees confirmed that the Arba Minch case is no exception: "NGOs apply for some grants, usually, for the grants of the international donor organizations. NGOs are core actors or players in utilization of funds of the international organizations and implementing these funds for the farmers. . . . Because NGOs [are] not government organizations . . . they need funds to implement the programs. And the funds come from the providing people, from some government program, from the international organization" (AR, interview, October 26, 2017).

The case study and additional interviews revealed that NGOs are facilitators of implementation, rather than political activists in the Global South. They communicate and implement already defined standards on the ground, such as organic production standards, instead of representing the demands of Southern producers in global decision making—for example, the demand for higher prices for their produce (AM, group discussions, September 4 and 5, 2017). NGOs such as PAN Ethiopia are accountable to their donors, not to the affected people. In consequence, as found by Nygren (2015), NGO certification initiatives risk paralyzing and even disempowering affected people, especially in the Global South. Western consumers tend to make choices that producers have to follow. Certification initiatives do not overcome the artificial divide between consumers and producers and the respective asymmetries (Hoskins 2014, 192). Analogies, such as GMOs (Western techniques) being like Porsches, even though there are no highways in countries of the Global South (WB, interview, November 13, 2017), demonstrate the reproduction of narratives surrounding certification initiatives about the Global North being advanced and the Global South being delayed. Such narratives harm countries like Ethiopia that are trying to attract foreign investment (while the interviewee who used this analogy missed the fact that Porsche cars represent an unsustainable, fossil-fuel-based system). In consequence, some critics consider voluntary certification to be simply a new way to depoliticize resource flows (Murphy 2000; Levidow 2013).

Nevertheless, in the cases of both GOTS and CmiA, individual producers and certification schemes in Ethiopia gained additional resources and capabilities. For example, farmers learned from the training provided by certification schemes and were able to significantly increase their harvests and income (Amera 2016). The Arba Minch project of certified cotton from Ethiopia provides evidence of empowerment. The certification initiative gave the farmers the impetus to organize among themselves and to negotiate higher cotton prices. Political pioneer schemes, such as IFOAM and FLO, hence demonstrate the ability to unite, engage, educate, and inspire people all over the world, even in least-developed countries such as Ethiopia. However, this impetus comes from the Global North. There is thus a reproduction of North–South asymmetries through certification.

3.3.3   Well Meant, Hardly Implemented

Does voluntary certification stand for *power with* others to pursue collective norms? As outlined in chapter 2, some IR scholars argue that actors are not continuously selfish (Janusch 2016; Manners 2015). I found this perspective confirmed with regard to some private governance initiatives. Movements and NGOs have promoted certification for the sake of environmental protection and fairness in world trade. Pioneering initiatives were clearly driven by spiritual and unselfish motives (Paull 2010). The first fair-trade groups were born in a Christian environment that aimed to overcome the "unfair" world trade system still based on the colonial division of labor between the Global South and North (Solidaridad 2017). Socially motivated individuals who organized Worldshops and established fair marketing organizations in support of Southern producers often work without payment (Barratt Brown 2007). In contrast to environmental movements, which aim for benefits such as forest protection that are widely spread across the world's population, fair-trade movements have mainly directed their efforts toward specific groups of beneficiaries other than themselves—for instance, Western consumers purchasing coffee at fair-trade premiums paid to Southern smallholders (Koenig-Archibugi and Macdonald 2013).

NGOs, such as Greenpeace and Solidaridad, were the main drivers behind the first global certification standards, and they would have failed without charitable funding, both in the creation and in the implementation of the standards (Bartley 2007, 321). This was exemplified in the case of the Arba Minch organic cotton project, in which international donors funded the NGO facilitation and paid for seeds and accreditation. Through the FSC, environmental NGOs obviously created situations in which they, as power-holders from the Global North, did not exercise power over but

with affected people in the south, finding common ground among allegedly conflicting interests, developing shared values, and creating collective
strength (Bartley 2007; Chan and Pattberg 2008). The creation of industry-
driven certification schemes, such as PEFC, was a response to NGOs' pressure (Dingwerth and Pattberg 2009). Haufler (2003) and others outline
how, under public pressure, TNCs began to accept responsibility for the
labor practices and human rights abuses of their foreign subcontractors.
They started to "export" human rights.

While TNCs are the "trailblazers and profiteers" (Sachs and Santarius
2007, 183) of the free-trade world order, they have started to acknowledge
global responsibilities by committing to voluntary certification schemes
that apply in foreign countries (Partzsch and Vlaskamp 2016). Conscious
consumers increasingly acknowledge their responsibilities for environmental pollution and exploitation of workers and communities that produce
their goods, regardless of whether they, as consumers, are citizens of the
exporting state or a foreign state (Segerlund 2010; Partzsch and Vlaskamp
2016). There is a growing demand for and offering of certified goods like
sustainable timber and ethical fashion (Sneyd 2014). If suppliers refuse to
disclose information and to certify their products, it becomes more difficult for them to find buyers and products receive lower prices. Noncertified
products receive lower prices, and noncertification may hence endanger
the financial viability of the suppliers (Koenig-Archibugi and Macdonald
2013). Private regulations generally pursue universal norms, such as human
rights, but also take a stance on controversial issues, like the prohibition or
introduction of Bt cotton in Ethiopia (BW, interview, September 2, 2017;
PAN, group discussion, September 2, 2018).

From a classical IR perspective, the EU and the United States encourage
certification to maximize utility based on their material capabilities and
economic gains (Quark 2013, 5). Although certification is voluntary and
hence a *soft power*, it effectively limits Southern producers' access to global
markets (Du 2018) and hence translates into a *hard power* (Nye 2011). In
the case of timber, countries in the Global North, such as Austria, may only
have championed normative standards of sustainable forestry and tropical forest protection to protect their domestic timber industry from less
expensive competitors from the Global South (Leipold et al. 2016). Private
regulation does not recognize nor deliberately accept unequal starting positions of companies in the Global North and South. However, as outlined in

chapter 2, classical IR power concepts assume that state actors, such as the US and EU governments, continue to be in the driver's seat. They ignore the detail that governments' hands are tied under the WTO and that, in parallel, the relative attachment of individuals to a particular nation-state is dissolving.

My findings show that TNCs are not simply an arm of their countries of origin. The phaseout of the MFA and the application of WTO rules in the textile sector make producers compete against each other on a global scale, and the few remaining global merchants and retailers search for the best deal without national preferences (Quark 2013). The case of cotton production in Ethiopia demonstrates that foreign companies investing in certified cotton and textiles do not only stem from the EU and the United States (but also from Turkey and India, in particular). As we will discuss in chapters 4 and 5, companies logging timber illegally in countries of the Global South—for example, in the Democratic Republic of the Congo and Indonesia—are often based in but not necessarily supported by governments of the Global North (Fishman and Obidzinski 2014; Maryudi 2016).

3.4 Summary

To what extent has private regulation made a difference? Is this a viable alternative to multilateralism? Obviously, noble intentions behind private regulation, such as stopping forest decline and introducing a fair world trade order, have failed so far. Despite the hopes of certification advocates, green markets have not washed away contradictions between domestic governance priorities. Certified products are only offered in niches. Therefore, Swilling and Annecke (2012, 191) reject these initiatives as "minor adjustments" and not a viable option to address "blood consumption." Besides the limited outreach and producers' niche existence, certification has adverse effects by stealing movements' thunder. As corporate leaders have adopted voluntary mechanisms to avoid legal liability (Haufler 2003, 50), we can assume that this has effectively prevented stricter command and control types of regulation (Levy and Newell 2004). This affects, in particular, countries with weaker regulation—countries of the Global South. My study of cotton/textile certification and Ethiopia confirms such early considerations made in the literature.

In Ethiopia, NGOs such as PAN Ethiopia are upholding projects such as the organic cotton cooperative in Arba Minch, while in parallel Abiy Ahmed continues the conventional path of the developmental state and has lifted the ban on Bt cotton (Fikade 2018; Lefort 2012). NGOs do not aim to oppose the persistent enthusiasm for modern agriculture, including the use of pesticides and synthetic fertilizers in a country (Planel 2012; Partzsch, Zander, and Robinson 2019). We have seen hardly any international advances on social and environmental issues over the last two decades. In contrast, voluntary certification tends to legitimize the status quo, including the persistent resource flows from producer to consumer countries (Dauvergne 2018a; Levidow 2013). Therefore, many activists refuse certification schemes per se and demand more radical approaches instead (Hoskins 2014, 183; Swilling and Annecke 2012, 191). Although it may have been well-meaning, certification is hardly implemented in a satisfying way (Nygren 2015; Pattberg and Widerberg 2016). In 2018, after twenty-five years, Greenpeace International announced it would not renew its membership in the FSC, which has been pioneering private regulation at a global scale (Greenpeace International 2018; Cashore, Auld, and Newsom 2004, x). This decision reflects growing rejection of private regulation in the international NGO scene and a dynamic to return to state actors. With regard to cotton and textiles, a Greenpeace interviewee underlined the responsibility of states: "We think organic [EU Organic] is the best standard. The other standards might have some benefit in the short term, but we really believe that, if we want a transformation of the agriculture system, we need to work for the best standard possible. And . . . *governments need to put policies [in place]* to advance those production systems that are more beneficial for the environment" (RT, interview, November 3, 2017, emphasis added).

In sum, my research confirms that voluntary certification has been driven by political pressure, rather than market incentives. It offered an obvious possibility to circumvent GATT rules and prevent WTO sanctions in order to regulate production processes around the world—that is, outside the territory of the initiating state. However, the "procedural turn" (Gupta 2008) of private regulation on non-product-related process and production methods (npr-PPM) is only happening in niche markets. The uptake of voluntary schemes as a response to the withdrawal of the state has remained limited. In addition, this ultimately disadvantages producers from the Global South who effectively have no access to new, high-priced niche markets. While certification initiatives might be well-intended, labeling products can only improve social and environmental conditions for a limited number of suppliers in global chains. Certified niche markets hardly have the ability to outbalance an ever-growing economy with unequal settings and continuously mounting environmental externalities. Most businesses involved in international trade have been and still are accepting nonsustainable and illegal practices throughout their global supply chains.

4   The Return of the State

There is a new trend toward public supply-chain-related laws. These domestic laws demand information from import companies regarding the environmental and social circumstances of production in foreign countries (Bartley 2014; Sarfaty 2015). For example, companies face regulatory requirements regarding illegal logging in their supply chains when importing timber (products) to Australia, the EU, and the United States (Bartley 2014; Leipold et al. 2016). Following the US Dodd-Frank Act Section 1502, which has been threatened by the Trump administration, the EU also introduced mandatory due diligence checks on importers of tantalum, tin, tungsten, and gold (3T&G) to stop the financing of armed groups through the trade of these minerals, in particular in the Democratic Republic of the Congo (DRC). Conventional regulations often have implications for global supply chains, but only with these new laws have supply chains become the direct target of regulation (Sarfaty 2015, 427). Different from earlier supply chain laws (mainly anticorruption),[1] companies now need to report on an annual basis (Sarfaty 2015, 431).

In the United States, the Legal Timber Protection Act (LTPA), adopted in 2008, has already been applied to generate dissuasive penalties. For example, a Criminal Enforcement Agreement required Gibson Guitars to pay a fine of USD 350,000 in 2012 for importing illegally logged ebony from Madagascar (US Department of Justice 2012). In addition, Lumber Liquidators, the largest hardwood flooring retailer in the United States, had to pay a combined USD 13.2 million in 2015 for violations of the LTPA. The retailer imported flooring from China that was made from timber illegally harvested in Far Eastern Russia (US Department of Justice 2015).

For Bartley (2014; 2018, 258), mandatory import requirements represent a "re-centering of the state" that may potentially constrict private authority resulting from the increase of co- and self-regulating institutions since the 1990s (similar in Fishman and Obidzinski 2014; Montouroy 2016). In some sectors, such as food, certification has become a "normative obligation" (Kalfagianni 2015). However, in other sectors, such as mining, NGOs have been unable to acquire consumer pressure considerable enough for companies to commit to voluntary certification beyond singular efforts at the firm level (Hilson 2014; Bloomfield 2017). Furthermore, in the textile sector, if less than 20 percent of global cotton produced is grown under voluntarily stricter social and environmental conditions (BCI 2018), as seen in chapter 3, this means that 80 percent of cotton farming potentially harms the environment and exploits people in producing countries (Brooks 2015; Sneyd 2011).

Mandatory requirements apply to all companies. Unlike earlier voluntary schemes, support is now emerging not just through consumer preferences for ethical products, but also through binding trade legislation by governments of importing countries (Sarfaty 2015). However, in forestry, the regulatory content remains weaker than some private schemes, such as the Forest Stewardship Council (FSC) and Programme for the Endorsement of Forest Certification (PEFC), which aim for both the sustainability and the legality of timber production. In principle, under the supply-chain-related laws insisting on legality, deforestation could continue even if all logging was done legally (Fishman and Obidzinski 2014, 259). Moreover, countries might weaken their legislation in order to allow exporting companies to more easily fulfill the legality requirements of importing countries.

This chapter discusses power dynamics resulting from the return of the state with public supply-chain-related laws, especially in the fields of forestry and minerals. In the first part of the chapter, I introduce the public supply-chain-related laws on timber and minerals in more detail, followed by a discussion of their new mandatory character. Although the new regulations are public law, they are based on private auditing. This aspect is important in order to understand their impact in the Global South, including reactions of exporting countries' governments. This part of the chapter is based on document analysis and literature review.

The US conflict minerals requirements focus on the DRC. Therefore, in the second part of this chapter, the DRC serves as a case study for a more detailed discussion of supply-chain-related laws. The Congolese Civil Wars began in 1996 and brought about the end of Mobutu Sese Seko's authoritarian regime (1965–1997). The wars ultimately involved nine African countries, multiple groups of UN peacekeepers, and twenty armed groups and claimed the lives of an estimated five million people (Le Billion 2013; Radley and Vogel 2015). Armed confrontations have continued, especially in the eastern part of the country (UN Security Council 2017). In addition to reviewing the few studies on the impact on the extraction of timber and minerals in the DRC, I comprehensively analyzed available policy documents (especially by NGOs) and conducted seventeen semi-structured interviews with all types of stakeholders (public, industry, and NGO representatives) involved in international resource trade with the DRC.

Finally, in a third part of this chapter, I discuss the return of the state against the backdrop of power dynamics outlined in chapter 2: the withdrawal of the state in the era of globalization, asymmetries between Northern consumers and Southern producers, and normative or ethical power in IR. Although we can observe an ongoing struggle regarding the implementation of new public supply chain laws, there is evidence that they might be effective in preventing conflict financing in the DRC.

4.1 Background: Public Supply-Chain-Related Laws

The new public supply-chain-related laws are imposing transparency standards that permit holding import companies legally accountable for their activities abroad. The United States has been a frontrunner in the fields of both timber and minerals. Established in 1900, the Lacey Act places the burden on US manufacturers to prohibit the import, export, sale, acquisition, or purchase of certain protected or illegal wildlife, fish, and plants. In 2008, the US Legal Timber Protection Act (LTPA) amended the Lacey Act to include illegally logged timber. In 2010, the EU followed with the Timber Regulation (EUTR; EC 995/2010), and in 2012 Australia adopted the Illegal Logging Prohibition Act (ILPA; Bartley 2014; Leipold et al. 2016).[2] In the field of minerals, in 2010, the United States adopted the Dodd-Frank Act, of which Section 1502 requires mandatory due diligence on potential conflict minerals from the DRC (Sarfaty 2015; Radley and Vogel 2015), and in 2017, the EU followed again with a similar regulation (EC 2017/821; Partzsch 2018). However, in 2017, the US president signed a draft executive order to suspend the act, reviving a debate on the intentions and impact of supply chain regulation (Geenen 2017; Koch and Kinsbergen 2018).

In the timber sector, mandatory requirements for importers focus on legality verification, meaning importers are responsible for ensuring resource extraction complies with the legal requirements in the place of production. According to the stated rationales behind the laws, curbing the illegal exploitation indirectly hinders deforestation (Fishman and Obidzinski 2014, 259). The external involvement of the Australian, EU, and US governments is justified on the grounds that illegal logging presents challenges not only to the countries where it happens, but to the international community as well. Beyond damaging the local environment, illegal logging contributes to the approximately 20 percent of global carbon emissions for which deforestation and forest degradation are responsible, threatens biodiversity, and undercuts international development efforts (Fishman and Obidzinski 2014, 261). Illegal logging deprives governments of USD 15 billion in revenue per year (Montouroy 2016, 59). The import of timber harvested in contravention to the laws of the country of origin is hence prohibited, and companies face penalties in case of offense not only in the country of origin, but also in the importing country. In addition, the US LTPA requires companies to exercise "due care" and importers to submit a Lacey Declaration at the port of entry, while the EUTR and ILPA require due diligence to mitigate the risk that inventories contain illegal timber (Fishman and Obidzinski 2014, 258).

Due care is defined as "that degree of care which a reasonably prudent person would exercise under the same or similar circumstances" (Saltzmann 2010, 4). It is applied differently to diverse categories of people with varying degrees of knowledge and responsibility. Greater knowledge requires more care. Hence, due care has to be defined individually for each prosecution case (Leipold and Winkel 2016, 44). The EUTR, in comparison to the US LTPA, requires importers and domestic operators to have a defined due diligence system in place (Fishman and Obidzinski 2014, 262). A due diligence system must consist of three elements inherent to risk management: access to information, risk assessment, and mitigation of the risk identified (EUTR, Preamble 17 and Article 6).

The EU due diligence provision, which specifies how illegality is to be determined, is critical to actualizing the import ban: "Instead of having to rely on unlikely rulings by courts in timber-exporting countries, European courts can make use of other evidence in deciding whether timber entering the EU has been harvested legally" (Fishman and Obidzinski 2014, 264).

However, despite the general provision, due diligence is also interpreted differently within the legal profession of EU member states; one court may consider someone to have shown due diligence where another court would not (Hoare 2008, 2). In addition, member states have wide discretion to choose the form and severity of the penalties they will apply within their borders (Fishman and Obidzinski 2014, 263). For example, in Germany, operators have faced very few sanctions, and these sanctions were mostly in the form of minor civil penalty fines, with a maximum fine of EUR 50,000 (around USD 56,000)—compared to USD 13.2 million in the case of Lumber Liquidators for violations of the LTPA in the United States (Leipold 2017, 44).

In Australia, domestic producers of raw logs have no specific due diligence requirements, whereas it is required from domestic processors and importers (Australian Government 2012). Importers have to declare in written form whether or not due diligence has been undertaken for the respective good. Unlike the EU and US laws, however, the ILPA officially recognizes third-party-certification schemes to prove compliance.[3] Indonesia has asserted that the Australian law therefore violates WTO rules (Fishman and Obidzinski 2014, 265), but several Southeast Asian countries introduced their own legality verification schemes to allow their exporters to comply with the ILPA's provisions (Overdevest and Zeitlin 2014). In particular, China is developing a timber legality framework, also in response to the EU and US laws (Partzsch and Vlaskamp 2016, 981). In addition, several private schemes specializing in legal verification have emerged, including NGO initiatives, such as SmartWood, which was initiated in 1989 by the Rainforest Alliance, an international NGO, and transitioned to NEPCon (Nature Economy and People Connected), another nonprofit organization, in 2018 (Rainforest Alliance 2018).

In the field of minerals, supply-chain-related laws in both the EU and, for the first time, the United States prescribe due diligence; however, the two laws focus on mandatory reporting only (no legality verification). In contrast to timber laws, mineral laws address the problem of international trade financing armed groups in conflict regions (Callaway 2017, 4). Australian and also Chinese authorities published official guidelines on the matter (Australian Government 2015; OECD 2015). The stated rationale is that curbing the illegitimate exploitation of natural resources by state and nonstate armed groups indirectly hinders financing of the ongoing conflicts (Sarfaty 2015, 440). Although Section 1502 of the US Dodd-Frank

Act was passed in 2010, the Securities and Exchange Commission (SEC)[4] issued a final rule in 2012 following a long public comment period (Sarfaty 2015, 438). This provision became effective in 2013. It requires due diligence from importers of 3T&G, which find their way into medical equipment, phones, computers, cars, and jewelry. Companies registered with the SEC (including foreign issuers) need to ensure that 3T&G originating in the DRC or its bordering countries are not benefiting armed groups in the area. Section 1502 imposes penalties on companies for not reporting or complying in good faith. Liability is attached for any false or misleading statement (Sarfaty 2015, 439).

After the adoption of Section 1502 of the Dodd-Frank Act, the Organization for Economic Cooperation and Development (OECD) Due Diligence Guidance for Responsible Supply Chains of Minerals from Conflict-Affected and High-Risk Areas was adopted in 2011 and revised in 2013 and 2016. Like the EUTR, the guidance gives detailed instructions to extraction companies on how to mitigate the risk of buying conflict minerals. It incorporates a five-step, risk-based due-diligence procedure: (1) establish strong company management systems, (2) identify and assess risks in the supply chain, (3) design and implement a strategy to respond to identified risks, (4) carry out independent third-party audits of supply chain due diligence at identified points of the supply chain, and (5) report on supply chain due diligence (Sarfaty 2015).

The OECD guidance serves businesses as a formula for the implementation of Section 1502. However, in addition, nonstate actors, such as the Enough Project and Responsible Sourcing Network, have published best practices (Sarfaty 2015, 443), and several voluntary certification and auditing schemes emerged after the adoption of the Dodd-Frank Act (Manhart and Schleicher 2013). These schemes focus specifically on the financing of armed conflicts (in contrast to forest programs, which focus on sustainability and/or legality). An illustrative example is the Conflict-Free Smelter Program (CFSP), which was established after the adoption of Section 1502 in 2010, and in 2017 changed its name to the Responsible Minerals Assurance Process, the flagship program of the Responsible Minerals Initiative (RMI), after the adoption of the EU Conflict Minerals Regulation in the same year (RMI 2018).

The EU Conflict Minerals Regulation (EC 2017/821) requires due diligence from importers and smelters or refineries of minerals or metals, based on the OECD rules, from January 2021 on. It goes beyond Section 1502 of the Dodd-Frank Act by considering any high-risk area, rather than applying only to the DRC and its bordering states. However, in contrast to the US law, the EU regulation refers only to the import of raw materials, and it does not apply to products that include processed minerals or metals. Furthermore, while the US government requires businesses to shed light on the whole supply chain, the EU only obliges actors from the upstream part of the supply chain to report on their due diligence efforts. The upstream part encompasses suppliers from the extraction sites to the smelters and refiners, and most smelters and refiners are located outside Europe (RK, interview, October 24, 2015). In consequence, for example, European car producers only face obligations if they import raw minerals and metals themselves (and if they do not export their cars to the United States, in which case they would be subject to the Dodd-Frank Act). The car producers are off the hook if they import processed component products, such as doors and seats, and/or if they purchase raw minerals and metals from other companies (which are often invisible to final consumers and hence are unlikely to fear reputational damage from reporting about conflict finance). Besides that, the EU obligation includes importers of primary minerals only above certain volume thresholds (for example, 100 kg of gold, "unwrought or in semi-manufactured forms, or in powder form with a gold concentration of 99.5 percent or higher that has passed the refining stage"; see annex 1 of the regulation).

Although there are considerable differences between the timber and minerals sectors, as well as between the adopting countries, public supply chain laws have some features in common. Most importantly, they all include mandatory requirements for importers in order to address circumstances of resource extraction and production, especially in the Global South.

4.1.1   Mandatory Requirements for Importers

With the new public supply-chain-related laws, Australian, EU, and US public authorities (with presumably less corruption and stronger law enforcement) hold import companies liable for the circumstances of production upstream in the supply chains (in host countries with presumably weak legal institutions). Governments of import countries hence use importers to enforce norms, such as sustainability and peace, in third countries. Therefore, as the supply-chain-related laws do affect business not only domestically, but also on a global scale, they can be considered an innovative alternative to international law (Sarfaty 2015). At the same time, supply-chain-related laws signify a shift away from the prevailing model of voluntary (private) regulation (Sarfaty 2015, 419).

In order to comply with—or, rather, circumvent—WTO rules, the timber and mineral laws are formulated in a very sophisticated way. First, like voluntary certification, the legality requirements continue to rely on the principle of information disclosure (Haufler 2010). Importers have to trace the origin of their timber to guarantee law compliance. In the field of minerals, the new supply-chain-related laws do not go beyond this mandatory due diligence. There is no explicit prohibition on the import of conflict minerals to the EU and the United States, only an obligation to execute due diligence and to disclose the origins of the minerals used (Kim 2015). In consequence, almost 80 percent of SEC-registered companies in the United States admitted that they were unable to determine the country of origin, and only 1 percent could certify themselves conflict-free with certainty beyond reasonable doubt (in 2015; see Kim and Davis 2016). However, as already mentioned, the timber laws are based on a second "trick" by requiring *legality*, unlike earlier voluntary initiatives, such as the FSC and PEFC, that have guaranteed *sustainability* of timber products (see table 4.1). Thus the laws are not imposing their own substantive requirements on third countries but seeking to limit trade on the basis of foreign definitions of legality (Fishman and Obidzinski 2014, 265).

This focus on legality developed after the voluntary sustainability schemes had been established in the 1990s (Montouroy 2016, 59). One of the most significant early efforts was the World Bank's Forest Law Enforcement and Governance (FLEG) program. Launched in 2001, FLEG was comprised of regional processes in which governments joined together in making policy commitments, which they failed to implement (Fishman and Obidzinski 2014, 260). Building on the trend of curbing illegal logging, in 2003, the EU adopted the Forest Law Enforcement, Governance, and Trade Action Plan (FLEGT) and its associated bilateral Voluntary Partnership Agreements (VPAs; see Gereffi, Humphrey, and Sturgeon 2005; Gulbrandsen 2014). In this context, the EU propelled several tropical timber-exporting countries to negotiate VPAs. VPAs are bilateral agreements accompanied by EU aid to reform domestic policies in third countries. This entails drawing up a wide-ranging forestry code and a national forest program (NFP) through

Table 4.1
Timber legality verification and minerals certification

Scheme	Initiator	Year founded	Type of certification	Number of certified projects in DRC (world total)	Countries
Timber sustainability certification					
Forest Stewardship Council (FSC)	Greenpeace and WWF	1993 (chain of custody certification since 2004)	Forest management certification; chain of custody (CoC) certification	0 (1,630)	All
Programme for the Endorsement of Forest Certification (PEFC)	European forest industry	1999 (chain of custody certification since 2001)	Forest management certification; CoC certification	0 (19,800)	All
Timber legality verification					
CertiSource Legality Verification System (CLAS)	CertiSource	2007	Verification of legal origin (VLO); Verification of legal compliance (VLC); CoC	0 (16 sawmills)	Indonesia
GFS Legal Verification Service (LVS) and Wood Tracking Program (WTP)	Global Forestry Services	2004	Forest management and CoC	0 (137 LVS; 158 WTP)	China, Malaysia, Philippines

Table 4.1 (continued)

Scheme	Initiator	Year founded	Type of certification	Number of certified projects in DRC (world total)	Countries
Legal Harvest Verification (LHV)	Scientific Certification Systems (SCS)	2010	Forest management and legal harvest verification	0 (8)	Brazil, China, Indonesia, Singapore, Suriname
Origine et Légalité du Bois (OLB)	Eurocertifor (now part of Bureau Veritas Certification)	2004	Legality; forest management certification; CoC	0 (61)	Austria, Belgium, Cameroon, Cote D'Ivoire, France, Italy, the Netherlands, Republic of Congo, Spain, Switzerland, Tunisia, UAE, USA
NEPCon LegalSource Standard (LS)	NEPCon	2013	Legality; due diligence	0 (58)	Austria, Ecuador, Gabon, Indonesia, Ireland, Latvia, Lithuania, Malaysia, the Netherlands, Poland, Switzerland, UK
SmartWood	Rainforest Alliance (now managed by NEPCon)	Launched 1989; VLO and VLC developed 2007; transitioned to NEPCon 2018	VLO; VLC	N/A	N/A

Timber Legality & Traceability Verification (TLTV)	SGS	2005	VLO; VLC; Chain of custody (CoC)	N/A	Indonesia, Malaysia, Papua New Guinea, Republic of Congo, Cameroon, Democratic Republic of the Congo, Tanzania, Australia, Belgium, Canada, Czech Republic, Denmark, France, Germany, the Netherlands, Switzerland, UK, USA
Woodmark Forest Verification of Legal Compliance (FVLC)	Soil Association	2015	Due diligence system (DDS) and VLC	N/A	N/A
Minerals certification					
Aluminium Stewardship Initiative (ASI) Standards	Aluminium Stewardship Initiative	2009	Performance and chain of custody (CoC) certification for aluminium (upstream)	N/A (9)	Austria, Germany, Norway, Switzerland, UK*
Analytical Fingerprint (AFP)	German Federal Institute for Geosciences and Natural Resources (BGR)	2006	Proof of origin documentation for tin, tungsten, and tantalum (3T) shipments	N/A	Burundi, DRC, Rwanda
Better Sourcing Program (BSP)	Resource Consulting Services, Ltd.	2014	Upstream assurance and validation of 3T, gold, cobalt, and gemstones from mines	N/A (30)	DRC, Rwanda

Table 4.1 (continued)

Scheme	Initiator	Year founded	Type of certification	Number of certified projects in DRC (world total)	Countries
Certified Trading Chains (CTC) Standards Certification	German Federal Institute for Geosciences and Natural Resources (BGR)	2007	Traceability, transparency and responsible mining certification for 3T and gold (upstream)	N/A	DRC, Rwanda
Conflict-Free Gold Standard	World Gold Council	2012	Responsible and conflict-free mining assurance certification for gold (upstream)	N/A	Australia, Canada, Mexico, Peru, South Africa, Tanzania, USA*
Conflict-Free Tin Initiative (CFTI) (no longer exists)	Dutch Government	2012–2014	Conflict-free sourcing certification for tin (upstream)	N/A	DRC, Malaysia
CRAFT Code of the Alliance for Responsible Mining	Alliance for Responsible Mining, RESOLVE, European Partnership for Responsible Minerals (EPRM)	2018	Due diligence and transparency framework for artisanal and small-scale mining (ASM) of gold upstream and throughout the supply chain	N/A	Colombia (pilot project), plus coalition members in Peru, Guyana, Burkina Faso, Senegal
Fairmined Gold Standard	Alliance for Responsible Mining	2009	Traceability, assurance and sustainability standard for ASM gold and precious metals for producers and suppliers	N/A (10)	Colombia, Peru, Bolivia, Mongolia

Fairtrade Gold Standard	Alliance for Responsible Mining in partnership with the Fairtrade Labelling Organizations International (FLO)	2010	Responsible mining and due diligence certification for gold and precious metals with an emphasis on upstream ASM	N/A (3)	Kenya, Peru, Uganda
ICGLR Regional Certification Mechanism (RCM)	ICGLR Regional Initiative against the Illegal Exploitation of Natural Resources (RINR)	2002	Conflict-free mine and CoC certification for 3T and gold	N/A	Great Lakes Region (Burundi, DRC, Kenya, Rwanda, Tanzania, Uganda)
Initiative for Responsible Mining Assurance (IRMA)	Coalition of NGOs, businesses, industry groups, labor unions and communities	2006	Responsible mining certification at the mine site level (not commodity-specific)	N/A	Canada, Colombia, France, Germany, Mexico, the Netherlands, South Africa, UK, USA*
International Cyanide Management Code	UNEP and International Council on Metals and the Environment (ICME)	2002	Compliance certification for the manufacture and transport of cyanide used in gold mining and production	N/A (269)	51 countries worldwide including Burkina Faso, Cote D'Ivoire, French Guiana, Ghana, Kenya, Liberia, Namibia, Niger, Senegal, South Africa, Suriname, Tanzania
Responsible Gold Guidance	London Bullion Market Association	2012	Human rights and conflict due diligence threshold for gold refiners	N/A (70)	30 countries worldwide including China, Indonesia, South Korea, Mexico, South Africa, the Netherlands, USA

Table 4.1 (continued)

Scheme	Initiator	Year founded	Type of certification	Number of certified projects in DRC (world total)	Countries
Responsible Jewellery Council	Coalition of industry organizations and jewellery retailers	2005	Code of practices (CoP) and chain of custody (CoC) certification for full diamond, gold and platinum supply chains	N/A (787)	71 countries worldwide
Responsible Minerals Assurance Process (RMAP) (formerly Conflict-Free Smelter Program)	Responsible Business Alliance; the Global e-Sustainability Initiative (GeSI)	2009	Upstream assurance and validation for smelters and refiner management systems of 3T, gold, and cobalt, and audits for downstream companies	N/A (256)	37 countries worldwide including Bolivia, Brazil, Canada, Chile, China, India, Indonesia, Malaysia, South Africa, Turkey, USA
SA 8000	Social Accountability International (SAI), affiliate of the Council on Economic Priorities	1997	Multisector social certification standard for factories, organizations, and companies	N/A (3,996)	64 represented countries worldwide
Tin Supply Chain Initiative (iTSCi)	International Tin Research Institute	2009	Responsible sourcing compliance for 3T and other minerals for large and small companies throughout the supply chain	N/A (2,948)	Great Lakes Region (Burundi, DRC, Kenya, Rwanda, Tanzania, Uganda)

*Headquarter locations of members and/or certified bodies; does not include locations of subsidiary companies, mines, smelters, etc.
Source: Author's compilation based on information provided on the homepages of and in personal communications by the certification schemes.

cooperation with the FAO's Committee on Forestry (COFO), as well as a clarification of legal forest practices and the institution of approved monitoring authorities with EU technical and funding support (Fishman and Obidzinski 2014, 260; Montouroy 2016, 70).

Furthermore, the 2005 FLEGT regulation established a licensing scheme that enabled countries to enter into VPAs with the EU, under which timber products can only be exported to the EU with a valid license issued by the country of origin (Fishman and Obidzinski 2014, 260). However, different from the later timber-supply-chain-related laws, only illegal timber from VPA partner countries could be excluded, and countries feared competitive disadvantages through compliance costs associated with entering VPAs. Countries without strict regulation and without a need for licenses continued to be more attractive to the timber industry (Fishman and Obidzinski 2014, 260). Only the 2010 EUTR, which followed the 2008 US LTPA, changed the rules of the game for EU timber importers. Because importers to those countries that adopted new timber laws are now exposed to the risk of penalty if found to be in violation of the ban on illegal timber or their due care/diligence obligations, countries that carry this risk of illegality become less attractive (Partzsch and Vlaskamp 2016, 981). Currently, Cameroon, Central African Republic, Ghana, Indonesia, Liberia, and the Republic of the Congo are implementing and Côte d'Ivoire, the Democratic Republic of the Congo, Gabon, Guyana, Honduras, Laos, Malaysia, Thailand, and Vietnam are negotiating VPAs with the EU (EU FLEGT 2018). However, there is some controversy regarding how serious governments of both exporting and importing countries are about implementation and enforcement. For instance, though there is increasing recognition that legality verification is overstraining the Indonesian national government, the EU cannot terminate the VPA for diplomatic reasons (MB, interview, August 16, 2018).

Sarfaty (2015) evaluates the first set of conflict minerals reports submitted to the SEC in 2014. Her sample consisted of nearly one thousand reports submitted in mid-2014. She studied the level of due diligence measures that companies have reported in their disclosures by checking whether companies fulfilled the different steps of the OECD Due Diligence Guidance and best practices outlined by the Enough Project and Responsible Sourcing Network. In addition, expert interviews and participatory observations helped her understand the effects of Section 1502 on corporate behavior toward supply chain transparency. Her results show a high level of weak and moderate due diligence (437). While the profitability of a company was statistically insignificant, companies delivered better reports if they had brand strength and/or participated in voluntary certification programs in parallel (446). In particular, reference to the CSFI (now renamed RMI) facilitated better compliance (447). Also, Sarfaty's results (448) suggest that large companies are more likely to perform better. For them, disclosure mitigates potential risks and enhances a company's reputation among consumers, investors, and NGOs (Hilson 2014; Sarfaty 2015, 459).

Experience from other sectors shows that the perception among enforcement officials is that there has been a substantial improvement in the quality of information reported over time (Hoare 2008, 5). Furthermore, as Sarfaty's (2015) results also indicate, there has not been any pronounced negative impact on the competitiveness of domestic businesses resulting from due diligence requirements because of the importance of other factors (e.g., level of service; Hoare 2008, 6). To the contrary, some companies see supply-chain-related laws benefitting their business from both efficiency and stability standpoints (Callaway 2017, 9). To this point, a business representative explained: "We believe [the EUTR] has a positive effect on companies getting certified and making more sure they now know where the wood they use is coming from" (UL, interview, September 29, 2017). Improved guidance, training, and information are particularly key for small businesses, which often do not have sufficient resources to keep abreast of new legislation and for which the costs of training and implementation are particularly high (Hoare 2008, 6).

However, businesses still feel the costs can be considerable (Hoare 2008, 5). In the case of the EUTR and the VPA with Indonesia, compliance costs for companies are estimated to be between USD 6,120 and 10,200, in addition to a complex administrative process that exceeds the management capacity of most small timber enterprises (Fishman and Obidzinski 2014, 260). In the case of the EU Conflict Minerals Regulation, compliance costs were estimated at USD 3–4 billion up front, and USD 200 million per year thereafter (European Commission 2014). Against this backdrop, an interviewee who represented European business warned of economic disadvantages: "You want to be the leader in sustainability and human rights and the other areas but, at the same time, you cannot jeopardize the competitive advantages of your own industry. . . . From our [European business] perspective involving the downstream into the regulation doesn't really add value because . . . you have to spend a lot of money on compliance" (SK, interview, November 20, 2015).

Koch and Kinsbergen (2018) assume that companies hoped to reduce compliance costs by intentionally promoting narratives about the negative unintended effects of the new minerals supply chain laws, without conveying the full story. Besides reviewing the academic literature, the authors analyzed the narratives used by major international journals and magazines, such as the *New York Times*, *Foreign Policy*, and the *Washington Post*. In addition, they studied primary data on actual mineral exports and military and rebel activity that was gathered from the Congolese Ministry of Mines and independent research institutes, such as IPIS Research in Belgium. They also reviewed a total of 281 comments that the SEC received when it launched the public comment period in early 2017. This analysis allows the two scholars to highlight how the situation in the DRC improved, despite the narrative of some actors regarding negative side-effects remaining the same.

4.1.2   Private Auditing to Fulfill Compliance

There is no doubt that domestic regulations on supply chains pose a unique compliance challenge to companies because these laws operate extraterritorially. Importers are more than just regulated entities; they impose standards on their third-party sources in other countries (Sarfaty 2015, 421). While timber is frequently exported to the EU or the United States as raw material (Montouroy 2016, 63), there are often seven or eight layers in the minerals supply chain between the original artisanal mine and the final consumer product (Sarfaty 2015, 431). Most electronic products, which always contain minerals, are channeled through China before reaching Western markets (Brühlhart Banyiyezako, August 26, 2015; Wellesley 2014). For these products, the supply chain can easily be fifty tiers deep, and importers had hardly any information on them when first confronted with US Dodd-Frank Act Section 1502 in 2010 (Sarfaty 2015, 431). Section 1502 directly requires due diligence from only about one thousand companies (Sarfaty 2015, 439), but it indirectly affects thousands of suppliers of these companies, including 150,000 to 200,000 European companies that have upstream minerals suppliers in the DRC area and downstream customers that export to the United States (European Commission 2014).

Therefore, most importers are overburdened with monitoring and enforcing compliance themselves, and they outsource compliance to third parties such as consulting firms or suppliers that audit the tiers of suppliers below them. So, again, we find an outsourcing of regulation to private certification schemes, as discussed in chapter 3.

In the field of timber, private sustainability schemes aligned their standards with the timber supply chain laws. The FSC has revised its controlled timber standard, developed for non-FSC-certified material used in FSC Mix products, to make it consistent with the new laws and to ensure that FSC certification meets the mandatory legality requirements (Gulbrandsen 2014, 87–88). In addition, several private systems of legal verification emerged after the adoption of the new laws, including Certisource Legality Verification System (CLAS) by Certisource, GFS Legal Verification Service (LVS) and Wood Tracking Program (WTP) by Global Forestry Services, Legal Harvest Verification (LHV) by Scientific Certification Systems (SCS), NEPCon LegalSource (LS) Standard by Nature Economy and People Connected (NEPCon), Origine et Légalité du Bois (OLB [Origin and Legality of Wood]) by Bureau Veritas (BV), SmartWood managed by NEPCon, Timber Legality & Traceability Verification (TLTV) by SGS, and Woodmark Forest Verification of Legal Compliance (FVLC) by the Soil Association (see table 4.1; Proforest 2011). Although these private initiatives can only guarantee protection from prosecution in Australia, they also serve EU and US timber importers by limiting the risk of illegal timber entering into the supply chain (Gulbrandsen 2014, 76).

SmartWood differentiates between two components of compliance: Verification of Legal Origin (VLO) and Verification of Legal Compliance (VLC) services for the sourcing of raw timber (Rainforest Alliance 2018). VLO verifies that timber comes from a known and licensed source and that the entity that carried out the harvest had a documented legal right to do so. VLC expands upon the basic component of VLO by verifying that timber harvesting and other relevant management activities in the forest where it was harvested comply with all applicable and relevant laws and regulations, including forest management, environment, labor and welfare, and health and safety requirements. VLO also requires compliance with legislation related to relevant taxes and royalties. Tenure or use rights for land and resources that may be affected by timber harvest rights must also be respected, in addition to compliance with requirements for trade and export procedures, including the Convention on International Trade in Endangered Species of Wild Fauna and Flora (CITES; Proforest 2011, 3; Rainforest Alliance 2018). SmartWood VLO is only allowed for a maximum of three years, at which point VLC must be achieved (this is decided on a case-by-case basis). VLC is likewise potentially only allowed for three years, at which point forest sustainability certification, such as FSC, should be sought (also decided on a case-by-case basis; Proforest 2011, 2).

Similarly, CertiSource's policy is to offer legality verification for a period of up to two years, at which point commitment to achieve FSC certification is required (Proforest 2011, 2). SCS emphasizes that the LHV is "a tangible first step toward a more comprehensive environmental and social responsibility standard such as FSC Forest Management or FSC Chain of Custody" (SCS Global Services 2018), and BV Certification, which was created by OLB, also offers FSC and PEFC certification to timber (processing) companies (BV 2018). Private auditing hence helps timber companies to fulfill mandatory requirements while channeling companies into private sustainability certification at the same time. These dynamics explain why voluntary timber certification continues to rise despite mandatory requirements only on legality in the sector (FSC 2019; PEFC 2018).

In the field of minerals, in contrast to timber, global standards of sustainability certification did not precede the mandatory requirements. Instead, while there were more ambitious efforts in response to social activism at the firm level (Bloomfield 2017), minerals certification has consistently focused only on transparency (Hilson 2014). However, after the adoption of Section 1502 of the US Dodd-Frank Act, private actors started to develop certification standards and sourcing initiatives that have aimed for conflict-free minerals extraction (see table 4.1; see Partzsch and Vlaskamp 2016). In 2011, a working group of companies, mostly members of the Electronic Industry Citizen Coalition and the Global e-Sustainability Initiative, formed the Conflict-Free Smelter Program (CFSP, now the Responsible Minerals Assurance Process [RMAP]). RMAP and the Responsible Minerals Initiative (RMI) use an independent third-party audit to identify smelters and refiners that have systems in place to ensure they source only conflict-free materials. The audit standard is based on the previously mentioned OECD Due Diligence Guidance (RMI 2018).

Alongside such general initiatives, there are resource-specific certification schemes, such as the Conflict-Free Tin Initiative (CFTI). Under the

CFTI, from 2012 to 2014, the Dutch government financed "best practice" upstream suppliers by working with mines in the DRC and Malaysia (CFTI 2018). As a direct result of the CFTI, in 2013, Philips arranged the production of fluorescent lamps containing Congolese conflict-free tin; the same year, the Fairphone company was founded in Amsterdam (*Sustainable Leader* 2014). Fairphone developed a mobile device that does not contain any conflict minerals and has "fair" labor conditions for the workforce along the supply chain. Conflict-free sourcing is guaranteed through cooperation with mines in the Eastern DRC (Fairphone 2017).

Fairphone has received a lot of public attention and sold more than one hundred thousand smartphones in its first three years of existence (Fairphone 2017). Again, however, different from the field of timber (see chapter 3), pioneers in the field of minerals do not aim for sustainability and fair trade, but only to avoid financing armed groups in conflict areas: "We are not a 100 percent fair phone. We are basically a movement aiming to include fair principles as much as possible in the making of the devices, but we are far from being completely 'fair' as there are millions of social and environmental issues in electronic supply chains to be addressed. It is really a step-by-step thing" (Laura Gerritsen from Fairphone, interview, October 29, 2015).

In sum, in the fields of both timber and minerals, we can observe the emergence of new voluntary schemes that respond to public requirements, especially in the EU and United States. Sarfaty (2015, 451–452), however, notes that "one wonders how much coordination or rather competition is actually occurring among the plethora of standards, initiatives, and certification providers." The various mineral standards are at odds over the definition of sustainability, legality, and precluded armed groups. For instance, RMI does not allow any armed groups to be present at mine sites, including state armed groups. By contrast, the industry-driven International Tin Research Institute (ITRI) Tin Supply Chain initiative (iTSCi) allows the presence of public and private security forces (including state armed groups) at a mine site, on the condition that they are not violating human rights (Sarfaty 2015, 453). For the field of minerals, Sarfaty (2015, 436) criticizes a "chain of outsourcing, involving layers of monitoring and enforcement, and often competing systems of incentive" that diminishes the impact of new public supply-chain-related laws in the Global South.

4.1.3 Impact in the Global South

Bartley (2018, 258) considers the return of the state to be an opportunity for more "place-conscious transnational governance." How to interpret and implement supply-chain-related laws on the ground is a major obstacle for affected companies, though. The more tiers a supply chain has and the less regulated the producing country of production, the more difficult it is for importers to implement the new laws (Montouroy 2016, 75; Sarfaty 2015, 424–425). While in the past companies may have been tempted to shift supply chains away from regulated regions (Sarfaty 2015, 433), mandatory due diligence requirements incentivize companies to source from "safe" countries, rather than high-risk areas that require more excessive due diligence requirements. In consequence, some critics claim that there is a "de facto effect of restricting trade" (Fishman and Obidzinski 2014, 266) or, in the case of the US Dodd-Frank Act, a "de facto embargo on mineral trade in the DRC" (Jeffrey 2012, 503–504; for a critical evaluation of the promotion of this narrative, see Koch and Kinsbergen 2018).

In the field of timber, the impact of regulation on developing countries is similar to that of voluntary certification. While compliance costs are high for all affected companies, they tend to disproportionally burden producers in the Global South, especially smallholders (McDermott, Irland, and Pacheco 2015). On paper, the ban on illegal timber and the due diligence requirements apply equally to imported and domestic timber. But, in application, timber harvested in Europe and the United States receives less scrutiny than imported timber, particularly if the latter originates in areas with high levels of illegal logging, such as the DRC or Indonesia: "On the one hand, this risk assessment criterion applies to all timber, and no additional due diligence requirements adhere to timber found to come from areas identified as being at high risk of illegality. On the other hand, timber from high risk areas may nonetheless experience de facto discrimination given that operators may hesitate to deal in such timber, which could reduce the timber's marketability even if it is in fact legal" (Fishman and Obidzinski 2014, 266).

Timber-exporting countries have indicated their displeasure with the new supply-chain-related laws. Members of the Asia-Pacific Economic Cooperation have agreed to a nonbinding accord to isolate the United States and Australia in retaliation for their illegal logging laws (Fishman and Obidzinski 2014, 265). The timber trade is lucrative, valued at over USD 150 billion per year. Some countries' gross domestic products (GDPs) are particularly tied to timber: in 2006, the forestry sector's contributions to the GDPs of the Central African Republic, Liberia, and the Solomon Islands were, respectively, 11.1 percent, 16.7 percent, and 17.7 percent. Compliance costs burden these countries' timber industries (Fishman and Obidzinski 2014, 260).

In the field of minerals, the US Dodd Frank Act Section 1502 focused exclusively on the DRC and its neighboring states. The stated rationale behind this law was to specifically cut arms-financing activities through the trade in minerals in this region (Sarfaty 2015, 440). In addition to concerns about high compliance costs, there are controversial discussions about whether the US law has improved the local human rights situation or hindered the economic development of the conflict region (Sarfaty 2015, 440; Koch and Kinsbergen 2018). As mentioned earlier, almost 80 percent of SEC-registered companies fulfilled mandatory requirements by simply reporting that they were unable to determine the country of origin (Kim and Davis 2016). Many scholars argue that to comply with the Dodd-Frank Act, it is easiest for US businesses not to import 3T&G originating in the African Great Lakes Region at all as minerals mined from outside the DRC and adjoining countries do not submit to the strict guidelines of Section 1502 (Jeffrey 2012; Manhart and Schleicher 2013). However, in my interviews, business representatives denied having refrained from importing from the DRC and demonstrated they were aware of the problem: "We do not want to boycott the local producers because, that way, you are destroying the local economy. People working in mining who might not have been involved in the conflict financing will lose jobs and lose incomes" (SK, interview, November 20, 2015).

Similar to the timber sector, compliance costs tend to disproportionally burden artisanal and small-scale miners (Hilson 2014; Radley and Vogel 2015), while Western companies, especially large ones, are able to potentially turn compliance into a competitive advantage (Sarfaty 2015, 448). In consequence, scholars have argued that the new public supply-chain-related laws in the fields of both timber and minerals are helping more affluent and capable suppliers to create new exclusive markets at the expense of the most vulnerable local actors in the Global South (Radley and Vogel 2015; McDermott, Irland, and Pacheco 2015).

4.2   Country Study: Conflict Resources and the DRC

The US Dodd-Frank Act focuses on the DRC (see figure 4.1). The DRC is also highly relevant for the new timber-supply-chain-related laws. While the UN estimates that organized crime in the DRC derived USD 40–120 million from gold, USD 7.5–22.6 million from 3T minerals, and USD 14.3–28 million from diamonds per annum, rebels may also have earned USD 16–48 million from timber and USD 12–35 from charcoal sales (UNEP-MONUSCO-OSESG 2015, 3–4). In particular, the Allied Democratic Forces (ADF), an Islamist

Figure 4.1
The DRC on map of Africa

rebel group proactive in North Kivu province with links to the Somali militant Islamist organization Al-Shabaab, is recorded to finance its activities through sales of conflict timber (Lawson 2014, 6). The UN Security Council (2003, 2016) has repeatedly called upon the international community to create appropriate institutions to control resource exploitation in the DRC. Currently, twenty thousand UN troops are present in the country (Sarfaty 2015, 452). At the same time, president Joseph Kabila has refused to cede power to a democratically elected successor within the timeframe mandated by the Congolese constitution (Callaway 2017, 9).

4.2.1 Conflict Resources from the DRC

The DRC is one of the world's richest countries in terms of natural resources, holding 70 percent of the world's coltan, a third of its cobalt and diamond reserves, and a tenth of its copper (Winter 2006). Forests cover an area of around one million hectares, which is more than half of the country's massive land area (Lawson 2014, 5). In 2016, the DRC officially exported 244.42 kg of gold, but real figures exceed these statistics (UN Security Council 2017, 23). Most of the gold went to Dubai (UN Security Council 2017, 2). Regarding timber, the DRC exports around five hundred thousand cubic meters per year (EU FLEGT 2018). In 2000, 100 percent of DRC's timber exports went to the EU (see figure 4.2), and until 2007, more than 90 percent of the DRC's timber exports were still destined for the EU. However, this proportion has since declined. In 2012, only 40 percent of timber exports went to the EU, and 40 percent went to China (Greenpeace Africa 2013, 10; Lawson 2014, 5). Immediately after the adoption of the EUTR, the exports to China increased from 57,500 tons (USD 33.2 million) in 2010 to 85,200 tons (USD 57.9 million) in 2011. They decreased again to 37,900 tons (USD 21.8 million) in 2016, while exports further dispersed to other Asian countries and Uganda (see figure 4.2). At least 10 percent is exported to neighboring countries (Lawson 2014, 24). There are rumors that, in addition to these exports, large volumes of illegally harvested timber from the Eastern DRC are smuggled to neighboring countries and further exported to China (Lawson 2014, 23). Similarly, China has become a bottleneck for the minerals-processing industry (SK, interview, November 20, 2015). While the timber and minerals processing capacities of the DRC itself tend to be limited, no official data is available for processed exports (Lawson 2014, 11).

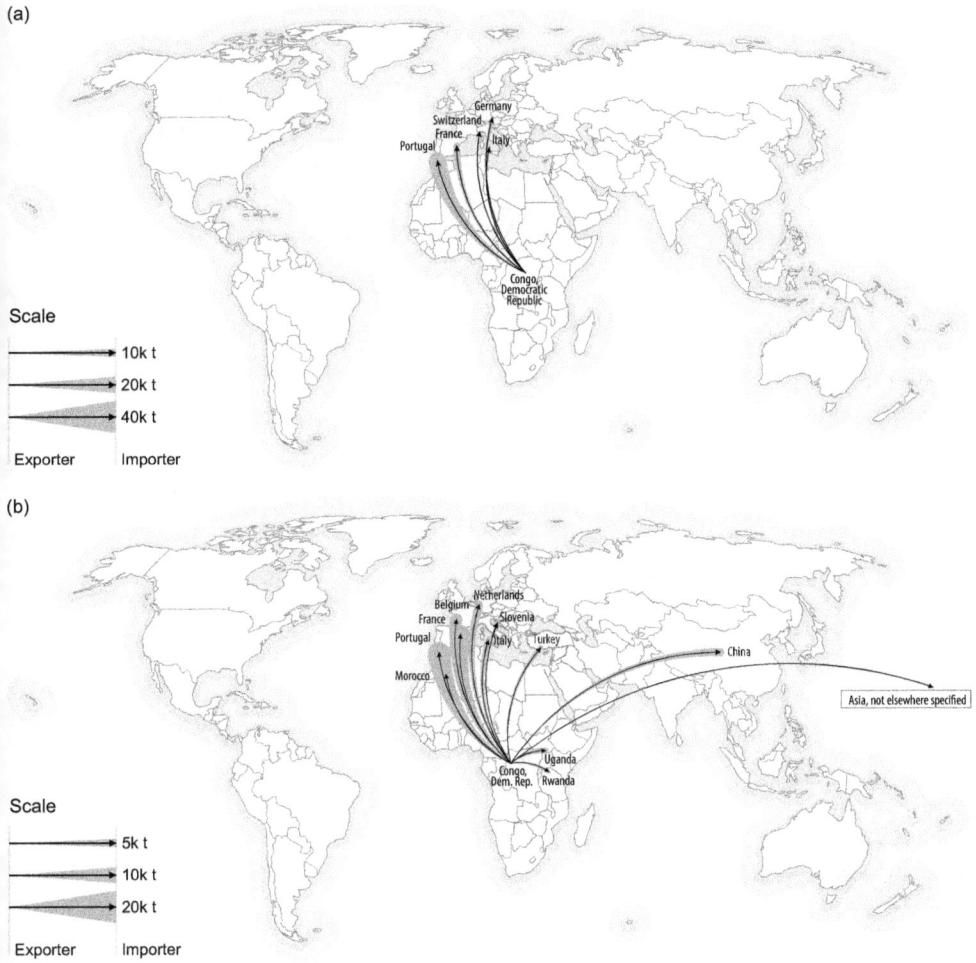

(a)

(b)

Figure 4.2
Timber (lumber and sawn wood) exports from the DRC in (a) 2000, (b) 2010, (c) 2011, and (d) 2016. *Source:* Chatham House 2019.

(c)

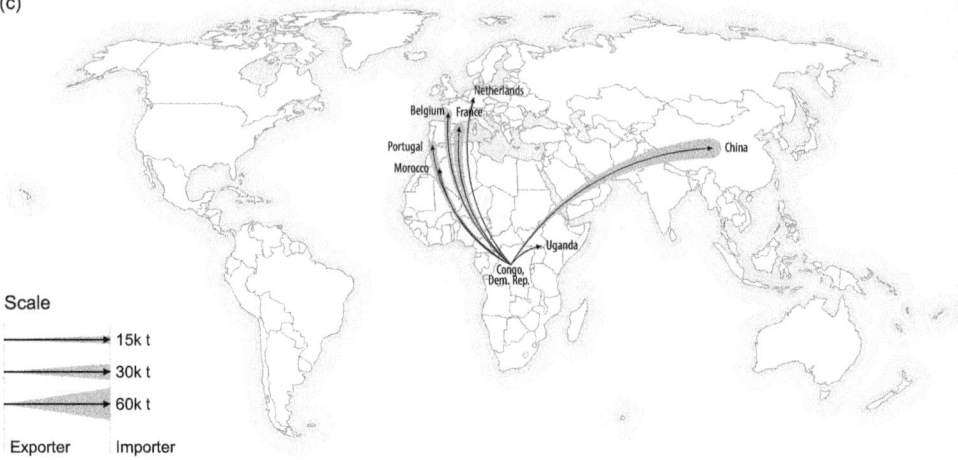

Scale

——————▶ 15k t

——————▶ 30k t

——————▶ 60k t

Exporter   Importer

(d)

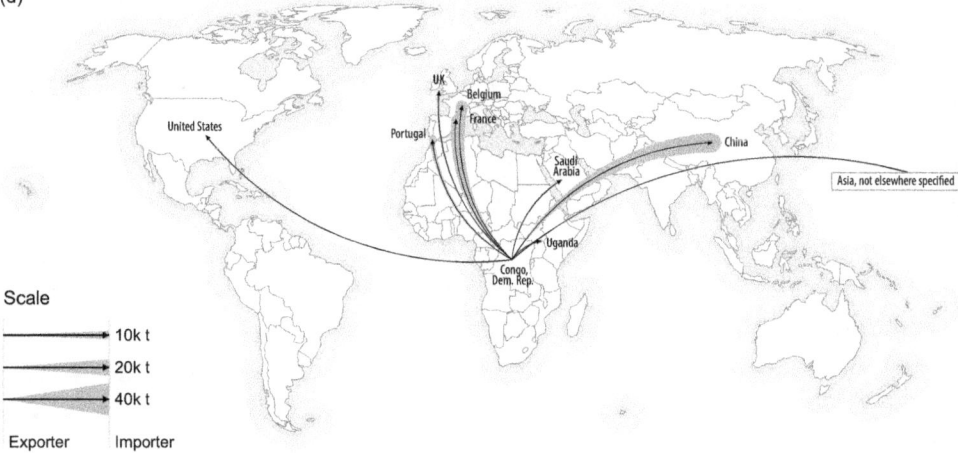

Scale

——————▶ 10k t

——————▶ 20k t

——————▶ 40k t

Exporter   Importer

Figure 4.2 (continued)

There is disagreement and a lack of clarity over how to map both minerals and timber sources in the DRC. The chaos of the Mobutu decades and
the failure to invest in infrastructure has meant that, up until now, relatively little of the DRC's forests have been industrially exploited (Counsell
2006, 7–8; Sarfaty 2015, 453). There is certainty, however, that the DRC has
the highest rate of forest degradation in the Congo Basin, with almost half
a million hectares of forest currently being lost each year (Lawson 2014, 6).
The adverse consequences are significant and widely felt, and include the

disruption of hydrological cycles, a reduction in biodiversity, and a contribution to rising atmospheric levels of greenhouse gases (Lawson 2014, 6). The DRC forests have spurred a high level of global interest due to a range of public good benefits, including weather-regulating services, habitat for biota, and sinks for carbon (Greenpeace Africa 2013). At the same time, some thirty-five million people (70 percent of the national population) depend on the forests for their livelihoods, especially Bantu farming people and Pygmy hunter-gatherers (around five hundred thousand people; see Counsell 2006, 7–8; Lawson 2014, 5).

Since the signing of peace accords in 2003, the international community has quickly moved to rebuild the country's political institutions and economy, and particularly to encourage foreign investment. In the field of timber, there have been major revisions to laws and regulations governing logging in the DRC, under pressure from, and with the assistance of, international donors. These efforts include a moratorium on new industrial logging permits since 2002 (Greenpeace Africa 2013, 2; REM 2013, 17).

The 2002 Forest Code sets out the basic framework for the DRC government's forest policy, specifically on forest ownership and user rights. However, there are several contradictions between this code and other relevant legislation, including laws governing oil and gas, water, mining, and agriculture. In particular, there are inconsistencies between the Forest Code and the 2006 Constitution with regard to the level of decentralization (Lawson 2014, 10). In addition, the Forest Code broadly recognizes the customary and traditional use rights of local and indigenous communities, but the lack of clarity over customary land rights has led to regular conflicts between communities over who has the authority to sign agreements (Lawson 2014, 11; REM 2013, 14). Furthermore, the Forest Code does not modify the 1973 Land Law and continues to assert state ownership over all areas of forest. It also broadly defines certain categories of forest as being for "(industrial) exploitation," "community use," and "conservation" (Counsell 2006, 11). Under the code, forestry concessions of up to five hundred thousand hectares can be granted, but not sold, rented, or exchanged. However, the operator of the land has the right to exploit all timber (Counsell 2006, 12). "Concessions" are subject to various stipulations set out in the code (Counsell 2006, 12). The total area of logging concessions fell from more than forty million hectares in 2000 to fewer than twelve million hectares a decade later (Lawson 2014, 6).

Nearly 90 percent of logging in the country is estimated to be illegal or informal (Lawson 2014, 2). Illegal artisanal permits are being used to circumvent the 2002 moratorium on new industrial logging permits. Ninety-four percent of these are allocated to companies (and not private individuals) in violation of the regulations (Greenpeace Africa 2013, 2; REM 2013, 13). Existing official maps of forest concessions do not take into account often complex user situations—in particular, parallel usage of areas by (Bantu) farming people and (Pygmy) hunter-gatherers (Counsell 2006). Artisanal loggers can only operate in local community forests on the basis of a written agreement or logging contract with these communities. As the boundaries of these local community forests are based primarily on habitual use, the communities' customary ownership is often imprecise. Hence, boundaries are a regular cause of dispute among different communities when trying to establish the person who has authority to sign agreements with artisanal loggers. Moreover, this issue is at the root of numerous intercommunal conflicts (REM 2013, 19).

Artisanal timber producers and traders largely fly under the radar in the whole region, and scholars see a clear need for policies and legal frameworks that incorporate their activities (Cerutti et al. 2018). However, Greenpeace (2013) finds that, though artisanal logging is a major problem, the worst offenders are TNCs that illegally use artisanal permits (Greenpeace Africa 2013, 4). Moreover, authorized felling volumes are not being respected, wood is not being properly marked, and quarterly production statements are not being submitted within the given timeframe (if at all; REM 2013, 17). Companies seldom pay taxes (permit tax, logging tax, reforestation tax; Greenpeace Africa 2013; REM 2013, 17), and if they do, they are extremely low and hardly ever reach local communities due to corruption (Counsell 2006, 19). Only considering legally harvested timber (10 percent of the timber harvest), it is estimated that at least USD 3.4 million in assessed taxes went uncollected in 2010 (representing 28 percent of all amounts due) and USD 1 million (7 percent of amounts due) in 2011. These discrepancies are arising from the government not invoicing the full amounts due, rather than companies failing to pay them (Lawson 2014, 17).

Although regulation requires that each logging concession is visited at least four times per year, very few visits actually take place, meaning that most concessions go unmonitored (Lawson 2014, 14). Furthermore, most enforcement officers are based in cities, many miles away from the logging concessions that they are meant to be monitoring (REM 2013, 20). Moreover, the quantitative distribution of permits by the Ministère de l'Environnement, Conservation de la Nature et Tourisme (Ministry of the Environment, Nature Conservation and Tourism [MECNT]) is not proportional to the forested land of a province (REM 2013, 19).

Based on data from the MENCT, Lawson (2014, 16) identified 255 illegal logging cases filed during 2012, of which only two (less than 1 percent) resulted in prosecution. Both cases involved companies to which artisanal logging licenses were issued illegally. Lawson (2014, 15) states that it is not clear what the other 253 cases were for or why they were not prosecuted. Enforcement officers often prefer not to send litigation files to court, allegedly so that they can retain control over the follow-up to the case. Thus, they demand that the offenders pay out-of-court fines directly. This practice, "akin to corruption" (REM 2013, 24), is in complete violation of the existing law. Even if prosecuted, however, penalties are usually below the value of the timber illegally harvested due to a lack of methodology for calculating damages in the DRC (Lawson 2014, 15; REM 2013, 25).

While the FSC and PEFC systems are only sparsely implemented in the Global South in general (Chan and Pattberg 2008), currently neither scheme has a single certified project in the DRC (FSC 2019). Greenpeace Africa (2013, 4) reported a 2011 case in which SIFORCO, a Swiss-owned company at the time, held FSC concessions (issued by SGS) while being involved in illegal logging activities in the country (see also REM 2013, 24–25). SIFORCO and SODEFOR are the DRC's two largest logging companies, which accounted for 60 percent of the industrial concession harvest in 2011 (Lawson 2014, 19). In response to Greenpeace's complaints, the FSC conducted several investigations and agreed with Greenpeace (FSC 2019). The FSC completely withdrew from the DRC after this complaint case, but the PEFC has widened its support to the country since 2011. The latter aims to promote uptake of forest certification in Central Africa—but without any realized certification in the DRC so far (PEFC 2018).

Utilizing donor funding, the international verification company SGS started to implement a new independent chain of custody system in the DRC in 2010 (Lawson 2014, 12). In addition, the World Resources Institute (WRI), an international NGO, has partnered with the DRC Ministry of Environment & Sustainable Development (MEDD) to develop an interactive forest map (WRI 2018). Lawson (2014, 18) reports that 8 percent of DRC timber is verified as legal (and none as sustainable by the FSC or PEFC). These legality verifications were issued only to SIFORCO and SODE-FOR. However, this timber cannot be considered risk-free, as the previously mentioned case of FSC disapproval demonstrates (Lawson 2014, 19).

With regard to minerals, state authorities themselves are sometimes responsible for perpetrating violence and hindering the mapping of mining sources (Sarfaty 2015, 452; UN Security Council 2017, 2). Despite emerging industrial production, much of the mineral production and trade is still artisanal and not formalized (i.e., small-scale mines run by independent miners not employed by a mining company), without consideration of any labor or environmental standards (de Haan and Geenen 2016; Sarfaty 2015, 453). It can be extremely dangerous, pose safety risks to women and children in particular, and have greater propensity to involve criminal networks and armed groups as traders, beneficiaries, or overseers (Callaway 2017, 19). Unlike the field of timber, voluntary certification initiatives are particularly active in the DRC. There are several in-region sourcing initiatives that are concurrently trying to track and monitor minerals from mine to smelter due to the specific geographical focus of the US Dodd-Frank Act Section 1502 (Callaway 2017; Sarfaty 2015, 452). The Responsible Minerals Initiative (RMI) lists many companies as members who are sourcing in the DRC (RMI 2018). Also, Fairphone runs two mines in the DRC (Tin mine, Tin ore, N2, Kalehe, and Tantalum mine, Tantalum ore, Numbi, as of February 2017).[5] Although local governments lack the capacity to curb violence, cross-border smuggling, and corruption (Sarfaty 2015, 452), clearly there is an emerging number of private and international initiatives working on the issue of conflict resources in the DRC. This is a major difference from the field of timber.

4.2.2   Reactions of the DRC and Neighboring Countries

When the new supply-chain-related laws in the fields of both timber and minerals were adopted in 2008, 2010, and 2012, and in 2010 and 2017, respectively, there was an immediate response by the exporting countries. In particular, VPA negotiations between the DRC and the EU started immediately after the adoption of the EUTR (EU FLEGT 2018). In the field of minerals, in response to the US Dodd-Frank Act, the DRC government has required exporters to exercise due diligence in accordance with OECD Guidance. Noncompliance with OECD Guidance has been sanctioned with the suspension of trading licenses (Manhart and Schleicher 2013, 30).

Regarding the DRC-EU VPA negotiations, the process was halted between September 2011 and August 2012 for a number of reasons. With a significant delay, the EU and the DRC validated the first two of the six principles of the legality definition in 2014 (EU FLEGT 2018). The DRC struggles to fulfill the EU's demands. The most significant obstacles to signing an agreement are related to the institutional and legal context of transitional arrangements that contradict the 2002 Forest Code (REM 2013, 33–34).

As outlined earlier, 40 percent of DRC timber continues to be exported to the EU, while a further 40 percent goes to China (see the maps in figure 4.2; Greenpeace Africa 2013, 10; Lawson 2014, 5). If timber is processed in China and then continues to be exported to the EU or the United States, importers also have to fulfill due diligence (or due care) requirements. In response, China has "made considerable progress towards tackling the trade in illegal timber" (Wellesley 2014, 22) and, among other measures, is working on a national timber legality verification system (Partzsch and Vlaskamp 2016). However, reports consider it unlikely that any of the timber production in the DRC could meet EU due diligence requirements (Lawson 2014, 2). Although in a 2014 Chatham House survey 80 percent of respondents believed the VPA negotiations to have brought at least minor improvements, some NGO representatives considered the situation in the DRC to have actually worsened since the adoption of the new timber-supply-chain-related laws (Lawson 2014, 16).

International attention on illegal logging in the DRC increased to a unique high in 2012. This was driven by increased research and campaigning by international NGOs, including WWF, Greenpeace, and Global Witness (Lawson 2014, 9; Partzsch and Vlaskamp 2016). The DRC had a donor-funded Independent Observer of Forest Law Enforcement and Governance (OI-FLEG) in place between December 2010 and April 2013, which exposed large-scale illegal industrial artisanal logging in the country (REM 2013). These exposures were then picked up and publicized by NGOs in 2012 (Lawson 2014, 6, 9). In addition, SGS (developing a timber traceability system in the DRC since 2011) brought several cases of illegality to the authorities, but without consequences (Lawson 2014, 13). The OI-FLEG also organized civil society workshops in the DRC with Réseau Ressources Naturelles (RRN), a regional NGO (REM 2013, 29). Another NGO, Observatoire de la Gouvernance Forestière (OGF), was founded by people trained by the OI-FLEG (REM 2013, 30). There is also a Field Legality Advisory Group

(FLAG), a subregional organization with the aim of monitoring forest activities. Despite the workshop and the existence of these groups, national NGOs still lack necessary technical expertise and require capacity building to adequately fill a watchdog role (REM 2013, 30).

Due to the particular geographical focus of the Dodd-Frank Act Section 1502 on the DRC, President Kabila suspended artisanal mining activities in North Kivu, South Kivu, and Maniema from September 2010 to March 2011 (see figure 4.3; Matthysen and Zaragoza Montejano 2013). This led to a temporary collapse of the mining industry in these regions and was often interpreted as the predicted "de facto embargo" (while mining continued especially in the Katanga region; see Manhart and Schleicher 2013). As mentioned earlier, however, companies intentionally promoted narratives on such unintended effects in order to reduce their compliance costs (Koch and Kinsbergen 2018).

Furthermore, on part of the affected (exporting) countries, the International Conference on the Great Lakes Region (ICGLR), with twelve

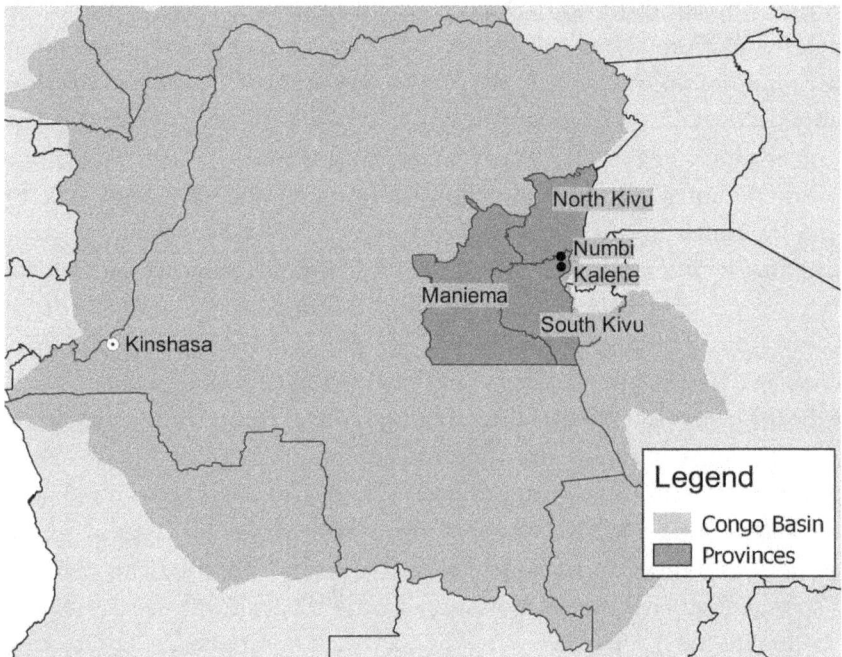

Figure 4.3
Map of the DRC

African member states, set up a Mineral Tracking and Certification Scheme in 2015, based on the OECD Due Diligence Guidance. This Scheme applies equally to US-based and other foreign companies. The ICGLR Regional Certification Mechanism is expected to eventually be integrated into the national law of its member states in the Great Lakes Region (Sarfaty 2015, 450). Local governments support the ICGLR mechanism because it is locally governed, while also responding to requirements of the importing states. Yet implementation by regional governments is weak because of minimal coordination between the ICGLR and national coordinators and the difficulties of translating and interpreting legal texts for agents on the ground (Sarfaty 2015, 456).

Regarding the charge of a de facto embargo, the mineral (processing) industry tries to avoid the impression it is avoiding sourcing from high-risk areas (SK, interview, November 20, 2015). Like in the field of timber, industry activities are accompanied by increased research and campaigning by international NGOs; in particular, the Washington-based Enough Project (Callaway 2017). While timber campaigns are based on the work of the donor-funded OI-FLEG, NGOs working on conflict minerals largely rely on and cite from public UN reports (UNEP-MONUSCO-OSESG 2015; UN Security Council 2017). This demonstrates public-private interlinkages. In addition, the US Agency for International Development (USAID) and EU governments support activities to improve infrastructure and institutional reforms to help enhance civilian control of the DRC's timber and mineral trade (EU FLEGT 2018; Sarfaty 2015, 456).

4.2.3   Impact on the Extraction of Timber and Minerals in the Eastern DRC

Assessing the impact of the new supply-chain-related laws is difficult. Inadequate local security and weak governance inhibit mapping and traceability in the DRC region (Cerutti et al. 2018; Sarfaty 2015, 452). Public supply-chain-related laws depend on importing firms to spend resources and to develop expertise to locate and regulate their suppliers (Sarfaty 2015, 452). At the same time, governments of importing countries have hardly any means to control the activities of these firms in exporting countries (besides, for example, sending independent observers). Prosecution very much depends on third parties, such as NGOs, to prove the neglect of due diligence obligations.

In the aforementioned cases of Gibson Guitar and Lumber Liquidators, WWF and the Environmental Investigation Agency, two international NGOs, had published reports on the companies' violations of the LTPA (Environmental Investigation Agency 2013; WWF 2013). Similar reports exist for violations in the DRC (e.g., Greenpeace Africa 2013), but neither importing countries nor the DRC authorities have opened prosecution cases. Also, NGOs did not take civil action through the courts (Lawson 2014, 10).

NGO reports disprove the assumption that new supply-chain-related laws restrict international trade. Neither timber nor minerals companies have refrained from sourcing in the DRC (Greenpeace Africa 2013; Callaway 2017, 12). Although a decreasing share of timber is exported to the EU and the United States (Lawson 2014, 20), Lawson (2014, 22) actually finds an intensification of the overall timber harvest after 2008 (when the LTPA was adopted). Likewise, there is no evidence for a de facto embargo (Jeffrey 2012, 504) against the DRC in response to the mineral-supply-chain-related laws (Callaway 2017; Koch and Kinsbergen 2018). NGOs demand a "conflict-free, not Congo-free" mineral supply (Callaway 2017, 11).

In 2017, the UN Group of Experts on the DRC reported to the UN Security Council that the implementation of mineral traceability "has considerably reduced instances of armed groups directly benefiting from the exploitation and trade of tin, tantalum and tungsten" (UN Security Council 2017, 2). As of April 2017, 420 mines in Congo had been verified as conflict-free. In 2010, no mines had received this designation (Callaway 2017, 4). This development corresponds with international and domestic NGOs reporting on the situation in the DRC (Callaway 2017, 9). When the US SEC requested public comments on the US mineral-supply-chain-related law, nearly twelve thousand comments were posted, and 99 percent of them called for enforcement and continued implementation of the law (Callaway 2017, 9). More than one hundred Congolese NGOs voiced their support for Dodd-Frank Act Section 1502. They outlined how it has helped increase rule of law in the DRC's mining sector and warned that any slowdown or reversal in implementation could lead back to violence and black market corruption (Callaway 2017, 9). In particular, thirty-one members of the Thematic Working Group on Mining and Natural Resources (2017, 2) noted in a letter to the SEC in 2017: "Despite being thousands of kilometers from Washington, the civil society organizations of South Kivu are among those most actively involved in speaking out in favor of the creation of a responsible mining industry and trade in minerals." However, assessments only refer to the aspect of conflict financing, neglecting to mention sustainability and legality issues.

4.2.4   Summary of Case Study Results

Public supply-chain-related laws are no panacea. This country study is original in examining public-private governance interactions on the ground through a comparison of the two fields of timber and minerals. While the timber laws focus on legality and the mineral laws address conflict finance, the DRC country study demonstrates how these different foci determine implementation. Although the request for legality seems to be an evident effort at first glance, a confused regulatory environment and lack of rule of law make legality verification almost impossible. In cases in which ownership is not clear, the Verification of Legal Origin (VLO) is hardly possible, not to mention the Verification of Legal Compliance (VLC). There is a deep contradiction between domestic regulative overlap and transnational requirements in the forest sector. In comparison, assessing the risk of financing armed groups, including state military units, is a feasible task. Companies need to source from areas free from armed groups' interferences. While private timber verification initiatives hesitate to and sustainability initiatives do not offer certification in the DRC, companies are more ambitious with regard to sourcing from conflict-free mines. In consequence, an increasing number of mines in the DRC is certified as conflict-free.

The DRC country study also demonstrated that, in both fields, the EU and US laws set a thief to catch a thief: TNCs, such as SIFORCO, demonstrably harvested timber illegally with the tolerance of the FSC's third-party auditor (Greenpeace Africa 2013, 4). NGOs are meant to control these private actors. However, NGOs have only shown to be able to act on the basis of publicly available data, in particular on the donor-funded OI-FLEG (timber) report. While Greenpeace accomplished the exclusion of a TNC from the FSC, on the basis of its own material, the EU and US public supply-chain-related laws have so far not allowed the NGOs to accomplish civil action through the courts against companies operating illegally or promoting conflict in the DRC.

4.3   Discussion: Reclaiming the State Monopoly

Governments of import countries use supply-chain-related laws to enforce norms, such as sustainability and peace, outside their own jurisdiction, especially in the Global South. In the following three sections, I discuss supply-chain-related laws against the three dominant perspectives on power in global supply chains found in chapter 2 and compare the power dynamics that the two forms of regulation trigger in global supply chains (chapter 3).

While new public supply-chain-related laws have been heralded as reclaiming the state monopoly on natural resources (timber) and armed forces (minerals; see Bartley 2014; Montouroy 2016; Sarfaty 2015), we have seen that when it comes to implementation, the laws have in fact caused further fragmentation and polycentrism. The first dominant perspective on power in global supply chains—that is, the withdrawal of the state at the expense of social and environmental considerations—is not necessarily contradicted by the fact that public supply-chain-related laws exist. A range of private actors is involved in due diligence and third-party auditing. Moreover, the public laws might affect all (import) companies but private regulation in niche markets is more ambitious with regard to environmental and social considerations—for instance, timber laws aiming only for *legal* instead of *sustainable* forestry. Hence, there is no overarching return of the state, but its limited return does not mean stricter social and environmental regulation.

There is also a mixed finding regarding the second dominant power perspective formulated in chapter 2. Although the laws are formulated in the Global North, they have the potential to strengthen the state's capacity in countries of the Global South. At the same time, the laws are seen as state intervention instead of the continuation of neoliberalism; in particular, Dodd-Frank Act Section 1502 is under attack in the United States for prioritizing peace over economic development and for risking a possible embargo on the DRC (Geenen 2017; Koch and Kinsbergen 2018). In the appendix, the fourth column summarizes my findings for the public supply-chain-related laws.

4.3.1   The Return of the State

An official US or EU embargo against the DRC would not be compatible with the WTO rules. The new supply-chain-related laws circumvent those rules and are consistently based on due diligence (or due care)—that is the principle of information disclosure (Haufler 2010)—and, in the case of timber, legality as defined by the exporting country (Fishman and Obidzinski 2014, 265). Liability is attached for any false or misleading statement (Sarfaty 2015). In contrast to private regulation, public supply-chain-related laws only partly depend on consumers' demand for environmentally and/or socially more ambitious products. Thus, at first glance, mandatory disclosure stands for a tricky "re-centering of the state" (Bartley 2014) or new "orchestrating" (Kleinschmit et al. 2018), especially in the timber sector, in which the request for legality also tends to strengthen governments of exporting countries vis-à-vis TNCs. After two and a half decades of global market deregulation and reliance on voluntary initiatives, public supply-chain-related laws promise to re-embed private rules in a state-driven arena (Montouroy 2016, 71). These laws would hence partly contradict the first central perspective found in the state-of-the-art research regarding power dynamics in a globalized world.

The new demand for intergovernmental VPAs after the adoption of the EUTR tends to account for a new state-driven dynamic as it is discussed in current research. Countries would lose much of the incentive to negotiate VPAs if the threat of the EUTR's due diligence requirements were to disappear. While enforcing regulation previously made exporting countries potentially less attractive to foreign investments in the timber sector, countries still hesitated to join VPAs with the EU. The new timber-supply-chain-related laws in Australia, the EU, and the United States have changed such dynamics. Now, countries with a weak government that carry a higher risk of illegality are rendered less attractive. In consequence, the number of timber-exporting countries negotiating VPAs has almost tripled (Partzsch and Vlaskamp 2016). In the field of minerals, the intergovernmental (nonprivate) OECD Due Diligence Guidance has become the key global metagovernance standard for new laws and private certification (Sarfaty 2015; Partzsch 2018). This development demonstrates a turn away from laissez-faire government. VPAs pledged to dispense with voluntary initiatives (Montouroy 2016). Existing initiatives, such as the FSC, revised their standards in response to the laws.

My empirical research confirms that in the two fields of timber and minerals, initiatives are increasingly guided by state-defined objectives. For timber, there are new initiatives that support companies in legality verification (e.g., SmartWood by the Rainforest Alliance and LHV by SCS); for minerals, there are diverse programs to ensure conflict-free sourcing (e.g., iTSCi and RMI; see Proforest 2011; Sarfaty 2015). Cashore and Stone (2014) argue that diverse public and private standard-setting projects can evolve in parallel and reinforce one another over time, such that an apparent weakening of standards in the short term can lead to stronger standards in the future. In other words, while we observe a rapid increase of competing standards for the moment, the "assemblage" (Overdevest and Zeitlin 2014) of international standards allows for learning, and only the most credible initiatives will survive in the long term (see also Gulbrandsen 2014, 86–87). Following these scholars, the new public laws might therefore lead to a greater centralization instead of further fragmentation (Montouroy 2016; Overdevest and Zeitlin 2014). However, in slight contradiction to these scholars, my empirical research shows that, at least for the moment, there is increased fragmentation due to diverse domestic laws in addition to existing and new private certification schemes.

The relation between the new timber laws and earlier voluntary certification programs is controversial (Montouroy 2016; Bartley 2014; Cashore and Stone 2014). Although the new legality laws—for example, the EUTR—represent a significant policy change regarding forest governance, a range of nonstate actors is involved in negotiating VPAs with timber-exporting countries (Montouroy 2016, 61). Previously export companies used to simply agree on standards, such as the PEFC, among themselves, but they now negotiate with domestic governments in order to have their own private instruments recognized as part of the VPAs. Therefore, Montouroy (2016, 70) argues that the new timber laws strengthened the position of state actors both in importing and exporting countries. In contrast to the VPAs, mandatory due diligence does not require this kind of interaction, but "only . . . the obligation on private actors to provide all the documents pertaining to shipment from the forest area to the European wood market in order to prove the legality of the imported wood and its traceability" (Montouroy 2016, 70).

Gulbrandsen (2014, 84) argues that, in combination with public procurement laws, international legality requirements have influenced and "traded up" certification standards; we can observe a continuously increasing commitment to the sustainability schemes of the FSC and PEFC (Gulbrandsen 2014, 87–88). However, new supply-chain-related laws have also essentially caused the emergence of new schemes that focus on legality and/or conflict finance and, hence, fall behind earlier ambitions of sustainability. Although, as outlined earlier, private auditing schemes such as SmartWood aim to channel companies from VLO and VLC ultimately to sustainability certification (Proforest 2011), there is no guarantee that companies do not simply remain with VLO or VLC. While at least 8 percent of the timber harvested in the DRC is verified as legal (Lawson 2014, 18), no timber from the DRC is certified as sustainable (FSC 2019; PEFC 2018). Moreover, due to international competition among countries for foreign investment, governments (of developing countries in particular) may even weaken their laws to make compliance with the legality provision easier for their companies, thereby gaining international competitiveness (Bartley 2014; McDermott, Irland, and Pacheco 2015).

The new laws also shift regulative authority to the private importers, which can chose to what degree they want to comply with the new laws as it is their responsibility to implement and enforce the laws exterritorially. Sarfaty (2015, 448) describes competition and overlap of the mineral certification initiatives in detail, and she finds that there is no added value when a company is involved in more than one initiative. Instead, she argues, many of the initiatives and standards suffer from a lack of transparency, such as RMI. RMI does not give out information on member companies, nor certified sites, "an irony given that their aim is to promote supply chain transparency" (Sarfaty 2015, 451). Without full disclosure regarding the activities and effects of companies in their supply chains, collective learning, as well as NGO monitoring and control, is difficult, if not impossible.

The case of the DRC clearly demonstrates that NGO monitoring and public pressure are essential for companies' compliance. NGOs and their capacities are key for the laws' effectiveness. Indeed, we find the "distinct model of outsourcing" of which Sarfaty (2015, 454) warned, and though public supply-chain-related laws do not completely depend on consumer demand for ethical products any longer, due to this model of outsourcing, they do depend on NGOs and their capacities to control the business sector abroad. NGOs participate in and monitor implementation in foreign countries (based on publicly available data). They are the most likely actors to take civil action through the courts in Australia, the EU, and the United States, as demonstrated by the LTPA cases of Gibson Guitar and Lumber Liquidators.

In sum, private actors abroad (usually in developing countries) would typically be beyond the reach of the Australian, US, and EU governments. Hence, with public supply-chain-related laws, the state has returned, but public policies still rely on nonstate actors, businesses and NGOs, to implement norms and standards in exporting countries. On the one hand, by forcing all self-regulation to converge on public principles such as legality and conflict-free production, the new laws "appear . . . as an attempt to recentralize the problem of definition and the choice of . . . policy tools" (Montouroy 2016, 74). On the other hand, the importing countries continue to depend on private initiatives to implement the public laws in exporting countries. In this vein, contrary to the first prevalent perspective on power, the state does not withdraw, but returns. However, there continues to be a dominance of private business at the expense of environmental and social consideration.

4.3.2 On Behalf of the Global South

The second perspective regarding power dynamics in a globalized world is that there are increasing asymmetries between actors in consuming countries of the Global North and actors in producing countries of the Global South. Public supply-chain-related laws allow consumer countries—in particular, Australia, the EU member states, and the United States—to enforce rules in producing countries. Increasing interest in bilateral cooperation as well as in private certification programs can be considered a demonstration that market incentives of the Global North work to strengthen institutions in the Global South. However, though, for example, the number of countries negotiating a VPA with the EU increased from six to fifteen countries after the adoption of the EUTR, only three bilateral agreements have been signed so far (with China in 2009, Indonesia in 2014, and Vietnam in 2017). Therefore, entering VPA negotiations could also represent stalling tactics of exporting countries. We should not necessarily assume an intrinsic motivation.

As mandatory due diligence requirements incentivize importers to source from "safe" countries, rather than high-risk areas that require more excessive due diligence requirements, some critics claimed that there are de facto embargos against exporting countries with weak institutions and/ or areas with armed conflicts in the Global South (Fishman and Obidzinski 2014, 266; Jeffrey 2012, 503). Indonesia has asserted that the ILPA violates

WTO rules, and exporting countries have indicated their displeasure with mandatory requirements for their exporters to the Australian, EU, and US markets. Compliance costs burden these countries' timber industries (Fishman and Obidzinski 2014, 260, 265).

Against this backdrop, public supply-chain-related laws, such as the EUTR, can be seen as a "new attempt by public actors [in the Global North] to dominate the regulation of a local natural resource [in the Global South] through its globalized trade and the informal economy" (Montouroy 2016, 62). Governments of exporting countries, such as the DRC, obviously do not share Western governments' ambition for legality and environmental NGOs' drive for forest protection. Outsourcing regulation to companies is a means by which states in the Global North can indirectly regulate firms in countries of the Global South, but this practice raises accountability concerns. Governments adopting supply-chain-related laws and businesses, especially those selling certified products from the Global South, claim to benefit local people. Private actors hence perform functions in these countries that are intended to be in the best interests of local people, but they are not decided by the local people themselves. By building upon legality defined by exporting countries, the laws support the self-determined agency of state actors in the Global South, but the importing governments set their own priorities by focusing on specific aspects (conflicts, deforestation, etc.). Public supply-chain-related laws thus strengthen law-abiding and/or certified actors in the Global South by providing market advantages to them while they limit capabilities of those disagreeing with their priorities. In this sense, however, I agree with Bartley (2018, 258) that the return of the state may lead to more "place-conscious transnational governance."

4.3.3   Ethical Power to Limit Blood Consumption

The third dominant perspective regarding power dynamics in a globalized world is that state and nonstate actors are not continuously selfish but exercise power with others to pursue collective norms of environmental sustainability and social justice. Countries of the Global North enforce the implementation of collective norms (international peace; forest and biodiversity conservation; climate mitigation; legality). Businesses in the EU and the United States did not question the normative priority behind the new laws (Partzsch 2018). For instance, while European businesses asked the European Commission for financial assistance in complying with respective standards, including the US Dodd-Frank Act (SK, interview, November 20, 2015), they basically supported EU Trade Commissioner Malmström (2017), who called the new Conflict Minerals Regulation a "good example of value-based trade."

The EU and other importing countries use TNCs to (re)claim the state monopoly in exporting countries. As we discussed in the previous section, while importing countries do not necessarily exercise power *with* governments and companies in exporting countries, the implementation of universal norms—for example, ending conflict finance—will definitely serve the people in exporting countries too. Importing countries use their market power to pursue environmental and social norms beyond their own territory. In this sense, public supply-chain-related laws are a hard power (Nye 2011; Damro 2012).

Southern governments and TNCs are coerced to cooperate by means of market power. Because the new laws render countries with strict regulation and enforcement more attractive, they clearly benefit domestic businesses in Australia, the EU, and the United States in comparison to businesses in countries with weak institutions in the Global South (McDermott, Irland, and Pacheco 2015). In this vein, scholars have argued that the public laws mainly serve the interests of the Global North, despite referring to universal norms, such as climate mitigation and biodiversity conservation. They have caused a de facto discrimination of Southern producers—in particular, small businesses without legal status, such as artisanal and small-scale miners (Leipold and Winkel 2016; Radley and Vogel 2015).

However, while this assumed intentionality is convincing with regard to the field of timber, where the importing countries have competing domestic businesses benefitting from the new laws (Leipold and Winkel 2016), these same countries very much depend on mineral imports from the Global South (70 percent of the world's coltan lies in the DRC alone; Winter 2006). The term *blood* or *conflict minerals* has become part of everyday speech. In the past, Swilling and Annecke (2012, 188) went so far as to blame consuming states for intentionally fueling armed conflicts in Africa and elsewhere to further access resources at "discounted prices." Besides potentially higher prices for conflict-free resources, businesses from consuming countries face additional direct compliance costs tied to the new laws (European Commission 2014; Burgis 2015). Thus, it is clear there is no EU or US market interest in having mineral-supply-chain-related laws. The argument that public supply-chain-related laws only serve selfish interests is not convincing.

4.4 Summary

Do public supply-chain-related laws increase prospects for environmental sustainability and social justice on a worldwide scale? Are they a better alternative to multilateralism compared to private governance? With their specific requirements, public supply-chain-related laws essentially recognize that the free-trade paradigm and economic globalization resulted in a lot of leeway for business operators to engage in illegal, conflict-promoting, and unsustainable activities, especially in countries of the Global South with weak state institutions. As opposed to earlier voluntary certification initiatives, which did not apply to the majority of companies (less than 20 percent of cotton production is certified and only 3 percent of cotton producers pay fair-trade prices; see chapter 3), mandatory schemes affect all companies importing to a particular regulatory state, as well as those companies' suppliers up the chain.

However, the new laws define only a minimum standard of stewardship—that is, legal or conflict-free production. In particular, US Dodd-Frank Act Section 1502 did not set the bar very high by requesting companies to only disclose measures taken to prevent conflict financing in the African Great Lakes region. The EU Conflict Minerals Regulation has expanded the geographical scale to "high-risk areas" but limited disclosure to the upstream part of the supply chain. Similarly, the Australian ILPA, the EUTR, and the US LTPA require *legality*, regardless of what this means in terms of environmental and social circumstances of production. Therefore, my interviewees have viewed the new supply-chain-related laws as only a first step toward more comprehensive sustainability (LG, interview, October 29, 2015; MR, interview, October 28, 2015). Nevertheless, with such first steps, the new public supply-chain-related laws turn away from global market deregulation and laissez-faire government. In this regard, public supply-chain-related laws may indeed lead to stricter regulation over time, as argued, for example, by Cashore and Stone (2014) and Overdevest and Zeitlin (2014).

5 Transnational Hybrid Governance

In the previous chapters, we saw that diverse public and private standard-setting projects are evolving in parallel. The EU-Eco-Regulation and the US National Organic Program (NOP) define what can be labeled Organic in their respective markets and are entirely voluntary. Supply-chain-related laws, such as the EU Timber Regulation and the US Legal Timber Protection Act (LTPA), have been giving further directions to the private sector by introducing mandatory due diligence/care and legality verification. At the same time, however, they have established a "distinct model of outsourcing" (Sarfaty 2015, 454). As consuming countries cannot directly implement rules outside their own territory, supply-chain-related laws continue to depend on compliance and enforcement by importing companies. This mix of public and private regulation is further advanced in the EU hybrid approach for "sustainable" biofuels (Ponte and Daugbjerg 2015). The EU Renewable Energy Directive (RED; 2009/28/EC) and its revised version (RED II; 2018/2001/EU) exemplify the pathway to polycentricism in global governance (Jordan et al. 2015). Here, in contrast to the timber-supply-chain-related laws, public and private regulation are deliberately entangled.

Japan, the EU, and the United States have been promoting biofuels as an alternative to fossil fuels as part of their contribution to climate-change-mitigation efforts since the early 2000s. European biofuels are receiving up to EUR 8.4 billion per year in subsidies (European Parliament 2015). Although only 8 percent of palm oil used in Europe was for biodiesel in 2010, this share grew to 45 percent in 2014 (Dings 2016). As consuming countries often do not have the domestic capacity to meet their growing demand for biofuels, supply chains have globalized (McNeely 2008). This development has severe economic, environmental, and social consequences for producing countries of the Global South (Levidow 2013; Bailis and Baka 2011). For example, the Indonesian palm oil sector has expanded drastically as a result of European demand, with severe environmental and social consequences (Mukama, Mustalahti, and Zahabu 2012; Silva-Castaneda 2012). Of Indonesian palm oil exports, 15.6 percent goes to the EU, where Indonesia has become the largest importer of palm oil, accounting for 23 percent of biodiesel imports (Chatham House 2019; European Commission 2018b).

The RED introduced a transnational hybrid governance approach to create a captive market for sustainable biofuels in 2009. On the one hand, the EU adopted mandatory biofuel targets for member states while, on the other hand, it is trying to prevent negative harms inside and outside its own territory, essentially utilizing private certification (Afionis and Stringer 2012). RED requires that at least 20 percent of total energy needs to be from renewables by 2020, of which at least 10 percent must come from renewable transport fuels. RED II strengthened the overall renewable energy target to at least 32 percent by 2030, with a clause for a possible upward revision by 2023. Biofuels are seen as instrumental in reaching the original 10 percent target in the transport sector, but they may only count if they meet certain sustainability criteria (Ponte and Daugbjerg 2015). Thus, the EU makes these sustainable criteria de facto mandatory because if biofuels do not contribute to the renewable target, they are economically unviable in comparison to fossil fuels. The EU prescribes a meta-standard to which biofuel producers can demonstrate compliance through national systems of compliance, bilateral and multilateral agreements, or private certification (European Commission 2009, 2018a).

Similarly, in the United States, the Renewable Fuel Standard (RFS) has prescribed a mandatory and increasing share of biofuels in the overall energy mix, including transport fuels, since 2005. These biofuels also have to fulfill minimum requirements, including certain minimum thresholds of lifecycle greenhouse gas (GHG) emission reductions and land use restrictions (Schnepf 2013). The US Environmental Protection Agency (EPA) is administering the RFS and issued detailed compliance standards for fuel suppliers, including a tracking system (Schnepf 2013). Only the EU explicitly allows for private certification to prove compliance with the meta-standard, and the vast majority of biofuel producers rely on this option

(Moser, Hildebrandt, and Bailis 2014). In practice, for these producers, private certification has become de facto mandatory if serving the EU market. The private certification schemes must be approved by the European Commission, and for a scheme to be approved, it must meet RED meta-standard criteria but can choose whether or not to include additional criteria (European Commission 2009).

Despite criticism of this hybrid governance approach and scholars querying the normative intention behind the request for sustainability (Dauvergne 2018a; Levidow 2013), the European Commission (2016) proposed to increase the overall share of renewables by 2030. In a first response, the European Parliament voted in favor of excluding biofuels produced from palm oil from being counted toward this target (European Commission 2018b). Throughout the negotiations, it was not clear whether the EU would continue its hybrid approach, "whether they [the Europeans] will create a certification. In the original draft, it somehow says that the EU wants to have a single certification" (TS, interview, August 14, 2018). The final text, which was adopted in December 2018, stipulates the promotion of palm-oil-based biodiesel, but there are new limits regarding indirect land-use change (ILUC). ILUC occurs when biofuel cropland displaces other cropland, with negative consequences on food security. To prevent such harm, RED II requires biofuel certification initiatives to revise their criteria (European Commission 2018a).

In the following section, I will first describe the EU-RED hybrid approach to re-regulate biofuel supply chains in more detail. In the second section, in order to illustrate the consequences for and responses of producing countries, I use Indonesia as an illustrative case study. In the third section, I will then analyze the hybrid approach against the backdrop of power dynamics outlined in chapter 2—that is, the withdrawal of the state in the era of globalization, asymmetries between Northern consumers and Southern producers, and normative or ethical power in IR.

Methodologically, I reconstructed power dynamics in global biofuel supply chains by reviewing the literature and analyzing policy documents published by the European Commission and the EU-approved schemes certifying palm oil from Indonesia. Subsequently, I collected material published by international and domestic (Indonesian) NGO campaigns on palm oil in Indonesia. In addition, I conducted twenty-eight semi-structured interviews with key informants along the palm oil supply chain.

It is necessary to maintain interviewee anonymity against the backdrop of ongoing negotiations about RED II, as well as diplomatic consultations regarding the EU-Indonesian Voluntary Partnership Agreement (VPA; see chapter 4). I also used participatory observation in the annual meeting of the Forum on Sustainable Palm Oil (FONAP) in Berlin on September 27, 2017. The meeting gathered actors particularly from the EU, with only a few from palm-oil-exporting countries of the Global South. Because of this imbalanced representation, I complemented my empirical data collection with a field trip to Indonesia in August and September 2018.

This chapter shows that with EU-RED, power dynamics have changed among actors within the field of biofuels. Like private regulation and supply-chain-related laws, the hybrid regulation relies heavily on the commitment of nonstate actors. The de facto mandatory requirement for certification, however, gives more *power over* to NGOs vis-à-vis the biofuel industry and public authorities in exporting countries. The biofuel industry depends on NGOs in multistakeholder schemes, and grievance procedures allow NGOs to sanction companies in case of noncompliance. In essence, RED provides NGOs with a greater possibility to advocate for and enforce stricter environmental and social standards. With the empowerment of NGOs through RED, marginalized groups gain new resources and capabilities to make their voices heard. Against this backdrop, sustainability provides a new common ground for action. However, there are discrepancies in interpretation. To accomplish the sustainability of biofuels beyond climate mitigation, the EU would need to significantly strengthen the metastandard. This could eventually come at the price of importing less biomass and changing unsustainable patterns of consumption domestically. The European Commission would need to stop approving new private standards that are weaker than existing ones in order for the EU to support a regulative race to the top.

5.1   Background: The EU Hybrid Approach for Sustainable Biofuels

The EU hybrid governance structure incites the private sector to establish certification schemes for sustainable biofuels. Different from the cotton/textile sector (see chapter 3), private certification of biofuels does not target the final consumers in the EU. Car drivers and electricity users do not see whether the biofuels from the service station or the electricity from the socket come from certified biomass production. Moreover, in contrast to mandatory due diligence checks and legality verifications (see chapter 4), there is no general import requirement or ban on biofuels without reporting or certification, respectively. Certification is voluntary in the sense that the production and import of noncertified biofuels are not prohibited. This guarantees compatibility with the World Trade Organization's (WTO) rules (Ponte and Daugbjerg 2015). However, certification is required for biofuels to count toward the EU 10 percent renewables target in the transport sector. Thus, the EU provides financial incentives through the mandate system that makes biofuels economically unviable unless they can be produced at a lower price than fossil fuels. At the same time, relying on private certification systems helps the EU to apply regulative authority beyond its own borders (Kemper and Partzsch 2018; Ponte and Daugbjerg 2015). The Indonesian and Malaysian government therefore question RED's WTO compatibility (*Jakarta Post* 2017a, 2017b; Ching and Majid 2017).

5.1.1 Public Meta-Standard Plus Voluntary Add-On

The RED meta-standard, for which private certifiers approve compliance, initially required that biofuels achieve 35 percent GHG savings, which increased to 50 percent in January 2017 and 60 percent as of January 2018, for new installations (European Commission 2009). There are also several restrictions on the type of land that biofuels can be produced on: biofuels cannot be produced from raw material derived from land that has high biodiversity value, land that has high carbon stocks (such as wetlands), or peatland, unless it can be proven that cultivation and harvesting did not drain previously undrained soil (European Commission 2009). This applies to land that had these particular designations on or before January 2008, regardless of whether the designation is still in place (European Commission 2009). In an amendment in 2015, the EU put a cap of 7 percent on the contribution that biofuels produced from food crops (first generation) can make, which went into effect in 2017 (European Commission 2015). RED II, which was adopted in December 2018, requires biofuel certification initiatives to revise their criteria to lower ILUC risks in all biofuel production, including through oil palm plantations (European Commission 2018a).

The EU sustainability criteria for biofuels are considerably less ambitious compared to the EU requirements for organic certification defined by the Eco-Regulation (see chapter 3), although both are generally used to certify and label palm oil products in the EU market (Kalfagianni, Partzsch, and Beulting 2019). At the same time, requesting sustainability is more ambitious than legality verification, which is demanded by the EU Timber Regulation (see chapter 4), except for countries with very strict regulations regarding sustainability.

The RED sustainability criteria have a strong focus on GHG savings as peatlands and lands with high biodiversity value, such as rainforests, usually have high carbon storage capacities (Reijnders and Huijbregts 2008; Afionis and Stringer 2012). In order for biofuels to contribute to commitments under the UN Framework Convention on Climate Change (UNFCCC), it is a prerequisite that they have fewer GHG emissions than fossil fuels. The Kyoto Protocol obliged the EU as a whole to reduce GHG emissions by 6.7 percent. In October 2017, the EU was among the signatories of the Paris Agreement, and it has promised to reduce carbon output "as soon as possible" and to work hard to attempt to keep global warming "to well below 2 degrees C" (UNFCCC 2019). Interviewees confirmed that the RED metastandard intentionally focused on GHG emissions (JS, interviews, December 8, 2016; IP, interview, October 18, 2017): "The climate dimension has monopolized sustainability discussions and has had perverse effects. In the name of fighting climate change, you lose sight of equally important environmental concerns, and you have self-defeating policies. . . . Sustainability criteria are a reflection of a political compromise and of the dominant debate, which is about climate change. . . . So there is no match between what is politically important in terms of ensuring a sustainable future" (MH, interview, December 14, 2016).

Moreover, Ponte and Daugbjerg (2015, 105–108) explain that the European Parliament refrained from introducing a number of social sustainability criteria relating to land rights and workers' rights when producer countries claimed these social criteria to contradict WTO rules. Brazil and seven other biofuel-producing states from the Global South warned in 2008 that they could file a WTO complaint over what they considered to be unfair barriers being raised against their biofuels (Ponte and Daugbjerg 2015, 107). Therefore, the European Parliament negotiators backtracked on social sustainability and accepted that RED limited the European Commission's role to report on social sustainability issues every second year (Ponte and Daugbjerg 2015, 107). It was not until 2015 that the European Parliament established the cap of 7 percent on first-generation biofuels (European

Commission 2015). The cap implies that a maximum of 7 percent of biofuels contributing to the renewable energy targets could alternatively serve for food purposes. This amendment aims to prevent indirect land-use change. If biofuel cropland displaces other cropland, this has negative consequences on food security. When less food is produced locally, food prices rise, and rising food prices mainly affect poor people. The RED amendment therefore contributes to greater social justice. In addition, ILUC has also been shown to substantially increase GHG emissions for many biofuels, including palm oil from Indonesia in particular, through smallholders deforesting in order to regain land for food production (Bourguignon 2015).

Although scholars have continued to criticize the fact that emphasis lies on the ecological aspects of sustainability rather than on social sustainability, Kemper and Partzsch (2018) demonstrate that the meta-standard even falls short in terms of environmental considerations. For example, there are only indirect implications for water through biodiversity and peatland protection criteria (Kemper and Partzsch 2018). Furthermore, several interviewees pointed out that environmental issues were left out of the RED if they were not related to climate change mitigation: "Soil fertility and water issues are not so much linked to the climate issues, so this is perhaps why they were easier to be left on the weaker side" (JS, interviews, December 8, 2016).

Moreover, only a few private certification schemes address social and environmental issues beyond climate change (Moser, Hildebrandt, and Bailis 2014; Kemper and Partzsch 2018). Several scholars have drawn attention to human rights abuses, child labor, forced labor, and gender discrimination and food insecurity in and around plantations and mills (Nesadurai 2013; Silva-Castaneda 2012; Oosterveer et al. 2014). After a report by Amnesty International (2016), an international human rights NGO, certifiers started to seriously debate the consideration of additional social criteria in their standards (notes from FONAP, September 27, 2017, Berlin; Zudrags et al. 2015).

5.1.2 Private Certification to Prove Compliance

The Roundtable on Sustainable Palm Oil (RSPO) was the first multistakeholder scheme that offered certification to the biofuel industry. Currently, 20 percent of palm oil worldwide is RSPO certified (Efeca 2016, 2). The roundtable was founded in Switzerland in 2004 as a result of an informal meeting initiated by WWF two years earlier with Aarhus United UK Ltd., Golden Hope Plantations Berhad, Migros, Malaysian Palm Oil Association, Sainsbury's, and Unilever (Partzsch 2011). RSPO RED was approved by the European Commission in 2011 and can be used to prove compliance to the meta-standard (European Commission 2019). It provides certification to companies that produce, source and/or use palm oil (RSPO 2019). From the beginning, (European) corporations and international NGOs have dominated the scheme. The Indonesian government and GAPKI (Gabungan Asosiasi Pengusaha Kelapa Sawit Indonesia), the Indonesian Palm Oil Association (with over six hundred members), withdrew their memberships in 2011. This occurred when the Indonesian government announced its own certification standard, Indonesian Sustainable Palm Oil (ISPO). Due to underrepresentation of actors from biofuel-producing countries, there is a need for the RSPO to legitimize its dominant position in the market (Hospes et al. 2017, 81; Wijaya and Glasbergen 2016).

Before and in parallel to the RED negotiations, European governments had pushed the creation and development of private certification schemes. In the Netherlands, Jacqueline Cramer, minister of housing, spatial planning, and the environment (2007–2010), chaired the Sustainable Production of Biomass project group. She invited a wide range of stakeholders to formulate criteria for sustainable biomass production and processing (Partzsch 2011). The results of the Cramer Commission (2006–2007) contributed to the setting of the Netherlands Technical Agreement (NTA) 8080 and Better Biomass certificate (Ponte and Daugbjerg 2015, 104). While the Cramer Commission was closely linked to Utrecht University, where Cramer is a professor of sustainability innovation, another multistakeholder standard was initiated at a university in Switzerland. A group at the Swiss École polytechnique fédérale de Lausanne (EPFL) initiated the Roundtable on Sustainable Biofuels (RSB; RSB 2016). Both multistakeholder schemes, NTA 8080 and RSB, were approved by the European Commission to prove compliance to the meta-standard. While NTA 8080's approval expired in August 2017, the RSB is still issuing certifications (European Commission 2019). In addition to the RSPO and the RSB, the International Sustainability and Carbon Certification (ISCC) was developed by a German consultancy with support from the German Federal Ministry of Food, Agriculture, and Consumer Protection (Ponte and Daugbjerg 2015, 103). The scheme includes only one NGO (WWF Germany). Therefore, some argue that although the ISCC has a formal multistakeholder structure, it was originally developed as a business-driven scheme (Ponte 2014, 269; IP, interview, October 18, 2017).

Against the backdrop of the severe negative and social impacts of biofuels, it remains controversial among NGOs whether their participation matters, or whether they only serve to greenwash biofuels (Lin 2012; Kemper and Partzsch 2018). For international NGOs, engaging in certification is advantageous because it expands their playing field and provides them with status and influence in an industry. In return, they provide credibility to the schemes and legitimize the expansion of biofuels—in particular, of oil palm plantations. Some NGOs, such as Friends of the Earth, Greenpeace, and Amnesty International, therefore refuse to participate in palm oil certification and have generally lobbied against biofuels (Partzsch 2011; Silva-Castaneda 2012; Cheyns 2014). However, Kemper and Partzsch (2018) find that the higher the number of NGOs involved in a scheme, the more ambitious the sustainability criteria. In contrast, as complying with additional criteria creates additional costs, biofuel companies tend to go for a scheme requiring the least effort. For example, the RSPO, which has high NGO participation, formulated considerably stricter criteria in comparison with the ISCC, which has only one NGO member (Kemper and Partzsch 2018).

Since 2011, the European Commission has approved sixteen certification schemes (European Commission 2019). After the adoption of RED in 2009, biofuel companies started to create their own certification schemes, which were developed and operated solely by members of the biofuel industry, without NGO participation. One such example is the HVO Renewable Diesel Scheme (HVO RD; Ponte 2014; Pacini et al. 2013). HVO RD fulfills only the minimum requirements defined by the EU-RED meta-standard and helps companies to completely circumvent NGO demands regarding sustainability certification (Kemper and Partzsch 2018). In consequence, on the one hand, we have less costly business schemes, and on the other hand, these schemes compete with more ambitious and more credible multistakeholder schemes. As one interviewee pointed out: "When I think about RED, I actually think a lot about RED in the way ISCC or RSPO are using it. . . . I think that's why it kind of serves the purpose of the industry because they can always say, 'Well, it's sustainable.' Industry is going to take the easiest way and they are not, like, in the attention of the public. . . . Everybody is hitting on RSPO; even ISCC is not getting that much criticism" (IP, interview, October 18, 2017).

Public certification is a third option; however, it is not directly related to RED, nor is it approved by the European Commission to fulfill the EU meta-standard. In response to RED and the de facto exclusion of noncertified palm oil from the EU market, the Indonesian and Malaysian governments launched their own public certification schemes for palm oil (UNDP, MoA, and RSPO 2015; Wijaya and Glasbergen 2016). The two countries account together for 90 percent of global palm oil production. The Indonesian Sustainable Palm Oil (ISPO) program was the first national standard of its kind established in 2011 (Wijaya and Glasbergen 2016; Chen Chen and Xin Yi 2016). The Malaysian Sustainable Palm Oil (MSPO) standard was created by the Malaysian government in 2013 and was officially implemented in 2015. Both ISPO and MSPO verify legality, which means that they confirm that a company followed all legislation related to its business practices (see also chapter 4). In Indonesia, the ISPO certification system is officially compulsory (except for independent smallholders, who are not required to comply until 2020; see UNDP, MoA, and RSPO 2015; Wijaya and Glasbergen 2016). In contrast, the MSPO is currently not mandatory. According to the Malaysian Palm Oil Board (MPOB), which oversees it, the standard was launched to help small and mid-range cultivators, who historically could not afford RSPO certification, operate sustainably (Efeca 2016).

Private (multistakeholder and business-driven) and public schemes for biofuel certification are completely integrated in the conventional palm oil market. Certification schemes allow for mass balance and book and claim approaches. *Mass balance* means that a company's overall share of certified biofuels needs to be consistent with, but not identical to, the share of the material from certified production; *book and claim* approaches allow companies to replace purchasing sustainable palm oil in physical volumes with electronic Green Palm certificates (Pesqueira and Glasbergen 2013, 302). In chapter 3, we noted that organic and fair-trade movements oppose such approaches as they aim to prevent the expansion of conventional agriculture and the reproduction of North–South asymmetries in world trade. Instead, they set up completely independent and alternative supply chains in which only certified products (or products with a minimum share of certified raw materials) are traded. This way, downstream producers pull their suppliers out of the conventional system and into alternative markets. There is no such pull effect resulting from mass balance and book and claim approaches. In the biofuel sector, companies are forced into certification by the EU's de facto mandatory approach: "Businesses are there because they are looking at it as an opportunity. Most of them are cost-risk calculated. Most of them calculate. They look at is as 'Oh, there is a big market.' The market had been *created by an act of law*. So, somebody, with the stroke of a pen, created a market overnight. It's not a natural market" (VV, interview, September 26, 2017; emphasis added).

We need to acknowledge that palm oil certification only occurred after the adoption of RED in 2009. The EU is more than simply "orchestrating" (Schleifer 2013) the daily business of certification initiatives. There would not be a 20 percent share of certified palm oil in the global market without the RED hybrid approach (Efeca 2016, 2).

5.1.3   Impact in the Global South

Diverse scholars have claimed that the EU-RED is forcing private actors to take over public functions in the Global South through a process called "roundtabling sustainability" (Ponte 2014; Wijaya and Glasbergen 2016). In practice, biofuel producers often commit to several schemes in parallel (Bundesregierung 2011). While the commitment to multistakeholder standards, such as the RSPO, provides them with credibility to the outside, the business-driven schemes provide a safety net. If companies lose the certification of one scheme due to an auditor's notification of lack of compliance, for example, they can continue to sell their product to the EU based upon compliance with other, supposedly less ambitious certification schemes. One of the few examples of a large producer that saw its certification temporarily withdrawn is the Malaysian IOI Group (RSPO 2019). After a complaint, investigations and audits showed severe noncompliance with the RSPO principles and criteria, including issues of labor rights violations and deforestation, and reported a number of conflicts with local communities and NGOs. However, after six months of suspension, the plans of IOI to resolve conflicts were deemed sufficient to lift the suspension of RSPO certification (notes from FONAP, September 27, 2017, Berlin; Cuff 2016). During the period in which IOI Group's RSPO certification was suspended, the plantations continued to be certified by ISCC, which neglected to start any further investigations (BV, interview, September 27, 2017).

Transnational hybrid regulation—that is, RED—is driven by the Global North—that is, EU member states in cooperation with private actors mainly from the downstream parts of supply chains (e.g., in the RSPO, as discussed ahead; see Wijaya and Glasbergen 2016, 220). Southern governments had expected a much higher demand for biomass such as palm oil, in particular, after the adoption of RED (VV, interview, September 26, 2017). In this context, private sustainability standards need to be understood "as external initiatives from the top of the value chain, which are channeled downward as new conditions for production to producing, often developing, countries" (Wijaya and Glasbergen 2016, 221). The EU-RED and its demand for voluntary certification make market access more difficult for third (non-EU-member) countries (TS, interview, August 14, 2018; VV, interview, September 26, 2017).

The Indonesian and Malaysian governments called EU-RED a form of a nontrade barrier used to stimulate the production of European plant oils (Ribka 2017b). The EU also got into diplomatic controversies with Argentina (VV, interview, September 26, 2017). As the EU does not have the domestic capacity to meet its own biofuel and related climate-mitigation targets without importing biomass (McNeely 2008), some scholars argue that there is a "North–South co-dependence" (Pesqueira and Glasbergen 2013, 301). Developing countries produce palm oil and depend on the demand from consuming countries. However, while European farmers receive subsidies and also benefit from the growing demand for their produce, there is a more intense "drive . . . to produce and get as much money as possible" (VV, interview, September 26, 2017) in developing countries exporting their biomass to the EU.

The gold rush metaphor is frequently used to describe the development of biofuels (Balkema and Pols 2015). Biofuel business, like gold mining, is unprofitable for most of society, or diggers and mine owners, respectively. A win-win rhetoric can make a person believe that they can achieve abundant wealth almost instantly and become an "energy sheik" (Rathke and Diepenbrock 2006, author's translation), but only a few actually make large fortunes. Several studies carve out the central role of knowledge and framing in this context (Baka and Bailis 2014; Hunsberger 2010; Kuchler and Linnér 2012). Social and political problems emerge through and by means of certain rationalities. In this vein, Levidow (2013, 221) outlines how the EU pursues global leadership for *sustainable* biofuels *because* it can then continue importing resources from the Global South, not *although* (see also Dauvergne 2018a).

Against the backdrop of North–South dichotomies, several scholars have analyzed the impact of the promotion of biofuels in exporting countries. They highlight detrimental consequences of the biofuel boom. For example, Hunsberger (2010) argues that the expansion of Jatropha for biofuel purposes in Kenya has been rolled out as a development strategy driven by multiple discourses that often (though not always) differ from the priorities of smallholders who are actually growing the crop. Baka and Bailis (2014) demonstrate that the Indian government supported the cultivation of Jatropha for biofuel purposes on so-called wastelands (degraded land; see country case ahead). However, these lands served local people before to harvest Prosopis as fuelwood with several times more useful energy. Replacing Prosopis with jatropha hence engendered changes in economic and property relations (Baka and Bailis 2014). Li (2017) describes that what comes after such a land grab is even more devastating for smallholders. She identifies a "mafia system" that is "an extended, densely networked, predatory system in which everyone in a plantation zone must participate in order get somewhere, or simply to survive. . . . Anyone who does not become mafia—become both defensive and predatory—is simply prey" (Li 2017, 2).

In this context, it comes as no surprise that if there are incidences of breach of law, like human rights violations in the previously mentioned IOI case, people turn to private certification schemes instead of calling for public law enforcement. Southern governments' self-determination is hence challenged twice, both by the foreign voluntary standards competing with domestic legislation and by their own citizens' demand for private regulation (Haufler 2003; Wijaya and Glasbergen 2016). In consequence, Wijaya and Glasbergen (2016) argue that there has been a five-stage process in Southern governments' response to private standards from the North.

First, there was a process of learning, in which Southern governments became aware of the relevance of sustainability standards for international trade. Similar to how we can explain business participation in voluntary certification schemes as a result of "the twin threats"' (Haufler 2003, 248; see chapter 3), Southern governments supported certification because this created a good image at the international level. For instance, by supporting the RSPO, the Indonesian government considered that the country might be able to address the negative campaigns of international NGOs against the environmental effects of the palm oil industry (Wijaya and Glasbergen 2016, 230). Related to this reputational threat, in the shadow of hierarchy or negotiations with international donor institutions, certification demonstrates good governance, which conveys transparency, accountability, and efficiency. Supporting certification initiatives indicated that governments were willing to leave behind bad governance practices, such as corruption and mismanagement of natural resources. Moreover, certification sometimes resulted in transfer of technology, knowledge, and skills; induction of more efficient market-management systems; and, therefore, upgrades of agricultural market conditions in developing countries (Wijaya and Glasbergen 2016, 222).

Second, following this phase of supporting certification, Southern governments started to reconsider the enforcement of their own regulations on environmental and social issues in the field of the production of agricultural commodities. Asymmetric power relations between Northern and Southern countries due to imbalances of power and competitiveness became less accepted (Wijaya and Glasbergen 2016, 240). A few national NGOs also believe that the establishment of the ISPO was a reaction of the Indonesian government to muffle negative campaigns of international NGOs on oil palm plantations because support of the RSPO was not able to reduce those campaigns (Wijaya and Glasbergen 2016, 231).

Third, due to "feelings of disadvantage and exclusion" (Wijaya and Glasbergen 2016, 240), exporting countries' governments decided to develop their own national standards. The increasing number of private standards similar to the RSPO created doubts about the logic of the private regulatory system as a whole (Wijaya and Glasbergen 2016, 240). In particular, the Indonesian and Malaysian governments have begun to resist voluntary schemes, with resistance taking the form of their public standards, ISPO and MSPO (Efeca 2016).

Fourth, while the private standards from the North were developed in close cooperation between businesses and NGOs, the Southern standards evolved from close cooperation, with potentially corporatist governance characteristics, between producer organizations and the government (Wijaya and Glasbergen 2016). In consequence, the Southern standards tend to emphasize economic prospects rather than social and environmental protections. The central Indonesian government frames this approach as paying more attention and respect to the specific conditions of production and preferences in the local or national context (Wijaya and Glasbergen 2016).

Fifth, Southern governments redirect their trade of agricultural commodities to parts of the world other than Europe and the United States. For example, China and India are not interested or at least are less interested in compliance with private sustainability standards as a prerequisite for a trade relationship (TS, interview, August 14, 2018; Wijaya and Glasbergen 2016, 240). Further, the Indonesian and Malaysian governments announced a plan to merge their two national sustainability standards—ISPO and MSPO—to form the Council of Palm Oil Producing Countries (CPOPC), with the aim of coordinating control of the palm oil market (Efeca 2016). However, another scenario that might be even more likely would consist of ISPO cooperating more closely with the RSPO in the future (UNDP, MoA, and RSPO 2015; Wijaya and Glasbergen 2016, 232).

5.2 Case Study: Palm Oil and Indonesia

Indonesia is the largest producer of palm oil in the world and produces thirty-five million tons per year (Amnesty International 2016, 3). Therefore, due to its significance, the country serves as a case study in this chapter (see figure 5.1). After the adoption of mandatory biofuel targets in the EU, palm oil imports from Indonesia increased by 117 percent from 2010 to 2011 alone (Mukherjee and Sovacool 2014), and the EU is now the second-biggest importer of Indonesian palm oil after India (and before China and Pakistan; European Commission 2018b; UNDP, MoA, and RSPO 2015). As mentioned earlier, in response to EU-RED and private certification, such as the RSPO, the Indonesian Minister of Agriculture launched the ISPO, the country's own national certification standard, in 2011 (UNDP, MoA, and RSPO 2015; Wijaya and Glasbergen 2016; Sahide et al. 2015).

In the following section, I will first explain in more detail the environmental and social challenges of palm oil production in Indonesia. Second, I will look more closely at certification, using the example of the RSPO as a voluntary scheme approved by the EU-RED and ISPO as a public response scheme by the Indonesian government. Finally, I will sum up this section on Indonesia by comparing the two certification schemes against the backdrop of the literature review in the background part of this chapter.

Figure 5.1
Indonesia on map of Southeast Asia

5.2.1 Environmental and Social Challenges of Palm Oil Production in Indonesia

Oil palm (Elaeis guineensis) is originally from West Africa and was introduced to Indonesia in 1911 by the Dutch colonial administration (Susanti
and Budidarsono 2014, 120). The Indonesian government began to stimulate oil palm expansion in the 1970s. However, production only really took
off in the 1990s, with an average of 10 percent annual growth in oil palm
plantations as a result of expanded Indonesian trade, economic liberalization, and policy deregulation to attract investment (see figure 5.2; Susanti
and Budidarsono 2014, 121; Wijaya and Glasbergen 2016). Compared to
other vegetable oils, palm oil has the highest production yield per hectare
at a lower price point (UNDP, MoA, and RSPO 2015, 5).

The Indonesian government categorizes oil palm plantations into smallholders (twenty-five hectares max.) and large estates (one hundred thousand hectares max.), with the exception of Papua, where ceiling limits are
twice as large (Susanti and Budidarsono 2014, 122). Smallholders account
for around 35 to 40 percent of all palm oil production in Indonesia compared to 55 percent for large-scale private companies and 10 percent for
state-owned companies (OECD 2012, 229). In 2010, ten companies owned
67 percent of all large-scale plantations, including Astra Astro Legari, Musim
Mas, Cargill, Asian Agri, Wilmar, Golden Agri, and Kadin Indonesia (OECD

(a)

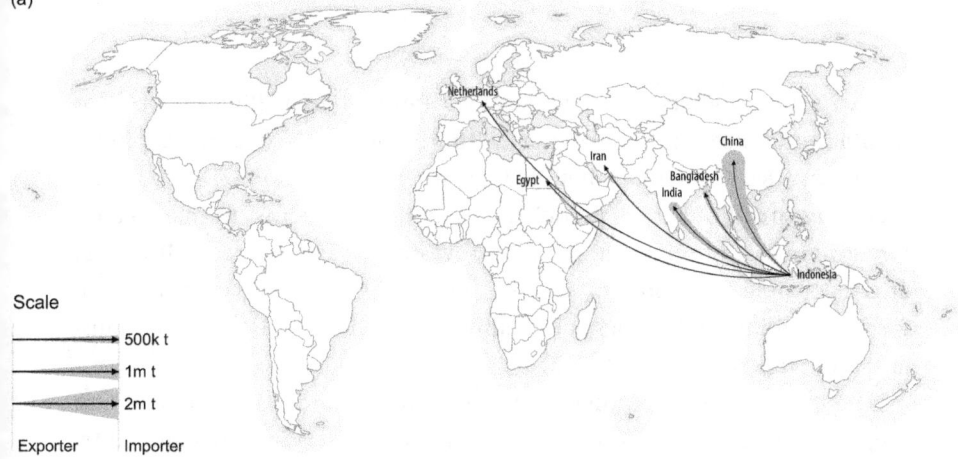

(b)

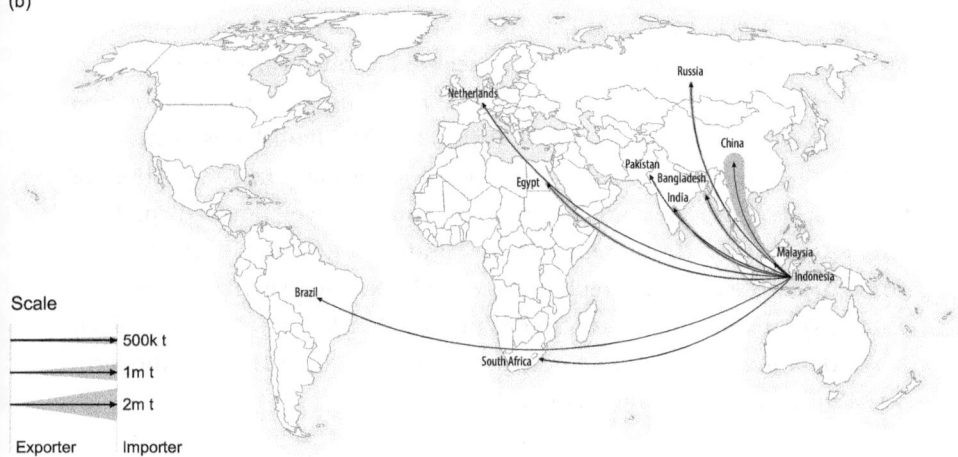

(c)

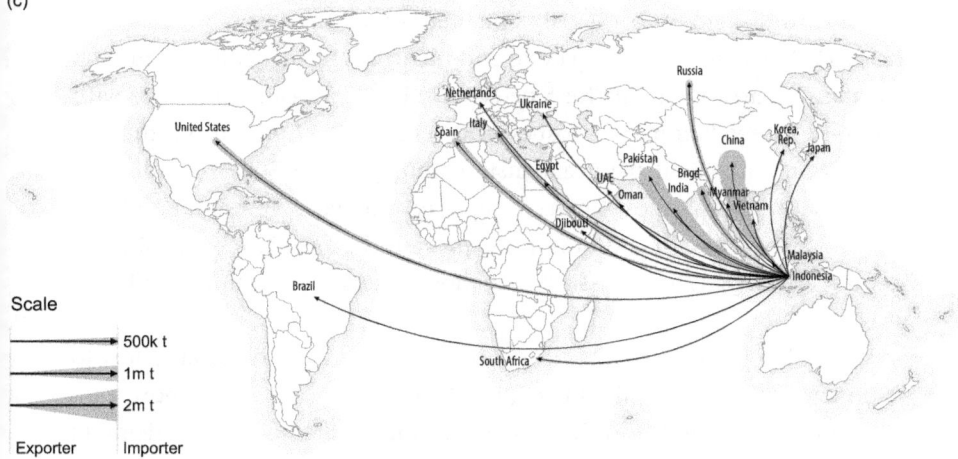

Figure 5.2
Palm oil (or fractions simply refined) exports from Indonesia in (a) 2009, (b) 2011, and (c) 2016. *Source:* Chatham House 2019.

2012, 229). Foreigners or foreign legal entities that are willing to apply for plantation licenses must collaborate with Indonesian citizens or legal Indonesian entities. Therefore, there is high interest from domestic investors, including smallholders, to participate in land investments. In many cases, foreign entities provide the required investment, but domestic investors are responsible for approximately 60 percent of the total investment in oil palm plantations in Indonesia, including government-funded projects (Susanti and Budidarsono 2014, 122).

The Indonesian government's priorities are economic development and preparing the industry to meet the sustainability standards demanded by the global market (Pramudya, Hospes, and Termeer 2017, 72). In the Master Plan for Acceleration and Expansion of Indonesian Economic Development (2011–2025), palm oil has been selected as one of the key economic activities in so-called economic corridors. The palm oil corridors are to be developed in Sumatra, Kalimantan, Papua, and Maluku Islands. Sumatra is already hosting most oil palm plantations, particularly in North Sumatra and Riau Province. In comparison, Kalimantan's development is particularly less advanced thus far (Susanti and Budidarsono 2014, 122). The government aims to support replanting, mainly on the existing smallholder estates, yet it also intends to support new estates developed on "degraded land" (Pramudya, Hospes, and Termeer 2017, 72; for critique of the term *degraded land*, see Baka and Bailis 2014).

Large-scale oil palm expansion has generated substantial land use change, and increasingly smallholders from all over Indonesia are involved in converting land into oil palm plantations (Susanti and Budidarsono 2014, 119). There are incompatible and inconsistent regulations and land use maps (there is data only for 5 percent of the total area of Indonesia with many errors; see Pramudya, Hospes, and Termeer 2017, 69). It is estimated that 56 percent of oil palm expansion from 1990 to 2005 in Indonesia replaced forest areas and 44 percent replaced crop lands (Susanti and Budidarsono 2014, 124). In addition, ILUC prevents biofuels from contributing toward achieving GHG emission reduction targets (European Commission 2018b).

Where land rights are not clear, land is often purchased in an effort to capture water resources (Mehta, Veldwisch, and Franco 2012). A report commissioned by the European Commission found that an increase in demand for bioenergy poses the risk of shifting water problems to third countries, which is particularly prevalent in palm oil production in Indonesia and Malaysia (Diaz-Chavez et al. 2013). There have been several grievances filed in Indonesia about toxins in drinking water, drying up of wells, declining fish stocks, and instances of drought in other community land next to plantations (Larsen et al. 2014). In addition, palm oil processing also produces approximately 0.75 tons of palm oil mill effluent (POME) per ton of crude palm oil, which is frequently emitted into natural water sources (Mukherjee and Sovacool 2014). Palm oil production is also extremely chemical-intensive. High pesticide, herbicide, and fertilizer levels contaminate water sources and render river water unsafe for daily uses (Obidzinski et al. 2012). Furthermore, to develop palm oil plantations, natural drainage is often destroyed and peatlands are frequently drained (Obidzinski et al. 2012; Tan et al. 2009). Besides contributing to biodiversity loss, palm oil production can therefore exacerbate droughts and floods in Indonesia (Obidzinski et al. 2012). Women and other socially marginalized groups are particularly affected by such environmental degradation (Basnet, Gnych, and Anandi 2016; Li 2014).

Smallholders (women), who often have no official land rights, are principally vulnerable. Investors, as well as certifiers and auditors, often only recognize titled land ownership and fail to recognize the wide range of property rights that exist and the complexity of men's and women's rights and responsibilities in communities (Basnet, Gnych, and Anandi 2016, 2; Silva-Castaneda 2012). Without formal land rights, smallholders face difficulties accessing funding to expand oil palm cultivation (Pramudya, Hospes, and Termeer 2017). Although both women and men were involved in all aspects of the smallholder economy prior to the arrival of large-scale oil palm plantations, Basnet, Gnych, and Anandi (2016, 2) found the smallholder oil palm plots allocated by the Indonesian government were generally registered in the name of the male head of household. Women were not represented in the smallholder cooperatives, and the monthly income from sale of the oil palm fruit was paid to men (Basnet, Gnych, and Anandi 2016, 3). In addition, as "shadow workers" or working at the provincial minimum wage, women were denied independent access to agricultural inputs, training, and credit (Basnet, Gnych, and Anandi 2016, 3).

In sum, the Indonesian palm oil sector can be linked to deforestation, biodiversity loss, and increased food insecurity, among other negative consequences that lead to further marginalization of (women) smallholders.

However, the government of Indonesia plans to further expand oil palm production, especially for exports to the EU and China, which is argued to serve national and regional incomes and provide employment for rural populations (Susanti and Budidarsono 2014, 120; Schleifer and Sun 2018). Voluntary certification schemes, enhanced by the EU-RED, as well as ISPO, are efforts to address the biofuel's negative environmental and social impacts.

5.2.2   Private Certification of Palm Oil from Indonesia: The Roundtable on Sustainable Palm Oil

The Roundtable on Sustainable Palm Oil (RSPO) takes a pioneering position in Indonesia regarding the private certification of palm oil (UNDP, MoA, and RSPO 2015). It has certified more than 2,500 projects in Indonesia, in addition to about eighty thousand smallholders (RSPO 2019). In total, there are six EU-approved schemes that offer certification for palm oil produced in the country (Kemper and Partzsch 2018). These include three multistakeholder schemes: the RSB, RSPO, and ISCC. In addition, there are three business schemes: the HVO RD, the Grain and Feed Trade Association Trade Assurance Scheme (GTAS), and RED Bioenergy Sustainability Assurance (RBSA; see table 5.1). In addition, Indonesia's largest palm oil producers (Astra Astro Legari, Musim Mas, Cargill, Asian Agri, Wilmar, Golden Agri, and Kadin Indonesia) set up their own partnership, the Indonesian Palm Oil Pledge (IPOP), for sustainable palm oil in 2014, but the Indonesian government instructed them to dissolve their organization in 2016 (SK, interview, August 21, 2018). Reportedly, the IPOP sustainability standard was more ambitious than the ISPO program (Chen Chen and Xin Yi 2016). This resulted in tensions between state agencies and IPOP and was followed by a public announcement by the IPOP signatories explaining that that the platform would dissolve in order to better support the ISPO program (Indonesian Palm Oil Pledge 2016; SK, interview, August 21, 2018).

Out of 3,872 members, the RSPO has only 124 members in Indonesia (RSPO 2019). Scholars have repeatedly criticized the fact that the region with the largest number of members is Europe, where no oil palm is grown (Wijaya and Glasbergen 2016). This circumstance reflects the supply-chain-related character of the scheme, of course. However, besides international NGOs, such as WWF and the Rainforest Alliance, who both have local offices in Indonesia, a number of local NGOs, such

Table 5.1
Palm oil certification schemes in Indonesia

Scheme	Type	Initiator	Members in Indonesia (Total)	Projects in Indonesia (Total)	Timing	Feedstock
Grain and Feed Trade Association Trade Assurance Scheme (GTAS)	Industry	Grain and Feed Trade Association	12 (871)	1 (297)	Initiated prior RED Operational in 2005 RED-approved in 2014	Palm oil and others
HVO Renewable Diesel Scheme (HVO RD)	Industry	Neste Oil	0 (1)	0 (6)	Initiated after RED Operational in 2014 RED-approved in 2014	Palm oil and others
International Sustainability and Carbon Certification (ISCC)	Multistakeholder	Meo Carbon Solutions Consulting	1 (102)	1,015 (18,592)	Initiated prior to RED Operational in 2011 RED-approved in 2011	All
RED Bioenergy Sustainability Assurance Scheme (RBSA)	Industry	Abengoa Bioenergy	0 (1)	0 (52)	Initiated after RED Operational in 2011 RED-approved in 2011	All
Roundtable on Sustainable Biomaterials (RSB)	Multistakeholder	Various; hosted by the Swiss Federal Institute of Technology in Lausanne	0 (86)	0 (35)	Initiated prior to RED Operational in 2011 RED-approved in 2011	All
Roundtable on Sustainable Palm Oil (RSPO)	Multistakeholder	WWF with Aarhus United, Migros, MPOA, and Unilever, among others	124 (3,872)	269* (2,508)	Initiated prior to RED Operational in 2010 RED-approved in 2012	Palm oil
Indonesian Sustainable Palm Oil (ISPO)	Public	Ministry of Agriculture of the Republic of Indonesia (MoA)	N/A	646 (N/A)	Initiated in 2011	Palm oil

*Does not include certified smallholders; total with smallholders = 88,753 (July 2018). *Source:* Homepages of certification schemes.

as Sawit Watch from Indonesia, have joined the RSPO in recent years (Silva-Castaneda 2012, 365).

The RSPO members agree to its process of certification and follow a set of principles and criteria with the proclaimed aim of producing and using palm oil in a sustainable way (see textbox 5.1). The principles and criteria focus on environmental sustainability, planning, and implementation for the long-term socioeconomic well-being and continuous improvement of the sector (RSPO 2013). Several studies highlight the RSPO's High Conservation Value (HCV) approach. The RSPO requires that HCV areas be maintained or enhanced (while minimum requirements for maintaining HCV areas are subjective; Efeca 2016, 3; UNDP, MoA, and RSPO 2015, 30–37; Wijaya and Glasbergen 2016, 232). The RSPO uses the HCV approach to fulfill the EU-RED meta-standard regarding biodiversity and peatland protection (discussed earlier). Studies also highlight that the second RSPO principle implies compliance with applicable laws and regulations in the countries of production (Efeca 2016; UNDP, MoA, and RSPO 2015). Wijaya and Glasbergen (2016, 228) consider this principle to be a direct result of the Indonesian government's influence on the RSPO. They argue that the government stipulated an indirect role as the legal provider of requirements that need to be fulfilled to receive RSPO certification.

Textbox 5.1
Principles of the Roundtable on Sustainable Palm Oil (RSPO)

- Commitment to transparency
- Compliance with applicable laws and regulations [in countries of production]
- Commitment to long-term economic and financial viability
- Use of appropriate best practices by growers and millers
- Environmental responsibility and conservation of natural resources and biodiversity
- Responsible consideration of employees, and of individuals and communities affected by growers and mills
- Responsible development of new plantings
- Commitment to continuous improvement in key areas of activity

---

Source: RSPO 2013, 6.

The RSPO is funded mainly through membership fees (RSPO 2019). Some member organizations receive public and/or donor funding; for example, German development aid is channeled through GIZ, or UK aid through Oxfam (MR, interview, September 4, 2018). This means that there is a conflict of interests: On the one hand, the RSPO has an interest in maintaining a high number of members to preserve funding. On the other hand, it has to safeguard the proper implementation of its principles and criteria. To conduct the certification audits, Accreditation Services International (ASI) accredits third party-auditors on behalf of the RSPO. Currently, there are twenty-three different institutions that control practices at plantations and in mills to define whether certification can be accredited based upon the RSPO's principles and criteria. An auditor must prove that he or she has not worked for the company being audited for at least five years in order to safeguard objectivity, and the ASI is mandated to suspend auditors if necessary (UNDP, MoA, and RSPO 2015). However, while the RSPO is based on the commitment to transparency and ethical conduct in business operations and transactions, like other voluntary certification schemes (see chapter 3), NGOs found strong indications of corruption (EIA and Grassroots 2015, 3). They criticize the RSPO's weak ability to implement measures against its own members, who frequently do not comply with criteria (Voge and Hütz-Adams 2014, 24). Too much leeway for interpretations of principles and criteria complicates the process of excluding noncompliant members and hampers the RSPO's effectiveness in achieving its goals (Ruysschaert and Salles 2014).

Third-party auditors are financially dependent on their clients (first-party companies). If state regulation in favor of plantation companies conflicts with customary law, auditors are likely to decide in favor of their clients and at the expense of local communities. In particular, regarding land issues, "auditors rarely recognize as valid evidence the forms of proof put forward by local communities. As a result, the whole process risks compounding local power imbalances" (Silva-Castaneda 2012, 362). Silva-Castaneda (2012, 362) emphasizes such "reverse effects" of certification and demands that the RSPO recognize customary law and respective proofs of legality in practice too. However, she conducted her study before the RSPO recognized the Free, Prior, and Informed Consent (FPIC) principle. FPIC ensures that a community has the right to give or withhold its consent to proposed projects that may affect the lands they customarily own, occupy, or otherwise use (FFP 2018; Pesqueira and Glasbergen 2013, 300).

Moreover, the RSPO has a grievance procedure that mandates that members develop a response and a corrective action if a complaint is judged to have validity (without juridical consequences, even if the second principle is not applied—i.e., noncompliance with domestic laws and regulations). There are twelve people on the complaints panel, including NGO and business members.[1] It does not matter whether a complaint is issued by a member or an outsider (RSPO 2019). In total, almost ninety complaints have been filed by diverse international and local NGOs (July 2018), including several complaints against IOI, including the above-mentioned grievance that led to the temporary suspension of one of the largest plantation groups from the certification scheme (RSPO 2019). (However, as IOI remained an ISCC member, the group could continue to export to the EU.)

In general, the structure of the RSPO is characterized by a balance of interests between business on one side and NGOs on the other side. As mentioned, the Indonesian government and GAPKI, the Indonesian Palm Oil Association, withdrew their memberships from the RSPO in 2011 (when ISPO was announced). Although NGOs still make up only 5 percent of the RSPO General Assembly, they have a strong ability to affect decision making due to a mutually beneficial alignment with downstream manufacturers and retailers (Nesadurai 2017). Moreover, NGOs are more committed and participate in meetings on a more frequent basis (notes from FONAP, September 27, 2017, Berlin). In addition to individual donor funding, NGOs often receive public funding for their participation in schemes—for example, from the UK Department of International Development (DFID). However, domestic NGOs in Indonesia face particular challenges regarding the costs of participation (KSP, interview, August 20, 2018; SK, interview, August 21, 2018). An industry representative argued that despite being underrepresented in overall numbers, NGOs play a very strong role in decision making: "Looking at the general assembly of the RSPO, the NGOs are very often overrepresented. Out of those fifty NGOs, at least half of them are attending all the general assemblies. Mainly another fifty supply chain members are participating at this general assembly, out of 2,500, because many of them are not interested in the process" (DM, interview, October 9, 2017).

Another industry representative argued that NGOs "only saw the negative" and described them as "total idiots" in regard to their demands to strengthen social aspects in certification standards (VV, interview,

September 26, 2017). An NGO representative confirmed this discussion and respective tensions between NGO and business representatives in the RPSO: "There are some producers who think that NGOs should not have such a high impact on the RSPO, and they think our voice is heard way too much. Of course, we think it's not heard enough! The producers do have a lot of power over the RSPO, if not the most power. . . . Everything depends on them" (IL, interview, October 18, 2017).

On the one hand, many NGO representatives question whether there is such a thing as sustainable palm oil at all and hence whether they should continue participating in certification schemes, especially since they are a minority position in all schemes (e.g., SM, interview, September 26, 2017; KSP, interview, August 20, 2018). On the other hand, interviewees emphasized that without NGO participation, certification standards would be less ambitious and not as well implemented (VV, interview, September 26, 2017; IP, interview, October 18, 2017; SK, interview, August 21, 2018). Several interviewees expressed the desire to pursue a multistranded strategy, in which certification is only one means among others. For example, Sawit Watch participates in the RSPO, while Walhi—a domestic partner NGO—criticizes the scheme "from the outside" (MR, interview, September 4, 2018).

A general challenge is the representation of (women) smallholders inside the schemes due to the costs associated with membership and certification (Cheyns 2014; Basnet, Gnych, and Anandi 2016). Many farmers do not see sustainability standards as mechanisms that will benefit their livelihoods (Wijaya and Glasbergen 2016, 239). While the Indonesian government fixes a price each year that smallholders should receive, there are intermediaries who further reduce the price actually paid to the smallholders themselves. In 2018, a smallholder farmer received IDR 300 (USD 0.02), compared to the fixed price of IDR 1,300 (USD 0.10), per kilogram of fresh fruits bunch (FFB, *tandan buah segar*; MR, interview, September 4, 2018). This amounted to a monthly average income of about IDR 2–3 million (USD 100) per smallholder. At the same time, the expenditure for auditing was about IDR 20 million (USD 1,300) per smallholder for a five-year period (SP, interview, September 5, 2018). Therefore, it is very difficult for smallholders to pay for certification themselves. Instead, they acquire the certification as part of externally funded NGO projects. Once these projects are over, many smallholders do not follow the standards anymore, and, for example, an interviewee estimated that about 20 percent of the smallholders leave the RSPO once the NGO projects have culminated (VB, interview, August 28, 2018).

The RSPO now works with 88,753 individual smallholders—both male and female—and 336,841 hectares of smallholder-certified area (RSPO 2019). In order to empower this marginalized group to participate in the arrangement and to ensure that their local demands are linked to global processes, the RSPO established a Smallholder Task Force, funded by a group of Dutch NGOs (Oxfam Novib, Hivos, Cordaid, and Stichting Doen) and the Dutch government (Pesqueira and Glasbergen 2013, 300). Sawit Watch, an Indonesian NGO, and the Forest Peoples Program (FFP), an international NGO with a focus on Indonesian forests, led the task force on their behalf. FFP and other NGOs also ensured that the RSPO recognizes the FPIC principle (FFP 2018; Pesqueira and Glasbergen 2013, 300).

Scholars emphasize that the RSPO structures allow for a wide range of organizations to participate in certification. Oxfam and Sawit Watch often serve as examples of NGOs that voice the interests of marginalized people in the RSPO (Wijaya and Glasbergen 2016, 236; Silva-Castaneda 2012). However, in the cases of both international and local NGOs, Pesqueira and Glasbergen (2013, 302) find that "the RSPO . . . only deal[s] with issues *about* smallholders. Hence, failing to make smallholders constitutive participants of the governance arrangement. . . . The creation of new spaces of participation, such as FPIC, the Smallholder Task Force, and the Dispute Settlement Facility, needs to be appraised within the context in which they have been created. Although most participatory spaces within the RSPO have been created collaboratively by various stakeholders, none of them have been demanded through collective action and mobilization from 'below.'"

Local entities and especially women struggle to be heard in the RSPO (Basnet, Gnych, and Anandi 2016). Cheyns (2014) argues that the RSPO is based on a liberal format of participation that discredits voices of smallholders and local communities, who come with a desire to raise and solve critical issues of injustices and/or engage in the most familiar attachments of their daily lives, sometimes with strong emotions. Local NGOs, which could build bridges, are often overshadowed by the large international organizations (Cheyns 2014). They often see the international NGOs as donors who fund particular implementation projects, which may serve certification, but which they themselves conduct in the first place to help smallholders and local communities (SA, interview, September 5, 2018). An interviewee explained this situation as follows: "If a new, local NGO gets involved, it's a bit harder to get in at the beginning to figure out how it works. . . . Language is . . . a problem because most of the stuff is in English. The RSPO is getting better with having stuff in Bahaza and Spanish and all the other kinds of languages, but (local NGOs) are heard. . . . There's also a community of (local) NGOs, so that we align ourselves and help each other. . . . The local NGOs . . . have to get organized and you need staff and resources to get involved. And knowledge!" (IL, interview, October 18, 2017).

In sum, the RSPO faces major challenges in terms of representation, rigorousness/flexibility, and implementation. NGOs have manifested themselves both as members inside and critical voices outside the RSPO, but there continues to be a discussion about how rigorous or flexible the certification standard should be, especially with regard to smallholders. So far, though there are some rigorous criteria in place, the scheme does not effectively sanction its own members. Some Indonesian NGOs expressed their appreciation that the RSPO acts on behalf of smallholders and the environment (KSP, interview, August 21, 2018; SOE, interview, September 5, 2018). However, as most of the RSPO members are non-Indonesian, the standard is also seen as an illustration of European consumer power and hence external power undermining the sovereignty of the palm-oil-producing country (Wijaya and Glasbergen 2016, 233). Thus, the ISPO standard was usually mentioned in tandem with the RSPO (e.g., KSP, interview, August 21, 2018; TS, interview, August 14, 2018).

5.2.3 Public Certification: Indonesian Sustainable Palm Oil (ISPO)

The Indonesian government launched the Indonesian Sustainable Palm Oil (ISPO) standard through the Ministry of Agriculture of the Republic of Indonesia in 2011 (and updated it in 2015). Based on existing Indonesian legislation, it aims to improve the sustainability and competitiveness of the Indonesian palm oil industry while contributing to the Indonesian government's commitment to reducing GHG emissions (UNDP, MoA, and RSPO 2015, 7). ISPO is also referred to as Indonesia's "legality standard" for palm oil (Efeca 2016, 1). The system relies heavily on AMDAL, the Indonesian Environmental Feasibility Assessment, in its requirements (Efeca 2016, 1). If verified legal, palm oil is certified as sustainable (Efeca 2016). In other

Textbox 5.2
Principles of Indonesian Sustainable Palm Oil (ISPO)

- Licensing system and plantation management
- Technical guidelines for palm oil cultivation and processing
- Environmental management and monitoring
- Responsibilities for workers
- Social and community responsibility
- Strengthening community economic activities
- Sustainable business development

Source: Efeca 2016.

words, the Indonesian state equates legality with sustainability. ISPO neither refers to nor fulfills the EU-RED meta-standard (see textbox 5.2). For example, following the meta-standard, biofuels cannot be produced from raw material derived from peatland (European Commission 2009). In contrast, ISPO allows planting on peat under specified conditions: peat may not be developed where more than 70 percent of the concession is more than three meters deep, and adverse impacts need to be avoided and water levels maintained at specified levels (Efeca 2016, 4). Moreover, ISPO mentions transparency, but does not establish it as an explicit principle (Efeca 2016). Different from the RSPO, which introduced the FPIC principle, ISPO does not request companies to get consent for a project: "The . . . RSPO also requires the company to provide FPIC to confirm that there is no social conflict, but in ISPO we don't use the FPIC. I don't know about the future ISPO, but there was just a recognition for some group of people in the area which is not clearly stated how it can show that there is no conflict. RSPO is more difficult to comply" (MI, interview, August 15, 2018).

Essentially, unlike the RSPO, which is voluntary and complies with the EU-RED meta-standard (i.e., allows for EU market access), ISPO, as an Indonesian government regulation, is mandatory for all oil palm growers operating in Indonesia, from large plantation companies to smallholders, although requirements for each vary. Large producers were required to comply with ISPO by 2014 or face penalties and risk losing their license to operate. For smallholders, the standard is voluntary until 2020 (UNDP, MoA, and RSPO 2015; Efeca 2016; Ernah, Parvathi, and Waibel 2016). Most of the large palm oil growers in Indonesia are organized through GAPKI, and, as outlined earlier, the government has limited capacity in governing the economic actors (Pramudya, Hospes, and Termeer 2017, 74). ISPO is funded by the Indonesian state but developed in close cooperation with GAPKI (Wijaya and Glasbergen 2016, 228). This demonstrates GAPKI's influence on palm oil politics in Indonesia. An industry representative stated that "up to fifty million people's lives depend on palm oil in Indonesia. So, if 25 percent are voters? We have many votes already, if everybody votes palm oil party" (TS, interview, August 14, 2018).

In contrast to palm oil businesses, NGOs were not officially involved in the ISPO development process. While Wijaya and Glasbergen (2016, 236) state that ISPO unsuccessfully tried to invite NGOs at the implementation stage, some interviewees said that they were consulted informally (e.g., KSP, interview, August 20, 2018; SK, interview, August 21, 2018). Interviewees underlined that Indonesian NGOs have been closely following the ISPO development (e.g., MR, interview, September 4, 2018; SP, interview, September 5, 2018). While many NGOs were initially in favor of the ISPO scheme, despite being excluded, diverse Indonesian and local branches of international NGOs[2] published a letter in which they criticized the government for not implementing the recommended changes (Indonesian Civil Society 2017).

Scholars explain the creation of ISPO as a function of Indonesian "national pride" (Wijaya and Glasbergen 2016, 233). Indonesia wanted to assert its identity as a nation by establishing ISPO as a national standard (Wijaya and Glasbergen 2016, 233). At the same time, the RPSO made the Indonesian government recognize the need for better enforcement of many laws and regulations (Wijaya and Glasbergen 2016, 235). When announcing ISPO in 2011, the Indonesian Minister of Agriculture explained the need for a public certification scheme, claiming that private certification schemes had too little outreach (Hospes and Kentin 2014). However, while the RSPO is currently certifying at least 20 percent of global palm oil (Efeca 2016, 2), ISPO is less successful. Even though ISPO is mandatory for large-scale plantations, the authorities could only announce that 12 percent of the 11.9 million hectares of oil palm plantations in Indonesia had been certified in 2017 (since 2011). This accounts for around 266 oil palm plantations (no numbers for voluntarily certified smallholders are available; see table 5.1; see Efeca 2016; Ribka 2017a). In particular, smallholders have no economic incentive to get certified (Ernah, Parvathi, and Waibel 2016). Moreover, many of them lack the legal documents, for example, on land ownership, that allow them to proceed with the certification (KSP, interview, August 20, 2018; SW, interview, September 5, 2018). There is also a controversy over which land counts as forest and agricultural land (KPS, interview, August 20, 2018; TS, interview, August 14, 2018): "The problem is that the regulation is still not good to accommodate the situation. That is why there is so much abuse by many authorities in Indonesia. That's one of the causes of the deforestation because one authority says, 'This is a forest,' while the other says, 'This is the definition of forest'" (MI, interview, August 15, 2018).

ISPO certification is carried out by third-party auditors, like most private certification schemes, including the RSPO (see chapter 3). Auditors must have specific knowledge on palm oil farming and agricultural practices and must speak Indonesian and, if possible, local languages (there are 1,300 ethnic groups with 746 local languages in Indonesia).[3] They must also pass a training course. Moreover, auditors must prove they did not work for a company they audited in the last three years in order to avoid corruption (UNDP, MoA, and RSPO 2015; Wijaya and Glasbergen 2016, 231). However, again, the legal situation is not always clear, and according to NGOs, corruption is common among auditors (EIA and Grassroots 2015). While ISPO has established complaint procedures (Efeca 2016, 5), Indonesian laws are also enforceable through the country's juridical system.

The lack of implementation signifies a general dilemma for ISPO. For palm oil producers, the certification effort along the EU-RED standard is incentivized by European market access, while compliance with Indonesian law is not rewarded (different from timber-supply-chain-related laws, for which lack of legality verification precludes exporting to Australia, the EU, and the United States; see chapter 4). "The problem is that the law enforcement is not working, so when the government says that something is mandatory but without enforcement people ask, 'Why should we comply?' I think that's happening in many developing countries when you make regulations but don't put law enforcement. . . . After the centralization in Indonesia, since 1998, there are so many allies in the regions who protect the plantations in the region, even if they're doing bad things" (MI, interview, August 15, 2018).

Access to new markets where there is a demand for legally verified palm oil may give a new impetus to ISPO, in particular if China makes a similar request in the future (Schleifer and Sun 2018). In this regard, the Indonesian and Malaysian governments have the same intentions, which is demonstrated by discussions on merging ISPO and MSPO (Efeca 2016). At the same time, the RSPO is increasingly cooperating with ISPO and makes use of the state's legitimacy and at least limited resources to enforce compliance (UNDP, MoA, and RSPO 2015; Wijaya and Glasbergen 2016, 232). The Indonesian government faces the challenge of governing the palm oil sector in regard to environmental and social issues and, simultaneously, to follow its priority of economic development.

5.2.4 Summary of Case Study Results

Membership in the RSPO and in the ISPO is driven neither by companies' motivation to become sustainable nor by consumers' individual demand. Private certification is incentivized by European market access (i.e., the exclusion of noncertified palm oil to contribute to the EU target of 10 percent renewables in the transport sector by 2020). ISPO is compulsory for all plantations in Indonesia without further incentives or rewards. Although it was adopted in response to the increase of private certification in the country, ISPO simply equates legality with sustainability, without compliance to the EU-RED meta-standard. In contrast, the RSPO fulfills and even goes beyond the meta-standard—for example, by requiring FPIC, which prioritizes communities' interests in land conflicts over the interests of the central government and palm oil industry (FFP 2018; Pesqueira and Glasbergen 2013, 300).

Comparing the two schemes, RSPO and ISPO, supports Wijaya and Glasbergen's (2016) claim that Southern standards tend to emphasize economic prospects, rather than the social and environment consequences of the industry at hand. However, in contrast to the Indonesian government's framing of the issue (Wijaya and Glasbergen 2016), the study reveals that this does not generally reflect the specific conditions of production and preferences on the ground. Rather, the RSPO tends to be closer to marginalized people, as NGOs make those people's voices heard.

Both the RSPO and ISPO programs face serious implementation deficits. The case against IOI demonstrates that the RSPO cannot guarantee the legality of each certified project. At the same time, this case shows that Indonesian citizens, represented by NGOs, turn to the private grievance panel of the RSPO instead of to the Indonesian judiciary. Interviewees underlined that for NGOs, the private grievance procedure is only one strategy among others to achieve justice for local communities. They actually use grievance cases to record land conflicts vis-à-vis the Indonesian state authorities (MR, interview, September 4, 2018; SP, interview, September 5, 2018). At the same time, they need to provide legal documents to the private grievance panel. What looked like a competitive situation between the RSPO and ISPO, in particular with regard to the entitlement of land ownership, turned out to be a chicken-and-egg problem on the ground (MR, interview, September 4, 2018). Whereas the private sector challenges the public sector at a theoretical level, the RSPO and ISPO programs complement each other in practical terms.

5.3 Discussion: Joint First Steps to Make Business Sustainable

The hybrid governance approach of the EU-RED represents a deliberate entanglement of public and private regulation. Because biofuel producers need to prove compliance through private certification, there is an additional power shift (Mathews 1997) to the private sector. A closer look reveals that, with the hybrid approach, NGOs in particular gain new *power over* through their crucial role in standard-setting, enforcement, and monitoring. The RED hybrid approach helps NGOs to confront the biofuel industry and contributes to NGOs' ability to challenge and discipline public authorities in exporting countries. Moreover, regarding North–South asymmetries, through the empowerment of NGOs, marginalized groups gain new resources and capabilities to make their voices heard. Sustainability provides a new common ground for action. However, though the EU uses its market power to enforce its own meta-standard as a predefined interpretation of sustainability on a worldwide scale, it prevents exporting countries from setting their own priorities. In the appendix, the fifth column summarizes my findings for the RED approach of hybrid transnational governance.

5.3.1 The NGOs New Power over Business and State Actors
The first dominant perspective on power in global supply chains, which I formulated in chapter 2, states that there is a withdrawal of the state, and this withdrawal led to a new private power over nation-states at the expense of environmental and social considerations. Do hybrid approaches confirm

or contradict this perspective? The new hybrid governance approach reflects not only the shadow of the WTO, but also that of the UNFCCC. There is no official EU ban on biofuels that do not comply with the RED meta-standard (and the RFS in the United States); certification is voluntary in the sense that the EU does not prohibit the production and import of noncertified biofuels. Because certification does not further discriminate against products with a different country of origin, it thus does not conflict with GATT (Ponte and Daugbjerg 2015). At the same time, the increased use of renewables in the transport sector is supposed to contribute to the commitments of the EU and other Western states under the UNFCCC (2019). For this purpose, these states need to guarantee that biofuels effectively contribute to GHG emission reductions, including when the biofuels are produced abroad.

Therefore, in addition to the adoption of mandatory targets regarding the share of biofuels in the overall energy mix, the EU (and the United States) adopted minimum requirements. First of all, in terms of GHG emission reductions in the EU, compliance with the meta-standard is proven by private certification. Compared to public supply-chain-related laws (chapter 4), the private proof of compliance indicates a more explicit shift of regulative authority to the private sector. The EU excludes noncertified biofuels from the mandatory target and respective subsidies. This lack of market incentive makes private certification de facto mandatory for biofuels in the EU. In consequence, we have seen the emergence of several multistakeholder and business-driven certification schemes, approved by the European Commission to comply with RED. In addition, there are new public certification schemes created by exporting countries—and, in the future, potentially other importing countries as well (Ponte 2014; Moser, Hildebrandt, and Bailis 2014). In particular, China may develop its own regulation in partnership with ISPO (TS, interview, August 14, 2018). Therefore, the RED hybrid approach has clearly led to further fragmentation.

As mentioned previously, the EU-RED makes certification de facto mandatory for all biofuels. There is no dependence on individual consumers, and the dissemination of sustainability certification into mainstream business signifies a regulative race to the top in regard to production standards (Cashore and Stone 2014). Therefore, examples like the German government's support of ISCC demonstrate the active withdrawal of the state, handing over standard-setting capacities to private entities (Ponte and

Daugbjerg 2015). However, the shifting of sustainability certification into the mainstream comes at the price of lower standards. As outlined earlier, the meta-standard focuses only on GHG emission reductions that are required under the UNFCCC (Kemper and Partzsch 2018).

After the adoption of RED, many companies did not start to participate in the RSPO or other early and comparatively ambitious multistakeholder schemes (Kemper and Partzsch 2018; Stattman et al. 2018). Instead, they adopted less ambitious business-driven standards, such as the HVO RD, that fulfill only the RED meta-standard (Ponte 2014). The most recent schemes of ISPO and MSPO further lower entitlements by equating sustainability with legality (while they are not approved by the European Commission as compliant with RED). Thus, while RED caused more companies to be certified (race to the top), fragmentation in response to RED has caused a race to the bottom among certification schemes in terms of the overall sustainability content. Plans to harmonize the private schemes, or ISPO and MSPO, have so far only been discussed, not implemented (Wijaya and Glasbergen 2016, 232). A possible scenario is IPSO cooperating with the RSPO in future (MI, interview, August 15, 2018). Hence, we find a similar dynamic as with the public supply-chain-related laws discussed in chapter 4. States are recentering the problem of definition and the choice of policy tools (Montouroy 2016; Bartley 2014). At the same time, states are lowering the reference (meta)standards compared to earlier private schemes. Again, therefore, NGOs are crucial actors for both standard definition and implementation.

Although NGOs are not members of all certification schemes approved by the European Commission (nor by ISPO and MSPO), the hybrid approach of RED increases their *power over* the biofuel industry significantly. NGOs play a very strong role inside the multistakeholder schemes due to their alignment with downstream manufacturers and retailers (Nesadurai 2017) and their resolute presence in committees and working groups as outlined previously (DM, interview, October 9, 2017). Compared to public supply-chain-related laws, with the hybrid approach, NGOs are better equipped to exercise *power over* state and business actors, as they play a more crucial role in defining, enforcing, and monitoring standards. If companies are interested in certification by a more esteemed multistakeholder scheme, they depend on the NGOs' cooperation.

At the same time, though some NGOs are increasingly involved in biofuel certification, the same and other NGOs have continued to publicly campaign against biofuels. Due to these campaigns, an EU import ban of even certified palm oil became a viable option in the RED II negotiations for the post-2020 phase (European Commission 2018b). Moreover, NGOs make use of grievance procedures as provided by private certification. In the case of the RSPO, the NGOs have several members on the complaints panel, and NGOs (and local communities) issued the most complaints (RSPO 2019). This demonstrates that, like in the cases of private regulation and public supply-chain-related laws discussed in chapters 3 and 4, NGOs are key when it comes to monitoring. Moreover, NGOs' power to enforce (codefined) rules is more direct. If NGOs demonstrate noncompliance and companies lose their accreditations in consequence, this has immediate economic consequences for those companies, which are de facto losing access to the European market (if they are not certified by a second scheme, as happened in the case of the IOI suspension; BV, interview, September 27, 2017).

By taking over roles of standard setting, monitoring, and enforcement that were formerly associated with the state, NGOs contribute to undermining the authority of nation-state governments. It should be the state's role to use its sovereignty to protect natural resources in its territory. However, the Indonesian government prioritizes the country's economic development over social and especially environmental considerations (MR, interview, September 4, 2018). While NGOs cooperate with business in private schemes, such as the RSPO, they are not participating in but instead criticizing the public schemes, such as the ISPO program (Wijaya and Glasbergen 2016). NGOs are using the certifiers' grievance procedures instead of turning to the state judiciary. This is most obvious for conflicts over land between local communities and the central government (FFP 2018; Pesqueira and Glasbergen 2013, 300). Local interests may diverge from what international NGOs advocate for (Silva-Castaneda 2012; Cheyns 2014; Nesadurai 2013), but NGOs definitely promote greater recognition of marginalized communities in Indonesia. The RED hybrid approach helps them to do so.

In conclusion, by explicitly shifting biofuel governance to the private sphere, hybrid governance approaches most significantly increase the power of NGOs over biofuel business, either in line with or in opposition to Southern governments. In contrast to the first prevalent perspective on power dynamics in IR, globalization and the withdrawal, or rather push back, of the state in Indonesia have not necessarily led to the dominance of private business. The RED hybrid approach strengthens NGOs. If we assume power to be zero-sum, the new power of NGOs comes at the expense of biofuel business, which needs to fulfill additional environmental and social obligations, but potentially only at the expense of governments in exporting countries.

5.3.2 Marginalized Groups' Power to Participate

Regarding North–South asymmetries, at first sight, the governance of biofuels perfectly illustrates Sachs and Santarius's (2007, 36) observation of Northern states being "omnivores." As it is impossible for these consuming countries to meet their biofuel and related climate-mitigation targets based purely on the biomass grown on their own territory, these countries increasingly import and consume biomass of an amount beyond their fair share (Chatham House 2019). However, when environmental and social burden shifting to the Global South are on the agenda, the exporting countries insist on free-trade rules (Ponte and Daugbjerg 2015). Southern governments have been the ones keen on exporting biomass to the omnivores for the sake of exchange revenue and economic development (VV, interview, September 26, 2017; Wijaya and Glasbergen 2016).

The EU request for sustainability certification (and the US RFS request for GHG reductions and land use restrictions) limits Northern market access. Therefore, as was evident from my empirical research, it is seen as a direct offense to the development of the Global South (MB, interview, August 16, 2018; TS, interview, August 14, 2018). Southern countries hence warned they would file a WTO complaint over what they considered to be unfair barriers raised against their biofuels instead of make an effort for better environmental and social production conditions (in accordance with domestic rules and laws; Ponte and Daugbjerg 2015, 108). However, similar to the case of Austria, when the government had to rescind its antitropical timber law in the 1990s and instead funneled the money allocated for the implementation into the emerging Forest Stewardship Council (see chapter 3; Bartley 2007, 321), the EU's move to voluntary certification in the RED hybrid approach allowed it to effectively bypass the opposition of the biomass-exporting countries.

In this vein, scholars associate the creation of ISPO with an Indonesian attempt to limit foreign (or private) interference (Wijaya and Glasbergen 2016, 233; Chen Chen and Xin Yi 2016). The development of the ISPO program was followed in 2015 by the MSPO. The two programs demonstrate the new Southern governments' *power to* accomplish things without outside assistance.

All private schemes, not only the RSPO, are dominated by members from consuming countries (Partzsch 2011; Wijaya and Glasbergen 2016). However, these actors cooperate with local NGOs, such as FPP and Sawit, in representing the interests of marginalized groups in respective exporting countries. The NGOs bring forward issues of indigenous land rights and smallholders' well-being by means of private certification (Wijaya and Glasbergen 2016; Silva-Castaneda 2012). NGOs have the potential to prevent TNCs from taking advantage of inconsistent regulations and unclear land use maps. In particular, NGOs made the RSPO acknowledge the FPIC principle to prevent land grabs (FFP 2018; MI, interview, August 15, 2018). Moreover, if businesses accept decisions made by a nonstate grievance panel, this can potentially solve land conflicts in favor of marginalized groups in the Global South. However, following Wijaya and Glasbergen (2016, 228), the private schemes, such as the RSPO, depend on the governments in the countries of production for implementation and for filling "the blank space that could not be filled by the private actors" (Wijaya and Glasbergen 2016, 228).

RED further empowers NGOs, which are supposed to and de facto do counterbalance business interests (FFP 2018; MI, interview, August 15, 2018). Through NGOs, private certification offers marginalized groups new opportunities to make their voices heard. They gain new resources and capabilities to bring their issues into the political agenda. Private schemes hence strengthen NGOs vis-à-vis public authorities of the nation-state, but the main addressee of NGO advocacy and private grievance is the biofuel industry. By holding companies (and governments) accountable for environmental and social issues *on behalf* of the people living in the Global South, hybrid governance arrangements represent accountability by proxy (Koenig-Archibugi and Macdonald 2013). The request for certification can be seen as an attempt of the EU, on behalf of local communities, to create a more sustainable and fairer trade system. Due to RED, business has committed to new sustainability rules. However, the RED meta-standard is purely defined by the EU, and the private schemes are likewise dominated by actors from the Global North. So far, only those actors in line with respective definitions of sustainability gain additional resources and capabilities in the biofuel sector.

5.3.3   Sustainability as Common Ground for Joint Action

Sustainability provides a common ground for joint action in transnational biofuel governance. A third central perspective regarding power dynamics in a globalized world is that actors are not continuously selfish, but rather exercise power with others to pursue collective norms of environmental sustainability and social justice (see chapter 2). Afionis and Stringer (2012) apply the concept of *normative power Europe* (NPE; Manners 2002) to RED. At first glance, one may argue that this hybrid approach demonstrates NPE. Biofuel certification is supposed to serve sustainability as a common good (climate change mitigation, biodiversity protection, etc.). When demanding sustainability certification for biofuels, the EU exercises *power with* rather than *power over* affected parties, such as the biofuel industry, consumers, and small famers in the Global South (Partzsch 2017a). On the surface, sustainability certification is neither in the self-interest of the certifying producers nor the European Commission. To the contrary, certification increases costs of production, limits potential biomass imports for fossil fuel replacement, and hence may even risk European energy security. However, Afionis and Stringer (2012) find that the EU is only paying lip service with RED. By erecting barriers aimed at shielding its own inefficient domestic biofuels production, the authors argue, the EU is in essence placing trade competitiveness and economic growth above environmental protection, thus permitting sustainability concerns to be addressed only in part. Renckens, Skogstad, and Mondou (2017) support Afionis and Stringer (2012). Moreover, these authors argue that no other country adopted EU-like biofuel sustainability standards.

However, when Afionis and Stringer (2012) apply the NPE concept to RED, they define the EU as one single actor. In contrast, Kemper and Partzsch (2018) differentiate between public actors, the biofuel industry, and NGOs. These authors find that higher NGO presence in biofuel certification schemes correlates with stronger sustainability criteria. Interviews revealed that NGOs are indeed responsible for stricter criteria in multistakeholder schemes. Therefore, Kemper and Partzsch (2018) conclude that though the EU, as a whole, is not acting as a normative power, NGOs pursue norms of environmental sustainability and social justice.

In addition, in contrast to Renckens, Skogstad, and Mondou (2017), my case study of palm oil and Indonesia found the RED approach to have an impact on other actors and countries. The fact that the Indonesian and

Malaysian governments introduced their own certification schemes for sustainable palm oil, ISPO and MSPO, demonstrates that producing countries generally share sustainability norms—although potentially with less focus on environmental sustainability compared to international NGOs in particular.

Whereas the EU-RED meta-standard focuses on climate change mitigation (similar to RFS and the United States), ISPO equates sustainability with legality. This interpretative discrepancy demonstrates that the EU enforces its own predefined version of sustainability in third countries. Southern governments and TNCs are coerced to cooperate by means of the EU's market power (Damro 2012). Using a simple political economy logic, we find that sustainability certification serves mainly the Global North to continue its dominance in the Global South (Levidow 2013; Baka and Bailis 2014). Sustainability certification does not prevent the EU from importing ever-growing quantities of palm oil and other biomasses at "discounted prices" (Swilling and Annecke 2012, 188). We see that imports have been increasing since adoption of RED, with horrible consequences in exporting countries, as described by Li (2017) and others.

Sustainability provides a common ground for action. However, RED (and US RSF) represents hard power (Nye 2011) and effectively limits market access. Although the same requirements apply to producers inside and outside the EU, the request for certification impedes access to the European market for producers from the Global South, as seen for private regulation in chapter 3 and public supply-chain-related laws in chapter 4 (Lesniewska and McDermott 2014; McDermott, Irland, and Pacheco 2015).

5.4 Summary

In contrast to voluntary certification, discussed in chapter 3, biofuel certification is not voluntary but rather mandatory for companies exporting to the EU. Furthermore, unlike the public supply-chain-related laws discussed in chapter 4, RED does not only demand legality and disclosure. Therefore, under RED, companies may generally have no choice but to comply with private standards and accept decisions by private grievance. Otherwise, they lose their certification and access to the European market. This circumstance leaves not only NGOs but also marginalized groups in the Global South represented by NGOs with new *power to* participate in sustainability.

While the request for private certification in particular strengthens NGOs vis-à-vis the palm oil industry and public authorities in exporting countries, the EU-RED also risks undermining the authority of Southern governments. FPIC illustrates this dilemma most clearly. If marginalized groups gain new resources and capabilities through certification, they can use them to oppose the central government's position in many land conflicts. At the same time, we have to acknowledge that the RSPO, with NGO membership and grievance procedures, is an outstanding case among private certification schemes. While "everybody is hitting on RSPO" (IP, interview, October 18, 2017), biofuel companies also have their own business schemes without NGO participation and without grievance procedures, such as the HVO Renewable Diesel Scheme (HVO RD). These schemes fulfill only the minimum requirements defined by the EU-RED meta-standard (Kemper and Partzsch 2018; Ponte 2014). Their emergence after the adoption of RED in 2009 signifies a race to the bottom compared to earlier, more ambitious multistakeholder schemes. The EU should not have approved those more languorous, business-driven schemes in addition to the multistakeholder schemes in order to enable a regulative race to the top under RED.

In conclusion, the EU-RED hybrid approach uses sustainability as a new common ground for action. The approach demonstrates that the free-trade paradigm is not unconditionally prevailing anymore. However, the normative impetus is followed by different normative interpretations. With EU-RED, sustainability certification is de facto mandatory for all companies producing biofuels for the European market. However, RED is not effective in addressing negative social and environmental impact. The meta-standard would need to be essentially strengthened if sustainability was meant to mean more than climate mitigation.

6 Conclusions: Power of Alternatives in Global Supply Chains

There is no doubt about the need for greater social and environmental regulation in global supply chains. Because governments are unable to regulate beyond their national territory, they have increasingly joined nonstate actors in new and emerging forms of private (voluntary), public (mandatory), and hybrid (public-private) regulation. In this final chapter, I compare the findings of chapters 3–5 and draw general conclusions (see also the appendix). The questions that guided the research and the structure of this book are as follows:

- Do new forms of regulation increase private *power over* nation-states, and does this power shift support or undermine environmental and social considerations?
- Do new forms of environmental and social regulation allow actors in the Global South to exercise *power to* develop sustainably?
- Do new forms of regulation enable processes of *power with* others to pursue collective norms and ethical values?

6.1 New Private Power and the Failure to Change Mainstream Markets

A first perspective on power, outlined in chapter 2, is that globalization and the withdrawal of the state led to a new private power over nation-states at the expense of environmental and social considerations. All three empirical chapters indeed show that with new forms of private, public, and hybrid approaches to supply chain regulation, power dynamics have changed among actors. State actors have maintained importance, but governments bound themselves to the WTO and its free-trade paradigm. While new regulative approaches allow single governments and nonstate actors to circumvent collective WTO rules in favor of environmental and/or social considerations, the regulations indicate a withdrawal of the state. In order to comply with WTO rules, all three forms of regulation are essentially based on the principle of disclosure instead of prescribing specific rules. Only in the area of climate change, with the UN Framework Convention on Climate Change (UNFCCC), were states able to create a UN institution that competes with the WTO at the international level (similar to the World Environment Organization, as suggested by Biermann and Bauer 2016). The EU Renewable Energy Directive (RED) hybrid approach illustrates this struggle: the meta-standard reflects the EU's commitments to both the WTO and the UNFCCC.

There is no doubt that the new forms of regulation underline the withdrawal of the state, but my findings are more ambiguous with regard to what this means for environmental and social problems. The three types of regulation support neither a race to the bottom (Altvater and Mahnkopf 1999; Lucier and Gareau 2015) nor a race to the top (Jänicke 2005; Ruggie 2013). Instead, we observe an ongoing emphasis on private schemes that address environmental and social problems in global supply chains. The new schemes often emerge in direct response to both (inter)governmental action and withdrawal. For example, the emergence of cotton schemes coincided with the application of WTO rules to the textile sector in 2005. FLO started to certify cotton and textile products in 2005, and Cotton made in Africa (CmiA) was created in the same year (Better Cotton Initiative in 2010; EU Ecolabel for textiles in 2014; see chapter 3). Furthermore, the adoption of the US Dodd-Frank Act Section 1502 in 2010 triggered the release of minerals certification schemes, which, like Section 1502, exclusively focused on conflict financing in the DRC and neighboring states—for example, the Conflict-Free Smelter Program (CFSP) that was established in 2010. After the adoption of the EU Conflict Minerals Regulation in 2017, which had a broader focus than the US legislation, the CFSP changed its name to the Responsible Minerals Assurance Process (RMAP), the flagship program of the Responsible Minerals Initiative (RMI; see chapter 4). Finally, palm oil certification schemes also emerged in response to the adoption of RED in 2009. Even the Roundtable on Sustainable Palm Oil (RSPO), which had already been founded in 2004, only became operational when RED started to be implemented in 2010 (see chapter 5). This book uniquely demonstrates this codependence of private governance initiatives across sectors.

Furthermore, I illustrated that across sectors, alternatives to multilateralism change the rules of the game by rendering exporting countries less attractive, particularly if they carry higher risks of conflict financing (minerals), illegality (timber), and environmental unsustainability (biofuels). State actors in importing countries provide the general direction (as suggested by Montouroy 2016) by, for example, addressing conflict financing in the mining sector and reducing GHG emissions (sustainability) in the biofuel sector. With new mandatory and hybrid forms of regulation, certification no longer depends only on individual consumers' demands. Therefore, on the one hand, we may argue that there is a race to the top as we can observe the emergence of an increasing number of standards with more and more companies committing to them since the 1990s. However, on the other hand, the new laws provide importers with substantial leeway, and more recent private standards have become much less ambitious in terms of their content.

Very few schemes were initiated independent of the shadow of hierarchy or command and control types of regulation (as also emphasized by Bartley 2007, 2018). However, schemes that were initiated independently do exist. Organic movements have credibly used voluntary certification to resist the industrial expansion of agriculture since the 1920s (Paull 2010; Demeter 2018), and fair-trade movements have convincingly worked to improve the well-being of smallholders in the Global South (Auld 2015; Barratt Brown 2007). Across sectors, I demonstrated how environmentally and socially ambitious initiatives increasingly compete with less ambitious, often industry-driven schemes. In consequence, there is a race to the bottom among certification schemes in terms of the overall sustainability content. More recently adopted schemes hardly match the quality of early organic and fair-trade standards (Kemper and Partzsch 2019; Raynolds, Murray, and Heller 2007). For example, the Demeter label, which was created in 1928 and is one of the most often applied voluntary standards worldwide, is also one of the strictest standards in many regards (Demeter 2018; Paull 2010).

In addition to weaker standard content, schemes that were created more recently also favor mass balance and book and claim approaches (e.g., BCI and RSPO, which certify the worldwide bulk of cotton and palm oil, respectively). These approaches do not require segregated supply chains, and downstream companies do not have to exclusively purchase from certified suppliers further upstream. Hence, there are no business-to-business pull effects along the chain, and the continued existence of the mainstream market is accepted (and possibly even supported as there is less pressure from ethically conscious consumers who are satisfied in niches, as suggested by Hoskins 2014, among others).

Voluntary certification has become an essential element of branded marketing, and individual consumers' demand created ethical niches within an ever-growing conventional market. Fair-trade and organic-certified cotton together have a world market share of 3 percent (FLO 2015, 24, 127; Textile Exchange 2016, 127, 5), and including industry-driven certification initiatives, less than 20 percent of global cotton production is voluntarily grown under stricter social and environmental conditions (BCI 2018). This means that more than 80 percent of cotton farming still potentially harms the environment and exploits people in producing countries on an widespread basis (Brooks 2015; Sneyd 2011). Only 1 percent of SEC-registered companies in the United States claimed that they were conflict-free; the majority of companies simply disclosed that they were unable to determine the country of their minerals' origin (in 2015; Kim and Davis 2016). Palm oil exported to the EU (15.6 percent of the global market; see Chatham House 2019) needs to be sustainably certified according to the meta-standard (i.e., prove GHG emission reductions), but the majority of palm oil production is only supposed to comply with Indonesian law (for which there is no proper enforcement; UNDP, MoA, and RSPO 2015; Wijaya and Glasbergen 2016, 232). In other words, the next Rana Plaza type of tragedy is foreseeable and may occur at any time. The problem is not lack of effectiveness of individual projects and schemes, but rather failure of new regulative approaches to change mainstream markets.

My comparative study shows that, besides providing general (normative) directions, the three new forms of regulation have caused further fragmentation and, therefore, each of them exemplifies the often-cited pathway to polycentricism in global governance (Jordan et al. 2015). Fragmentation implies a power shift to nonstate actors. However, complementing earlier studies (Dauvergne 2018b; Fuchs 2007), the main beneficiaries here are not TNCs but NGOs, especially in the case of new mandatory (public) and de facto mandatory (hybrid) forms of regulation. In all cases, NGOs do not only act as counterparts to business; enforcement depends on their commitment to implementation and monitoring. Even in the case of public timber-supply-chain-related laws, which are essentially based on legality verification and hence the rules are defined by state actors of exporting countries, NGOs are de facto responsible for prosecuting illegal logging and taking legal action. For example, NGOs proved that Gibson Guitar and Lumber Liquidators had violated the US Legal Timber Protection Act (LTPA) in Madagascar and Siberia, respectively (Environmental Investigation Agency 2013; WWF 2013). Although NGOs inevitably face restrictions in standard enforcement due to their limited (financial) capacities, the two cases also demonstrate that there is not a zero-sum power shift away from states. In contrast, with the new regulative approaches, NGOs become the henchmen of state actors: they are supposed to compensate for state failure in the governance of global supply chains.

Furthermore, my research demonstrates that public and private regulations are not mutually exclusive. We have discussed throughout the book how governments have supported private re-regulation. Likewise, and this is something often neglected (e.g., by Fuchs 2007; Green 2013), many private schemes have adopted standards that oblige companies to fulfill or gradually improve fulfillment of public regulations in countries of production—for example, minimum wages and prohibition of forced and child labor (e.g., GOTS and CmiA). In this vein, none of the studied exporting states opposed private schemes (so long as they actually remained voluntary). On the ground, whether or not private or public actors chose to enforce standards, which improve environmental and social conditions but increase financial costs of production, often turned out to be a chicken-and-egg problem. The power shift to the private sector can be considered the cause, or the effect, of state failure. New regulative approaches with participation of nonstate actors support, rather than undermine, environmental and social considerations when applied in practice. However, so far, all studied regulative approaches have led to further fragmentation and failed to be used in such a way that they change, instead of only complementing, mainstream markets. Partly, but not fully, agreeing with the first power perspective, derived in chapter 2, I can conclude that *globalization and the withdrawal of the state led to a new private power over nation-states, and private regulation could only effectively respond to the consequent lack of environmental and social considerations in ethical niches.*

6.2   The Paradox of Northern Commitment and Southern Empowerment

A second central perspective on power in global supply chains focuses on increasing asymmetries between actors in consuming countries of the Global North and actors in producing countries of the Global South (see chapter 2). If we compare the findings on all three new forms of regulation—private (voluntary) regulation, public (mandatory) supply-chain-related laws, and hybrid approaches—we see that alternatives to multilateralism so far allow consumer countries in the Global North to effectively bypass the opposition of exporting countries in the Global South to international or bilateral agreements. The most illustrative encounter in this regard is the creation of the Forest Stewardship Council (FSC). Beforehand, due to the opposition of (tropical) timber-exporting countries, an international forest convention failed at the UNCED in 1992. Moreover, timber-exporting countries claimed that the Austrian ban on tropical timber imports constituted a protectionist nontariff barrier to trade under GATT and, in consequence, the Austrian government rescinded its law in 1993 (Bartley 2007, 321). In this situation, the FSC, as a voluntary scheme, was established and allowed actors to bypass Southern governments' opposition and to circumvent GATT rules. Although the impact with regard to forest protection is doubtful, it is impeding international trade in tropical timber and disadvantages exporters from countries of the Global South (McDermott, Irland, and Pacheco 2015; Haufler 2003, 246).

However, though different scholars have already outlined the increase of asymmetries (Du 2018; Levidow 2013; Sneyd 2015), these debates neglect the fact that private actors have likewise realized suggestions from Southern governments—in particular, to establish control schemes for world prices of agricultural commodities, such as coffee and cocoa. Nevertheless, the non-state actors who initiated these private regulations stem from the Global North. One such example is the Fairtrade Labelling Organizations International (FLO). FLO advocates for the interests of Southern governments but is headquartered in Bonn (Germany), and most of the twenty-seven member organizations are also based in the Global North[1] (Fairtrade 2017).

Although FSC is often cited as an example in the literature (Bartley 2007, 2018; Lauber 1997) and diverse scholars explain how new forms of regulation are disadvantaging the Global South (Du 2018; Levidow 2013; McDermott, Irland, and Pacheco 2015), my cross-sectoral study reveals these regulations to be principally in line with, and not contradicting, government policies in the Global South. For instance, I found that the Ethiopian government considers certification to be a means to adapt to global markets and promote exports in line with the developmental state (Lefort 2012). The International Conference on the Great Lakes Region (ICGLR) set up a Mineral Tracking and Certification Scheme in 2015, which is driven and supported by local governments in the region (Sarfaty 2015, 450). Southern governments only oppose requirements as unfair barriers if they are mandatory; for example, RED's de facto mandatory request for sustainability certification (*Jakarta Post* 2017a, 2017b; Ching and Majid 2017).

The WTO nondiscrimination principle treats all states as equals, which favors countries with higher capabilities, potentially at the expense of countries with lower capabilities. If supply chain regulation does not take North–South asymmetries into account (like private regulation in the case of the FSC, but unlike FLO, for example), it risks exacerbating negative effects in the Global South. Supply chain regulations incentivize companies to source from safe countries, rather than high-risk areas. They hence render countries with strict regulation and enforcement more attractive—that is, countries in the Global North (McDermott, Irland, and Pacheco 2015; Sarfaty 2015; Leipold et al. 2016). Although the new regulative approaches thus apply to producers inside and outside the countries that adopted the regulations, they impede Global South producers' access to Western markets—at least, so long as countries of the Global South are considered less safe compared to countries of the Global North. For this reason, for example, the vast majority of sustainably certified forest area can be found in the Global North (FSC 2019). (This also raises questions about additionality—that is, whether regulative approaches really created change on the ground or whether only projects that already fulfill higher standards receive certification and/or market access, as suggested by Nygren 2015, among others.) In contrast, the new regulative approaches often establish de facto restrictions on imports from countries of the Global South—in particular, a "de facto embargo on mineral trade in the DRC" in the case of the US Dodd-Frank Act Section 1502 (Jeffrey 2012, 503–504; for a critical evaluation, see Koch and Kinsbergen 2018).

Moreover, in line with this, McDermott, Irland, and Pacheco (2015; see also Lesniewska and McDermott 2014; Leipold et al. 2016) found forest certification and timber supply-chain-related laws to favor large producers and concentrated supply chains destined for external markets. They argue that costs of certification and extensive legal requirements are too high for smallholders, excluding them from the respective markets. Costs of certification were also an obstacle to smallholders in my case studies. Small-scale producers were not able to pay for the certification and/or auditing themselves—and they had trouble securing international donors (MK, interview, September 8, 2017; SP, interview, September 5, 2018). In general, small-scale producers acquire certification as part of externally funded projects by international NGOs (see also Sneyd 2011, 130). NGOs are facilitators that train smallholders and supplement capabilities they need assistance with. Moreover, NGOs and their donors often have knowledge required at a particular stage of the certification processes and make relevant decisions; in particular, they select the schemes for which the producers acquire certification. Therefore, once an NGO project ends, there is a very high risk that producers will no longer follow the standards or acquire certification (BW, interview, September 2, 2017; VB, interview, August 28, 2018).

New forms of supply chain regulation do not overcome the artificial divide between consumers and producers and respective asymmetries (Hoskins 2014, 192). Although NGOs raise "issues *about* smallholders" (Pesqueira and Glasbergen 2013, 302), small-scale producers, whether they are cotton farmers in Ethiopia, artisanal miners in the DRC, or oil palm growers in Indonesia, are themselves not constitutive participants of the new governance arrangement. Producers and local NGOs lack required forms of subjectivity. Smallholders therefore rely on NGOs. In consequence, particular subjectivities—as well as narratives about Southern producers—are reproduced (Tucker 2014; Nygren 2015), and smallholders depend on the NGOs—in addition to the smallholders' and NGOs' dependence on international donors, certifiers, and auditors, who have become crucial (foreign) gatekeepers to consumer markets in the Global North.

This development—greater dependence of producers in the Global South on private actors further down the chain—tends to be further strengthened by the fact that private schemes, such as the FSC and the RSPO, offer grievance procedures (RSPO 2019; Silva-Castaneda 2012). Haufler (2003, 251) notes that if citizens in developing countries turn to the private sector for governance rather than to their own governments, this undermines the strength and health of those governments. However, my interviews revealed that NGOs use private grievance procedures only in parallel to political activism aimed at, in particular, the central state government. For example, in the case of land conflicts, issuing a private grievance case helps local communities in the central state's legal structures to formally prove that there is a land conflict in Indonesia with a corporation and that, therefore, the central government must take legal action (MR, interview, September 4, 2018; SP, interview, September 5, 2018). These findings contradict earlier arguments that claim RED sustainability certification serves the EU as a means to depoliticize global resource flows (Levidow 2013). In contrast, I found that RED sustainability certification enables marginalized groups via NGOs to (re)politicize palm oil production and to make their conflicts visible. These Southern actors gain new *power to* develop sustainably (see chapter 5).

Although private certification and due diligence—more specifically, consuming countries' (de facto) mandatory request for both—obviously undermine governments in producing countries, this tends to be different for legality verification (chapter 4). Legality verification is based on Southern governments' own rules—for example, in the case of land conflicts, recognition of customary law. Importers are responsible for ensuring compliance with the legal requirements in the place of production. In consequence, one might argue that legality verification allows for new self-determined agency of Southern actors and governments. However, the rationale behind the legality verification laws in the timber sector is the claim that curbing illegal exploitation indirectly hinders deforestation (Fishman and Obidzinski 2014, 259). In this vein, the EU Timber Regulation (EUTR)/FLEGT programs are accompanied by aid to reform domestic policies in timber-exporting countries, such as the DRC (Fishman and Obidzinski 2014, 260; Montouroy 2016, 70). Although these programs very much resemble classic programs of official development aid, importing states add on market incentives by giving privileged market access to countries with Voluntary Partnership Agreements (VPAs) (Fishman and Obidzinski 2014, 260). Thus, after closer examination, legality laws are similar to other new regulative approaches. They utilize importing companies to enforce (or incite) particular conditions of production in exporting countries. Market rejections or incentives tend to be necessary because governments of exporting countries in the Global South have priorities that are different from those of countries in the Global North—for example, rapid economic growth instead of tropical forest protection and climate change mitigation.

However, though TNCs (which frequently come from consuming countries) often support government priorities in the Global South, economic growth alone does not serve all people in exporting countries (Lefort 2012; Li 2017; Wijaya and Glasbergen 2016). Against this backdrop, legality verification strengthens marginalized actors in exporting countries vis-à-vis governments and large corporations just as much as officially mandatory due diligence checks (chapter 4) and de facto mandatory sustainability certifications (chapter 5). In contrast, due diligence checks weaken actors benefitting from the trade in conflict minerals and illegally logged timber, including armed rebels, as well as large corporations buying from them and other informal suppliers. Furthermore, sustainability certification also increases the costs of palm oil production at the expense of all producers, but in favor of social and environmental considerations.

My conclusion therefore differs from those of McDermott, Irland, and Pacheco (2015), among others who studied only the forest sector, and Hilson (2014), who explored minerals certification. These scholars found that local communities do not benefit from and even suffer disadvantages due to private and public supply-chain-related regulations. In my case studies, including the organic cotton project in Ethiopia and RSPO certification in Indonesia, NGOs were able to facilitate external market access to smallholders by covering their costs of certification, for example, and helping smallholders to overcome this financial barrier. In addition, individual producers and certification initiatives gained additional resources and capabilities through new supply chain regulation. For example, producers benefitted from training provided to them by the NGOs within the context of certification. Voluntary certification initiatives, as such, clearly benefit from the de facto mandatory request on importers to purchase only sustainably certified palm oil for biodiesel exports to the EU.

In particular, pioneers such as International Federation of Organic Agriculture Movements (IFOAM) demonstrate an ability to engage and inspire people, including marginalized smallholders in remote areas, such as in Southern Ethiopia (as well as disadvantaged people in the Global North). However, even so, new types of supply chain regulation are initiated in the Global North. (Indonesian Sustainable Palm Oil [ISPO] and Malaysian Sustainable Palm Oil [MSPO] are public standards only applied domestically.) There is sympathy and support for new regulative approaches in the Global South, but this does not belie the paradox of Northern commitment and Southern empowerment. There are new transnational alliances in favor of environmental and social considerations beyond North–South divides. However, we need to admit that new forms of supply chain regulations do not serve the countries of the Global South per se. In this vein, we need to modify the second central perspective on power in global supply chains, formulated in chapter 2, as follows: *New regulative approaches address but do not overcome asymmetries between actors in consuming countries of the Global North and actors in producing countries of the Global South.*

6.3   Fading Supremacy of the Free-Trade Paradigm

Addressing social and environmental problems in global supply chains should be an ethical duty. Tragedies such as the collapse of the Rana Plaza factory building in 2013, during which over one thousand garment workers died, illustrate the burden shifting associated with international trade and the need to improve supply chain governance. A third central perspective on power in global supply chains sees state and nonstate actors as not continuously selfish. Instead, scholars assume that actors do also exercise *power with* others to pursue collective norms of environmental sustainability and social justice (see chapter 2). Although there are a few sectors, such as the timber sector, in which domestic business in the Global North might benefit economically from barriers to imports (Leipold et al. 2016; McDermott, Irland, and Pacheco 2015), consuming countries very much depend on imports of raw materials, such as cotton, and manufactured products, such as textiles, in order for the majority of people to maintain their lifestyles (Swilling and Annecke 2012; Sneyd 2011). The DRC alone holds 70 percent of the world's coltan, which is needed for electronic products such as cars and mobile phones (Winter 2006). Indonesia and Malaysia together account for 90 percent of global palm oil production (Wijaya and Glasbergen 2016).

Movements and NGOs from the Global North were the main drivers behind new regulative approaches in all studied sectors—for example, in the forestry sector, in which WWF and Greenpeace got FSC off the ground (Bartley 2007). Fair-trade and organic movements created separate supply chains in many sectors, including the cotton and textile sectors (see chapter 3). International attention on illegal logging and conflict financing through natural resource trade in the DRC, as well as on the negative impact of palm oil production, was driven by increased research and campaigning by international NGOs, including the Enough Project, Global Witness, Greenpeace, and WWF (chapters 4 and 5). Supply chain regulation increases costs for importing companies, their suppliers, and, hence, their customers (European Commission 2014). However, businesses in the EU and the United States did not question the normative priority behind new supply chain regulations, only the extent of commitment (Partzsch 2018; Haufler 2003). In this vein, governments of importing countries exercise *power with* TNCs to address social and environmental problems in global supply chains.

My research shows that new types of supply chain regulation stand for universal norms and values. Sustainability provides a common ground for action, which is shared by Southern governments too. This is demonstrated by the fact that ISPO and MSPO, the two public standards of the Indonesian and Malaysian government, claim to implement sustainability. Although the Indonesian and Malaysian countries' governments may have decided to develop their own national programs as an effort to resist foreign and/ or private standards (Wijaya and Glasbergen 2016; Efeca 2016), ISPO and MSPO do not challenge the normative content of the foreign standards as such. There are only discrepancies in interpretation. For example, regarding palm oil production, ISPO equates sustainability with legality, while the EU focuses on climate change mitigation (see chapter 5). Likewise, in other sectors, certification programs also take a stand on controversial issues such as GMOs and the expansion of irrigation agriculture in the case of cotton/ textile certification (see chapter 3).

Western regulative initiatives enforce their interpretation of universal norms on a worldwide scale, including in countries of the Global South, by impeding market access for those firms that do not comply. By making compliance mandatory for all importers, governments ask for more than just minor adjustments (Swilling and Annecke 2012, 191). Public supply-chain-related laws and hybrid approaches change the rules of the game that is at the core of blood consumption (Swilling and Annecke 2012, chapter 7): that is, governments prevent resource-intense Western lifestyles existing at the expense of people in Africa and elsewhere. All three regulations effectively limit Southern producers' access to global markets if producers do not provide certification or due diligence/care. Unfortunately, however, compliance costs are an obstacle even to those producers that actually comply with predefined standards. Small-scale producers that are without legal status may subsequently be excluded from global markets in particular (as shown by McDermott, Irland, and Pacheco 2015, among others).

The relation between normative and market power is controversial (Damro 2012; Manners 2015). Due to their strong consumer markets, the EU and the United States are able to exercise hard economic power in international relations (IR). The rise in VPA negotiations after the adoption of the EUTR and certification since RED demonstrate that sustainability norms are not implemented as a matter of course. It is self-evident for companies in the Global North to risk reputational and juridical consequences if they break the law and/or social and environmental norms, but the majority of companies in developing countries struggle to fulfill existing legislation. This struggle might be due to weak governments and contradicting laws, rather than companies purposefully breaking the rules—for example, in the case of the DRC. In this situation, however, supply chain regulations reassure universal norms. New import requirements incite companies involved in international trade to advocate for governmental reform, rather than continuously taking advantage of weak governments in countries of production.

Scholars have argued that corporate leaders have adopted voluntary mechanisms to avoid legal liability and stricter command and control types of regulation (Bartley 2018). However, with (de facto) mandatory requirements for all importing companies, we see an increasing interest in private initiatives advocating for compliance with existing legislation in exporting countries. The commitment of importing countries, however, remains limited to particular components of specific supply chains, such as GHG emissions reductions in palm oil production, instead of more fundamental transitions to sustainability in the transport sector. If the overall fuel consumption is rising in the EU (Radke 2017), there is an increase in GHG emissions even if 10 percent of fossil fuels are replaced with sustainably certified biomass-based fuel, such as palm-oil-based biodiesel.

Commitment to the collective norms of environmental sustainability and social justice is very selective. Again, if less than 20 percent of global cotton production is voluntarily grown under stricter social and environmental conditions (BCI 2018), this means that more than 80 percent of cotton farming and, very likely, all other steps of the textile production chain still harm the environment and exploit people in producing countries on a regular basis (Brooks 2015; Sneyd 2011). Blood consumption (Swilling and

Annecke 2012, chapter 7) is still the rule, rather than an exception. Moreover, even if all consumers started to voluntarily purchase only certified products and/or certification became de facto mandatory, like with RED, standards are still limited to particular aspects of production. In addition, asymmetries continue to exist due to the technological lead of industrialized countries (reproduced through patents, for example), sovereignty of quality definitions, subsidies and import tariffs, and other requirements, but also different levels of production costs in each country. However, though subsidies and import restrictions have been considered unacceptable in the past due to the free-trade paradigm (Quark 2013; Brooks 2015; Biermann 2001), norms are changing. For example, EU Trade Commissioner Malmström (2017) justified import requirements invoked by the Conflict Minerals Regulation with "value-based trade" (see chapter 4). The supremacy of free-trade norms is fading. Hence, I found some evidence for the third perspective on power: *State and nonstate actors are not continuously selfish but exercise power with others to pursue collective norms of environmental sustainability and social justice.*

6.4   Outlook and Future Research: Where to Go from Here?

New supply-chain-related regulative approaches contrast with global market deregulation and laissez-faire government. In this regard, they may indeed pave the way for value-based and ethical world trade (as suggested by Cashore and Stone 2014; Gulbrandsen 2014; Overdevest and Zeitlin 2014; among others). Interviewees have repeatedly viewed new regulative approaches as first steps toward more comprehensive sustainability (e.g., LG, interview, October 29, 2015; MR, interview, October 28, 2015). However, organic and fair-trade movements already took such first steps back in the 1920s (Demeter organic) and 1960s (Oxfam fair trade). The free-trade paradigm is presently fading in favor of environmental and social considerations, but why does supply chain regulation come so late? How can substantial differences between sectors and countries be justified on normative grounds? In this last section, I would like to highlight four of my cross-sectoral findings in this regard. These findings concern, first, public-private interrelations and the insufficient shadow of the state; second, missing involvement of smallholders in the Global South; third, excessive and conflicting demands on NGOs; and, fourth, the limits of using purchasing power for political purposes.

First, we have revealed throughout the book that new forms of regulation are deeply intertwined with intergovernmental and other state regulation, or the lack thereof, in our globalized economy. Those forms studied in this book have all intended to be socially and/or environmentally beneficial alternatives or accompaniments to existing state regulation. While some of them aim to replace the current system, others only complement and coexist with the mainstream. In the former sense, organic movements used voluntary certification to resist the industrial expansion of agriculture (IFOAM 2012; Paull 2010), and fair-trade movements aimed to overcome the colonial division of labor between producers in the Global South and consumers in the Global North (Barratt Brown 2007). In the latter sense, certification has become an element of branded marketing to target ethically conscious (and more affluent) consumers (Raynolds, Murray, and Heller 2007; Dingwerth and Pattberg 2009). The latter type of regulation is more prone to greenwashing (Partzsch, Zander, and Robinson 2019). It is crucial to understand that both types of approaches allow pioneer companies to economically benefit from the lack of social and environmental regulation in mainstream markets. If all companies had to fulfill stricter standards, pioneers would lose their unique selling points. However, while the first resistance type of regulation is embedded in broader political opposition (i.e., environmental and social justice movements), the latter does not only accept but instead also upholds the current system by cushioning its social and environmental harms.

Complementing other studies on new forms of regulation (Dingwerth and Pattberg 2009; Raynolds, Murray, and Heller 2007), I would like to highlight this difference between resistance, or transformative, and complementary, or system-stabilizing, types of alternatives. A lot of research focuses on system-stabilizing consequences and inherent greenwashing of new forms of regulation (Levidow 2013; McDermott, Irland, and Pacheco 2015; Sneyd 2015), but we need more research on the resistance type of alternatives and how the state's shadow supports, or rather hinders, their diffusion. Although they cover only niche markets (e.g., as noted in chapter 3, fair-trade and organic certified cotton together have a world market share of only 3 percent; see FLO 2015, 24, 127; Textile Exchange 2016, 127), studying these approaches in more detail will allow for new insights into how transformational change happens.

In this context, I would like to discuss premiums, which are paid to certified producers in addition to the normal market price. Many of my interviewees argued that if Western consumers insist on social and environmental standards, they should pay a higher price to certified producers. Currently, in contrast to the perceptions of most consumers (who pay increased prices for certified end products), farmers often do not receive higher prices for certified produce—for instance, in the case of organic cotton and sustainably certified palm fruits (MR, interview, September 4, 2018; SP, interview, September 5, 2018; Textile Exchange 2017, 34). The underlying assumption of demanding premiums is that social and environmental standards only complement conventional production. It perverts the "polluter pays" principle. Instead of making the party responsible for environmental (and social) damage pay for the reparation, premiums are paid by people who insist on socially and environmentally friendly production. Hence, the request for premiums assumes that conventional environmentally and socially harmful production is normal, and ethical production is only a complementary premium type of certification.

In a transformed system, as originally envisioned by organic and fair-trade movements, all producers would be able to receive higher prices because social and environmental costs would no longer be externalized. Those premiums currently paid by fair-trade initiatives are an effort to anticipate this transformation (Fairtrade 2017). Scholars have outlined the disadvantages of mixing fair trade and non–fair trade (Barratt Brown 2007, among others). An interviewee told me of smallholder cooperatives that sell to both fair-trade companies, which commit to pay more than world market prices, and TNCs, which partly purchase at the fixed fair-trade price (and label a share of their products accordingly), but bargain down the price of the rest of their purchase below world market price (FH, interview, January 13, 2017). With mass balance and book and claim approaches, such exceptions become the rule. For consumers aiming to resist the conventional system, there is thus no way around insisting on separate supply chains (as required by the EU Organic Regulation and US NOP).

The differentiation between resistance and system-stabilizing types of regulation is also linked to current debates in certification practice about *additionality*—that is, findings that only those projects that already fulfill higher standards receive certification and/or EU and US market access (SK, interview, August 21, 2018; VB, interview, August 28, 2018). Against this backdrop, scholars have warned that new alternative forms of regulation only privilege already existing projects with better social and environmental conditions, instead of really improving business performance at sites of implementation (see especially Nygren 2015). An illustrative example is Cotton made in Africa (CmiA) making consumers pay more for rain-fed agriculture, although its cotton is grown in a region of Ethiopia where irrigation infrastructure has not yet been developed (section 3.2.3). There is no additionality, or water-related improvement on the ground, resulting from this certification criterion. With this in mind, certifying best practice is not sufficient: we need additionality in the sense of tangible progress.

Second, a major challenge alternative forms of regulation face is the involvement of small-scale producers in the Global South (in addition to paying premiums, fair-trade initiatives originally differentiated themselves from others by exclusively working with smallholders; see chapter 3, section 3.1.2). Smallholder and family farms operate about 75 percent of the world's agricultural land (Lowder, Skoet, and Raney 2016). In Indonesia, smallholders account for about 35 to 40 percent of all palm oil production (OECD 2012, 229). In the DRC, artisanal mining comprises an estimated 90 percent of the mining sector (Geenen 2012). As the bulk of regulative initiatives focus on environmental issues, the economic and social consequences of supply-chain-related regulation are widely neglected (for critique, see Geenen 2017; McDermott, Irland, and Pacheco 2015; Sneyd 2011). However, fair-trade initiatives, which focus on economic and social aspects in the Global South, do exist. They have over fifty years of experience giving small-scale producers fair prices, training, advice, and funding (Barratt Brown 2007; Levi and Linton 2003). IFOAM demonstrates an ability to engage and people in and inspire people by organic farming, including smallholders in the Global South (see chapter 3, section 3.2.2). Furthermore, there are more recent schemes, such as CmiA, which adapt environmental ambitions to the local context—for instance, by providing purchase guarantees to smallholders (see chapter 3, section 3.2.3).

The increasingly obvious discrimination against producers from the Global South through alternative forms of regulation undermines more than just their credibility and legitimacy. Global business may have benefitted in the past from the exclusion of potential competitors, but the marginalization of small-scale producers now limits market growth, especially in sectors in which certification and due diligence have become de facto mandatory (chapters 4 and 5). Hence, there is a double need for smallholder involvement in new forms of regulation. In order to close this gap, further research is needed to more deeply understand existing fair-trade and other socially focused approaches and determine transferabilities to more environmentally focused initiatives.

Third, NGOs often claim to represent small-scale producers and local communities at sites of implementation, and my research found that they actually do so—although their policy instrument choices often deviate from those preferred by affected communities (chapters 3–5). A reason for this "broken telephone" (van der Ven 2019b, 82) that I see is that new forms of regulation extensively overstrain the capacities of NGOs. There are conflicting demands on them because they are supposed to take over legislative, executive, and juridical roles simultaneously.

In multistakeholder arrangements, NGOs participate in standard formulation. Here, when performing legislative functions, they are principally disadvantaged compared to business actors who have more resources available to advocate for their interests. This has been argued by diverse actors, in particular, with regard to local NGOs (Cheyns 2014; Sneyd 2011, 2015). Complementing these earlier findings, however, my case studies showed that in practice, NGOs can have a considerable influence due to their continual and engaged participation—in particular, international NGOs (see especially section 5.2.2).

Besides their participation in standard setting, a core activity of NGOs is to apply for, and often pass through, funding to implement projects on the ground. For example, this was true for PAN Ethiopia in the case of the Arba Minch cotton project. Confirming earlier research (Sneyd 2011, 2015), the NGO project was left at the mercy of donors. The NGO and donors ultimately decided on the EU Organic certification, although the primary interest of farmers was to receive higher prices for their yield (AM, group discussion, September 5, 2017), and organic cotton has not achieved higher prices compared to conventional production (Textile Exchange 2017, 34). Passing the auditing process and obtaining the certification served only the donors' expectation, instead of the farmers' needs (AM, group discussion, September 5, 2017).

There are similar problems in the palm oil sector. An interviewee estimated that about 20 percent of the smallholders leave the RSPO once externally funded NGO projects have culminated (VB, interview, August 28, 2018). However, in Arba Minch, for the sake of receiving the organic certification, farmers had to establish a cooperative, and this cooperative allowed them to negotiate a higher price for their yield (AM, group discussion, September 5, 2017). Hence, eventually, as the cooperative was a side-effect of certification, PAN Ethiopia supported the famers in accomplishing their prior interest in a higher income. Throughout my field research, I experienced NGO representatives searching for ways to compromise in the face of conflicting demands and interests.

Whereas earlier research already dealt with NGOs' role in standard setting and implementation, this book also delivers novel insights on the role of NGOs by highlighting their crucial juridical function (especially section 3.2.2; section 4.2.1; and section 5.2.2). Since the 1990s, an increasing number of NGOs has changed from strategies of naming and shaming to more collaborative approaches like multistakeholder certification (Bartley 2018; Haufler 2003). This means that NGOs, such as Greenpeace, fundamentally changed their strategy to accomplish stricter environmental standards (Bartley 2007). (However, Greenpeace International effectively reversed its stance in 2018 when it announced that it would not renew its FSC membership.)

Besides, or despite, their participation in standard setting and implementation, NGOs continue to be expected to monitor and enforce new forms of regulation. It is controversial whether NGOs are able to do so, given their dual (or tripartite) function (Lin 2012; Partzsch, Zander, and Robinson 2019). Some multistakeholder schemes, like the FSC and RSPO, maxed out conflicting demands on NGOs by setting up private grievance procedures, in which NGOs are actively involved in both the complainant and judging sides (FSC 2019; RSPO 2019).

In the case of voluntary certification, an accepted grievance and loss of certification and/or membership is assumed to imply reputational risks and hence loss of revenue among ethically conscious consumers (following Bartley 2018; Haufler 2010; among others). An example is the FSC grievance case of Greenpeace Africa against SIFORCO in the DRC (section 4.1.2). Greenpeace caused the company to lose its certification (for a limited period), but the NGO was also an FSC member at the time (Lawson 2014, 19; REM 2013, 24–25). SIFORCO demonstrably harvested timber illegally (Greenpeace Africa 2013, 4), but the NGO did not take civil action through the courts against the company, based on the EUTR, the US Lacey Act, or ILPA.

Despite scholarly assumptions of reputational loss resulting in revenue loss (Haufler 2010, among others), SIFORCO continued to be among the DRC's largest logging companies after the grievance case (Lawson 2014, 19). Therefore, we may not argue that the company was particularly harmed by the loss of FSC certification, and this actually contradicts assumptions made in the literature about companies' motivations to participate in private governance (Dauvergne 2018b; Haufler 2003). More research is needed here.

In the case of de facto mandatory certification with EU-RED, however, certification or membership withdrawal can result in exclusion from the EU biofuel market (see chapter 5). In order to prevent this risk, as I outlined for the RSPO IOI case (section 5.1.3), exporters hedge their bets by committing to several certification schemes in parallel. When IOI was suspended by the RSPO, it continued to be certified by the ISCC. NGOs would have needed to advocate for it to lose certification from other schemes too. However, like in the FSC SIFORCO case, the complainant NGO left it to one single grievance case, or first-instance private jurisdiction; that is, it did not take legal steps (section 5.3.1).

There is a general need for more research regarding the implications of governance fragmentation and overlap with regard to NGOs. In order to immediately close the described loophole created by companies committing to several schemes, the EU could cease to allow companies to contribute to its renewable energy targets if they are suspended by at least one of the accredited certification schemes (no matter whether or not another scheme continues to grant them certification). Moreover, NGOs could receive state aid for taking legal steps, instead of relying only on private grievance.

Finally, and fourth, what all studied alternative forms of regulation have in common is that they are based on purchasing power, and this has clear limits. Consuming countries and people enforce rules on actors further up their supply chains. Exporting countries support new regulative approaches, but they set different priorities; in particular, they prioritize rapid economic growth over environmental protection (see chapters 3–5).

Against this backdrop, new market incentives tend to be necessary to at least enforce environmental standards. As argued earlier, sustainability provides a common ground for action now. The new regulative approaches implement collective values.

For instance, in chapter 3, we noted that the Ethiopian government is encouraging cotton cultivation and exports in order to increase foreign exchange earnings to stabilize the country's currency, generate fiscal revenue, and provide inputs for import-substituting industries (AT, interview, September 7, 2017). The promotion of large-scale commercial agriculture became one of its core objectives, while environmental considerations have been delayed (Abbink 2011; Lefort 2012; NPC 2016). Likewise, we noted in chapters 4 and 5 that natural resource protection is again not a priority of either the DRC or the Indonesian government. In consequence, the majority of companies in developing countries is allowed not to fulfill even existing legislation, including TNCs originating from the Global North (section 3.2.1; section 4.2.1; and section 5.2.1). In this situation, new forms of regulation incite companies to improve their own performance and advocate for governmental reform in exporting countries. By making compliance mandatory for all importers, governments of consuming states ask for more than "minor adjustments" (Swilling and Annecke 2012, 191) in producing countries. Hence, I do not agree with earlier research that argues in this direction (Levidow 2013; Sneyd 2014; Swilling and Annecke 2012). Alternative regulation does exist and must be applied more consequently in order to prevent blood consumption. Further research is needed to provide more cross-sectoral learning and strategies for ways to overcome limitations.

Now it is time for a more fundamental reform of the world trade system. This book has demonstrated that states are not unable to regulate but that multilateralism does not work, and solutions are fragmented (private, mandatory, hybrid). There is not yet, and may never be, one single alternative. However, we need to bring together regulative approaches already used for governing different supply chains. For example, legality verification, which is mandatory only for timber, should be generally applied on a worldwide scale (see also Bartley 2018). Requirements could be systematically raised over time, as they were in the case of EU-RED. The RED metastandard initially required that biofuels achieve 35 percent GHG savings, which increased to 50 percent in 2017 and 60 percent as of 2018 for new installations (European Commission 2009); new requirements on ILUC were amended in 2015 and 2018 (European Commission 2015, 2018a). In comparison, while the EU Organic Regulation and US NOP already provide ambitious minimum requirements, they are still completely voluntary (see chapter 3). Similar to EU-RED, governments could introduce and continuously raise the mandatory share of organic products in the market. In parallel, governments should refrain from approving additional schemes that are less ambitious than existing ones, as seen in the biofuel sector (see chapter 5). In particular, the use of the fair-trade label should be legally restricted (e.g., in line with the FLO and/or ILO standard) and its market share should increase over time—at least, for those agricultural commodities for which world market prices repeatedly fell to a level that caused misery and poverty in the Global South, such as coffee and cocoa.

Diverse sectors provide illustrative examples of regulative alternatives to multilateralism. There is no need, or excuse, for any individual consumer, TNC, or Western country to purchase goods and services produced under unacceptable conditions. However, the voluntary purchase of only ethical products is obviously limited. Therefore, we need to better understand and more prudently combine private with public regulation in new hybrid arrangements. Social justice and environmental sustainability should have priority all along global supply chains.

Appendix

Overview of power dynamics through the new (re-)regulation of global supply chains

State of research perspective	Analytical questions for studying new regulation	Private regulation (voluntary certification)	Public supply-chain-related laws	Hybrid transnational governance
(1) Globalization and the withdrawal of the state led to a new private *power over* nation-states at the expense of environmental and social considerations.				
	• **Does the regulation comply with WTO rules: And if yes, how does it comply?**	• WTO acknowledges technical regulations so long as they do not discriminate against products with a different country of origin, or form an unnecessary obstacle to free trade.	• Mandatory requirements for importers are based on due diligence (or due care), i.e., the principle of disclosure. • Timber laws rely on definition of legality by exporting country. • Liability is attached for false statement.	• EU-RED reflects both the shadow of the WTO (no ban) and the UNFCCC (need for GHG emission reductions). • Mandatory share of biofuels in the overall energy mix, and these biofuels have to comply with meta-standard (proven by certification). • Lack of market incentive makes private certification de facto mandatory for biofuels in the EU.

State of research perspective	Analytical questions for studying new regulation	Private regulation (voluntary certification)	Public supply-chain-related laws	Hybrid transnational governance
	• Does the regulation support a race to the bottom regarding environmental and social considerations?	• Governments use voluntary certification to compensate for a lack of environmental regulation, e.g., Austria financing Forest Stewardship Council (FSC). • Public regulation is limited to voluntary use of term *organic* (e.g., EU Organic Regulation, US NOP) and protection of trademarks (e.g., FLO label). • Privatizing *up* in market niches occurs.	• Public laws change the rules of the game for all companies (race to the top). • Environmental and social considerations fall behind earlier ambitions of private regulation in voluntary niches (legal and/or conflict-free instead of sustainable and/or organic production; race to the bottom).	• EU-RED makes certification de facto mandatory for all biofuels; there is no dependence on individual consumers. • New private schemes are less ambitious compared to earlier schemes in defining sustainability standards. • New public schemes of exporting countries only verify legality (instead of sustainability).
	• Does the regulation lead to further centralization, or fragmentation and polycentrism of global governance?	• WTO faces an increasingly fragmented landscape of certification schemes.	• Further fragmentation is due to diverse domestic laws in addition to existing and new certification schemes	• Further fragmentation is due to additional private certification schemes to prove compliance and new public schemes from exporting countries in response.
	• Is there a zero-sum power shift to TNCs or other private actors?	• New authority of private collective and individual actors in defining standard contents ("sustainable forestry," "better cotton") occurs.	• Shift of regulative authority to the private importers who are supposed to enforce rules exterritorialy occurs.	• Shift of regulative authority to the private certification schemes occurs.

State of research perspective	Analytical questions for studying new regulation	Private regulation (voluntary certification)	Public supply-chain-related laws	Hybrid transnational governance
	• Are NGOs a counterpart to TNCs and/or are they themselves subject to a neoliberal discourse?	• NGOs is counterpart to businesses. • Ethically conscious consumerism replaces political activism.	• The laws depend on NGOs and their capacities to monitor and control the business sector abroad. • The laws are based on disclosure and partly depend on consumers' demand for environmentally and/or socially conscious products.	• NGOs are a counterpart to TNCs and state actors in producing countries.

(2) There are increasing asymmetries between actors in consuming countries of the Global North and actors in producing countries of the Global South.

| | • Are the regulations and/or WTO rules favoring countries of the Global North? | • Voluntary certification allows consuming countries to bypass the opposition of the producing countries in intergovernmental negotiations.
• WTO nondiscrimination principle does not recognize North–South inequalities. | • Public supply-chain-related laws allow consuming countries to enforce rules in producing countries
• Increasing interest in VPAs demonstrates that market incentives of the Global North work to strengthen public institutions in the Global South.
• De facto embargo against countries with weak institutions and/or areas with armed conflicts in the Global South occurs. | • Request for sustainability certification limits access to Northern markets.
• Southern countries warned to file a WTO complaint over unfair barriers against their biofuels. |

State of research perspective	Analytical questions for studying new regulation	Private regulation (voluntary certification)	Public supply-chain-related laws	Hybrid transnational governance
	• Are NGOs or other actors speaking on behalf of the Global South?	• NGOs speak on behalf of people in Global South but are accountable to donors in the Global North. • Certification depoliticizes resource flows from the South to the North.	• Governments adopting supply-chain-related laws and businesses, especially those selling certified products from the Global South, claim to benefit local people.	• NGOs and marginalized groups in the Global South gain new resources and capabilities for agenda-setting and stating grievances. • Private schemes, including grievance procedures, strengthen NGOs vis-à-vis public authorities of the Indonesian nation-state.
	• Is there self-determined agency among actors of the Global South?	• Political pioneer schemes are able to unite, engage, educate, and inspire people. • Developing countries' self-determination is further undermined, if their citizens turn to the private sector for governance instead of to their own governments.	• By building upon legality defined by exporting countries, the laws support state actors in the Global South.	• No, RED meta-standard is purely defined by Europeans, and private schemes are dominated by actors from the Global North.
	• Do actors in the Global South gain new resources and capacities from the regulation?	• Individual producers and certification initiatives gain additional resources and capabilities (e.g., farmers through training provided by certification initiatives).	• Law-abiding and/or certified actors gain market advantages.	• Actors in line with RED-defined sustainability gain additional resources and capabilities.

State of research perspective	Analytical questions for studying new regulation	Private regulation (voluntary certification)	Public supply-chain-related laws	Hybrid transnational governance

(3) State and nonstate actors are not continuously selfish but exercise power with others to pursue collective norms of environmental sustainability and social justice.

	• For which norms and values does the regulation stand?	• Movements and NGOs initiated certification schemes for collective norms of environmental protection and fairness in world trade.	• Countries of the Global North enforce the implementation of collective norms (international peace; forest and biodiversity conservation; climate mitigation; legality).	• NGOs exercise normative power by pursuing environmental protection and social justice (land reform). • EU pursues sustainability with a focus on climate change mitigation. • ISPO also aims for sustainability (while equating the concept to legality).
	• Are these commonly generated and shared norms (power with)?	• Private regulations generally pursue universal norms but also take a stance with regard to controversial issues such as GMOs.	• Ending blood consumption serves the people in resource-exporting countries.	• EU enforces international norms in the Global South but based on predefined interpretation.
	• Do actors that are more capable coerce and manipulate others in finding only supposedly common ground?	• Private regulation does not recognize unequal starting positions of companies in the Global North and South.	• Southern governments and TNCs are coerced to cooperate by means of market power.	• Southern governments and TNCs are coerced to cooperate by means of market power.
	• Is market power used to pursue environmental and social norms?	• Although certification is voluntary and hence soft power, it effectively limits Southern producers' access to global markets.	• Public supply-chain-related laws are hard power and effectively limit market access.	• RED (and US RSF) is hard power and effectively limits market access.

State of research perspective	Analytical questions for studying new regulation	Private regulation (voluntary certification)	Public supply-chain-related laws	Hybrid transnational governance
	• **Do universal norms and ethical values serve trade discrimination of Southern countries?**	• Businesses accept voluntary mechanisms to prevent state regulation, and this affects in particular countries with weaker regulation (in the Global South).	• De facto discrimination of Southern producers—in particular, small businesses without legal status occurs; there are also additional compliance costs for businesses from importing countries.	• Certification requirements impede access to the European market for producers from the Global South (but same requirements for producers inside the EU).

Notes

1 Introduction

1. China has an export share of 8 percent in the global market in terms of resources (1 billion tons), and 3.7 percent in terms of financial value (166 billion USD). Its resource import share is 21 percent (2.7 billion tons), with a financial value share of 12 percent (554 billion tons) (in 2016) (Chatham House 2019). China is the world's largest manufacturer. A large share of its resource imports continue to be exported in the form of processed products, especially to the EU and the United States, in the textile and timber sectors (Cashore and Stone 2014; West and Lansang 2018).

2. In November 2016, the European Commission initiated the revision of this Directive for the post-2020 period. The revised Renewable Energy Directive (EU 2018/2001) was adopted in December 2018, and the member states need to implement most elements by June 30, 2021. When I speak of "RED" in this book, I mean both the original and revised Directive (RED I and II).

2 Three Central Perspectives on Power in Global Supply Chains

1. Canada, France, Germany, Italy, Japan, the United Kingdom, and the United States.

2. Argentina, Australia, Brazil, Canada, China, France, Germany, India, Indonesia, Italy, Japan, Mexico, Russia, Saudi Arabia, South Africa, South Korea, Turkey, the United Kingdom, the United States, and the EU.

3. There were 77 founding members of the organization, but it has expanded to 134 member countries.

4. Sachs and Santorius's triad originally referred to the EU, the United States and Japan.

3 Private Regulation in Global Supply Chains

1. After China, India, the United States, and Pakistan.

2. The following fair trade labeling initiatives are or were FLO members (since 1997): Fairtrade Australia and New Zealand; Fairtrade Österreich (Austria); Fairtrade Belgium; Fairtrade Canada; The Czech Fairtrade Association (marketing organization); Max Havelaar Denmark; Fairtrade Estonia; Reilun kaupan edistämisyhdistys (Finland); Max Havelaar France; TransFair Deutschland (Germany); Fairtrade Hong Kong Foundation (marketing organization); Fairtrade Mark Ireland; Fairtrade Italia (Italy); TransFair Japan; Europe Korea Foundation (marketing organization); Fairtrade Latvia; Fairtrade Lithuania; TransFair-Minka Luxembourg; Mexico Comercio Justo México (associate member); Stichting Max Havelaar (The Netherlands); Fairtrade Max Havelaar Norge (Norway); Fair Trade Label South Africa (associate member) (South Africa); Asociación del Sello de Productos de Comercio Justo (Spain); Fairtrade Sverige (Sweden); Max Havelaar Foundation (Switzerland); The Fairtrade Foundation (UK); and Fairtrade America (United States). These labeling initiatives were joined in 2007 by three Fairtrade producer networks: Network of Asian and Pacific Producers (NAPP); Coordinadora Latinoamericana y del Caribe de Pequeños Productores de Comercio Justo (CLAC); and Fairtrade Africa.

3. In May 2018, Greenpeace International announced that it would not renew its FSC membership, because, after more than twenty-five years of experience, the NGO considers timber certification "a helpful but insufficient tool in the struggle to save our forests" (Greenpeace International 2018).

4. After China, India, the United States, and Pakistan.

5. In order to fulfill the EU Organic standard, the farmers had to change to organic seeds. The study does not consider the use of the potentially more advanced seeds.

6. Cotton Outlook publishes representative prices for the principal growths of raw cotton. The Cotlook A index is intended to be representative of the level of offering prices on the international raw cotton market. It considers the cottons most frequently traded.

4 The Return of the State

1. In the area of anti-corruption, the US Foreign Corrupt Practices Act (FCPA) extends the jurisdiction of US courts to enforce bribery charges extraterritorially. It requires that US companies avoid engaging in activity that violates the corruption standard contained in the Act itself (while the timber supply chain-related laws require compliance with the laws of the countries in which they do business) (Fishman and Obidzinski 2014, p. 265). The FCPA attaches liability to a company through

its supply chain vendors. Because of the high penalties attached to violations under the FCPA, according to Sarfaty (2015, p. 1427), this law has spurred companies to develop compliance policies and enforce contractual provisions on their third-party suppliers. In Europe, the UK Money Laundering Regulations of 2007 pioneered money laundering requirements. These Regulations include customer due diligence requirements, which obligate a business to verify the identity of a customer and determine the purpose and intended nature of their relationship with them. In addition, the Regulations require identifying any beneficial owners, i.e. those who own or control the business (directors, shareholders, etc.) (Hoare 2008, 4). Similar steps are required in Japan and New Zealand (Hoare 2008, p. 11).

2. In 2006, Japan amended its Green Procurement Law to restrict state purchases of forest products to those that have been harvested legally from sustainable sources (Hoare 2008).

3. Public procurement policies of most EU member states also accept FSC and PEFC certification as evidence of legal and sustainable timber from all regions and producers, while the United States has thus far not been willing to develop procurement policies for timber at all (Gulbrandsen 2014, 78–79).

4. The Securities and Exchange Commission (SEC) is an agency of the United States federal government. Companies need to register if traded at the nation's stock and options exchanges.

5. https://www.fairphone.com/en/how-we-work/mapping-phone-made/.

5   Transnational Hybrid Governance

1. Lim Sian Cho, Bumitama Agri Ltd; Frazer Lanier, Citibank; Marieke Leegwater, Solidaridad; Henry Barlow (Affiliate Member); Priya Gopalan, USB; Samantha Bramley, USB; Matthias Diemer, WWF Switzerland; Melizel Asuncion, Verite; Michelle Desilets, Orangutan Land Trust; Lanash Thanda; SEPA (Sabah Environmental Protection Association); Robert Kruger, African Agriculture Fund; Suzanne Hall, San Diego Zoo Global.

2. Palm Oil Farmers' Unions (SPKS), Indonesia Ecolabel Agency (LEI), Forest Watch Indonesia (FWI), Independent Forestry Monitoring Network (JPIK), Kaoem Telapak, Indonesia World Resources Foundation, Greenpeace Indonesia, Human and Nature for a Sustainable Indonesia Foundation, Partnership, Institute for Ecosoc Rights, GAIA, Tropical Forest Foundation (TFF), Padi Indonesia (East Kalimantan), Jasoil (West Papua), Uno Itam (Aceh), Lembaga Tiga Beradik (LTB–Jambi), Evergreen (Central Sulawesi), Yayasan Pusaka, Sayogyo Institute, Indonesia Center for Environmental Law, Kemitraan, GeRak Aceh, Stabil East Kalimantan, MATA Aceh, Perkumpulan Bantuan Hukum Kalimantan, PPLH Mangkubumi, JAPESDA Gorontalo, GRID East

Kalimantan, LPMA Borneo (South Kalimantan), Yayasan Peduli Nanggroe Atjeh (PeNA), and Jikalahari (Riau) .

3. https://www.icco-cooperation.org/en/countries/indonesia.

6 Conclusions

1. Australia and New Zealand; Austria; Belgium; Canada; Czech Republic; Denmark; Estonia; Finland; France; Germany; Hong Kong; Ireland; Italy; Japan; Korea; Latvia; Lithuania; Luxembourg; México (associate member); The Netherlands; Norway; South Africa (associate member); Spain; Sweden; Switzerland; UK; and United States.

References

Abbink, Jon. 2011. "Ethnic-Based Federalism and Ethnicity in Ethiopia: Reassessing the Experiment after 20 Years." *Journal of Eastern African Studies* 5 (4): 596–618. doi:10.1080/17531055.2011.642516.

Afionis, Stavros, and Lindsay C. Stringer. 2012. "European Union Leadership in Biofuels Regulation: Europe as a Normative Power?" *Journal of Cleaner Production* 32 (1): 114–123.

Aga, Asefa, and Berhanu Woldu. 2014. "The Challenges of Large Scale Cotton Farms and the Prospects of Sustainable Small Scale Farmer Cotton Production in Ethiopia: Ethiopian Cotton Producers, Ginners and Exporters Association." Bahir Dar University. Paper presented at the 3rd International Conference on Cotton Textile Value Chain in Africa.

Aggestam, Lisbeth. 2008. "Introduction: Ethical Power Europe?" *International Affairs* 84 (1): 1–11.

Allen, Amy. 1998. "Rethinking Power." *Hypatia* 13 (1): 21–40.

Alliance Experts. 2017. "Trends in the Textile Industry in Ethiopia." Accessed August 20, 2018. http://www.allianceexperts.com/en/knowledge/countries/africa/trends-in-the-textile-industry-in-ethiopia/.

Altmann, Philipp. 2017. "Macht und Theorie: Wie Macht erforschen?" *GAIA* 26 (2): 81–83.

Altvater, Elmar, and Birgit Mahnkopf. 1999. *Grenzen der Globalisierung: Ökonomie, Ökologie und Politik in der Weltgesellschaft.* 4th ed. Münster: Westfälisches Dampfboot.

Amera, Tadesse. 2016. *Cotton Farmers Do Better with IPM in Arba Minch, Ethiopia.* Addis Ababa. Accessed June 27, 2017. http://afsafrica.org/wp-content/uploads/2016/02/IPM-in-Arba-Minch-Ethiopia.pdf.

Amera, Tadesse. 2018. "Please Don't Stop Giving to Charity: These Ethiopian Farmers Show How Crucial It Is." Accessed October 20, 2018. https://www.theguardian.com/commentisfree/2018/feb/27/i-train-organic-farmers-ethiopia-depend-on-donations.

Amera, Tadesse, and Asferachew Abate. 2008. "An Assessment of the Pesticide Use, Practice and Hazards in the Ethiopian Rift Valley: Africa Stock Program." Accessed November 20, 2017. http://www.thenrgroup.net/theme/PAN-ecotox/pdf/annex_6_ethiopia _mini-project_report.pdf.

Amnesty International. 2016. "The Great Palm Oil Scandal: Labour Abuses behind Big Brand Names." Accessed June 20, 2018. https://www.amnesty.org/download/ Documents/ASA2152432016ENGLISH.PDF.

Andrée, Peter. 2011. "Civil Society and the Political Economy of GMO Failures in Canada: A Neo-Gramscian Analysis." *Environmental Politics* 20 (2): 173–191.

Arendt, Hannah. 1970. *Macht und Gewalt*. München: Piper.

Armedangels. 2016. "Join the Fashion Revolution." Video, 0:54. April 24, 2016. https://www.youtube.com/watch?v=9tMrRN_BtuA.

Armedangels. 2018. "Homepage." Accessed August 7, 2018. https://www.armedangels.de/ maennerbekleidung-shirts-t-shirt-solid-james-10251843-188.html.

Arts, Bas. 2003. "Non-state Actors in Global Governance: Three Faces of Power." Max-Planck-Projektgruppe, Recht der Gemeinschaftsgüter 003/4. http://homepage .coll.mpg.de/pdf_dat/2003_04online.pdf.

Auld, Graeme. 2015. *Constructing Private Governance: The Rise and Evolution of Forest, Coffee, and Fisheries Certification*. New Haven, CT: Yale University Press.

Australian Government. 2012. "Illegal Logging Prohibition Act: ILPA." Accessed December 20, 2015. https://www.comlaw.gov.au/Details/C2012A00166.

Australian Government. 2015. "Due Diligence Guidelines for the Responsible Supply Chain of Minerals from Red Flag Locations to Mitigate the Risk of Providing Direct or Indirect Support for Conflict in the Eastern Part of the Democratic Republic of the Congo." Accessed December 20, 2015. http://dfat.gov.au/international-relations/ security/sanctions/sanctions-regimes/congo/pages/due-diligence-guidelines-for-the-responsible-supply-chain-of-minerals-from-red-flag-locations-to-mitigate-the-risk-of-provi.aspx.

Azubuike, Eustace Chikere. 2018. "The Participation of Developing Countries in the World Trade Organization (WTO)." *Baku State University Law Review* 4 (2): 121–148.

Bachrach, Peter, and Morton S. Baratz. 1962. "Two Faces of Power." *American Political Science Review* 4 (56): 947–952.

Bailis, Robert, and Jennifer Baka. 2011. "Constructing Sustainable Biofuels: Governance of the Emerging Biofuel Economy." *Annals of the Association of American Geographers* 101 (4): 827–838.

Baka, Jennifer, and Robert Bailis. 2014. "Wasteland Energy-scapes: A Comparative Energy Flow Analysis of India's Biofuel and Biomass Economies." *Ecological Economics* 108:8–17. https://doi.org/10.1016/j.ecolecon.2014.09.022.

Baldwin, Richard. 2016. "The World Trade Organization and the Future of Multilateralism." *Journal of Economic Perspectives* 30 (1): 95–116. https://doi.org/10.1257/jep.30.1.95.

Balkema, Annelies, and Auke J. K. Pols. 2015. "Biofuels: Sustainable Innovation or Gold Rush? Identifying Responsibilities for Biofuel Innovations." In *Responsible Innovation 2: Concepts, Approaches, and Applications*, edited by B.-J. Koops, I. Oosterlaken, H. Romijn, T. Swierstra, and J. van den Hoven, 283–303. New York: Springer.

Bansard, Jennifer S., Philipp Pattberg, and Oscar Widerberg. 2017. "Cities to the Rescue? Assessing the Performance of Transnational Municipal Networks in Global Climate Governance." *International Environmental Agreements: Politics, Law and Economics* 17 (2): 229–246. https://doi.org/10.1007/s10784-016-9318-9.

Barnett, Michael. 2010. *The International Humanitarian Order*. London: Routledge.

Barnett, Michael, and Raymond Duvall. 2005. "Power in Global Governance." In *Power in Global Governance*, edited by Michael N. Barnett and Raymond Duvall, 1–32. Cambridge: Cambridge University Press.

Barratt Brown, Michael. 2007. "'Fair Trade' with Africa." *Review of African Political Economy* 34 (112): 267–277.

Bartley, Tim. 2007. "Institutional Emergence in an Era of Globalization: The Rise of Transnational Private Regulation of Labor and Environmental Conditions." *American Journal of Sociology* 113 (2): 297–351.

Bartley, Tim. 2014. "Transnational Governance and the Re-centered State: Sustainability or Legality?" *Regulation & Governance* 8 (1): 93–109.

Bartley, Tim. 2018. *Rules without Rights: Land, Labor, and Private Authority in the Global Economy*. Oxford: Oxford University Press.

Basnet, Bimbik Sijapati, Sophia Gnych, and Cut Augusta Mindry Anandi. 2016. *Transforming the Roundtable on Sustainable Palm Oil for Greater Gender Equality and Women's Empowerment*. Bogor: CIFOR—Center for International Forestry Research. Accessed May 15, 2018. https://www.cifor.org/library/6383/transforming-the-roundtable-on-sustainable-palm-oil-for-greater-gender-equality-and-womens-empowerment/.

Bassett, Thomas J. 2010. "Slim Pickings: Fairtrade Cotton in West Africa." *Geoforum* 41 (1): 44–55.

BCI. 2013. "The Better Cotton Assurance Program: Applicable from 2014 Harvest Season." Accessed May 15, 2018. https://bettercotton.org/wp-content/uploads/2014/01/Better-Cotton-Assurance-Program_final_eng_ext.pdf.

BCI. 2018. "Homepage: Better Cotton Initiative." Accessed May 10, 2018. http://bettercotton.org/.

Bedall, Philipp. 2011. "NGOs, soziale Bewegungen und Auseinandersetzungen um Hegemonie: Eine gesellschaftstheoretische Verortung in der Internationalen Politischen Ökonomie." In *Zivilisierung des Klimaregimes: NGOs und soziale Bewegungen in der nationalen, europäischen und internationalen Klimapolitik*, edited by Achim Brunnengräber, 59–84. Wiesbaden: VS Verlag für Sozialwissenschaften.

Berenskoetter, Felix, and M. J. Williams, eds. 2007. *Power in World Politics*. New York: Routledge.

Betsill, M. M. 2006. "Transnational Actors in International Environmental Politics." In *International Environmental Politics*, edited by M. M. Betsill, Kathryn Hochstetler, and Dimitris Stevis, 172–202. New York: Palgrave MacMillan.

Betsill, M. M., and Elisabeth Corell, eds. 2008. *NGO Diplomacy*. Cambridge, MA: MIT Press.

Beyene, Atakilte, and Emil Sandström. 2016. "Emerging Water Frontiers in Large-Scale Land Acquisitions and Implications for Food Security in Africa." In *A History of Water: Water and Food in Africa*, edited by Terje Tvedt, Terje Oestigaard, and Jostein Bakke, 502–520. London: IB Tauris.

Biermann, Frank. 2001. "The Rising Tide of Green Unilateralism in World Trade Law: Options for Reconciling the Emerging North–South Conflicts." *Journal of World Trade* 35 (3): 421–448.

Biermann, Frank, and Steffen Bauer. 2016. *A World Environment Organization: Solution or Threat for Effective International Environmental Governance?* London: Routledge.

Biermann, Frank, and Udo E. Simonis. 2000. "Institutionelle Reform der Weltumweltpolitik? Zur politischen Debatte um die Gründung einer 'Weltumweltorganisation.'" *Zeitschrift für Internationale Beziehungen* 7 (1): 163–184.

Bleiker, Roland. 2018. *Visual Global Politics*. Ann Arbor, MI: Routledge.

Bloomfield, Michael John. 2017. *Dirty Gold: How Activism Transformed the Jewelry Industry*. Cambridge, MA: MIT Press.

BMGF. 2018. "Fact Sheets: Bill & Melinda Gates Foundation." Accessed July 15, 2018. https://www.gatesfoundation.org/Who-We-Are/General-Information/Foundation-Factsheet.

Bob, Clifford. 2005. *The Marketing of Rebellion: Insurgents, Media, and International Activism*. Cambridge: Cambridge University Press.

Boltanski, Luc. 1999. *Distant Suffering: Morality, Media and Politics*. Cambridge: Cambridge University Press.

Börzel, Tanja, and Thomas Risse. 2005. "Public-Private Partnerships: Effective and Legitimate Tools of Transnational Governance?" In *Complex Sovereignty: Reconstituting Political Authority in the Twenty-First Century*, edited by Edgar Grande and Louis W. Pauly, 195–206. Toronto: University of Toronto Press.

Bourdieu, Pierre. 1987. *Sozialer Sinn: Kritik der theoretischen Vernunft.* Frankfurt a.M.: Suhrkamp.

Bourguignon, D. 2015. "EU Biofuels Policy: Dealing with Indirect Land Use Change." January 2015. https://www.europarl.europa.eu/RegData/etudes/BRIE/2015/545726/EPRS _BRI(2015)545726_REV1_EN.pdf.

Brooks, Andrew. 2015. *Clothing Poverty: The Hidden World of Fast Fashion and Second-Hand Clothing.* London: Zed Books.

Brühl, Tanja, Tobias Debiel, Brigitte Hamm, Hartwig Hummel, and Jens Martens, eds. 2001. *Die Privatisierung der Weltpolitik: Entstaatlichung und Kommerzialisierung im Globalisierungsprozess.* Bonn: Dietz.

Brühlhart Banyiyezako, Michèle. 2015. "Here Is What You Need to Know about China's New Conflict Minerals Guidelines." *RCS Global*, August 7, 2015. http://goxi.org/profiles/blogs/here-is-what-you-need-to-know-about-china-s-new-conflict-minerals.

Brülls, Maike. 2019. "Keine Flyer verteilen: Aktivist*innen von Extinction Rebellion ketten sich an Regierungsgebäude und kleben sich auf Straßen fest." *Missy Magazine* 4:52–53.

Brunnengräber, Achim. 2017. "Warum sich die Klimaforschung mit harten Machtverhältnissen beschäftigen muss." *GAIA* 26 (1): 13–15.

Bulkeley, Harriet, and M. M. Betsill. 2004. "Transnational Networks and Global Environmental Governance: The Cities for Climate Protection Program." *International Studies Quarterly* 48 (2): 471–493.

Bulkeley, Harriet, and M. M. Betsill. 2013. "Revisiting the Urban Politics of Climate Change." *Environmental Politics* 22 (1): 136–154.

Bundesregierung. 2011. *Antwort der Bundesregierung die Kleine Anfrage der Abgeordneten Niema Movassat, Sevim Dagdelen Andrej Hunko*, September 21, 2011. http://dipbt.bundestag.de/dip21/btd/17/070/1707045.pdf.

Burgis, Tom. 2015. "Dodd-Frank's Misadventures in the Democratic Republic of Congo." *Politico Magazine*, May 10, 2015. https://www.politico.com/magazine/story/2015/05/dodd-frank-democratic-republic-of-congo-117583.

Busby, Joshua William. 2007. "Bono Made Jesse Helms Cry: Jubilee 2000, Debt Relief, and Moral Action in International Politics." *International Studies Quarterly* 51 (2): 247–275.

BV. 2018. "Bureau Veritas: Homepage: Our Timber Services." Accessed February 20, 2018. https://www.bureauveritas.com/home/about-us/our-business/certification/sector -specific-solutions/forest-wood-products/our-services/default-content-our-services.

Callaway, Annie. 2017. "Demand the Supply: Ranking Consumer Electronics and Jewelry Retail Companies on Their Efforts to Develop Conflict-Free Minerals Supply Chains from Congo." November 2017. https://enoughproject.org/wp-content/ uploads/2017/11/DemandTheSupply_EnoughProject_2017Rankings_final.pdf.

Canovan, Margaret. 1978. "The Contradictions of Hannas Arendt's Political Thought." *Political Theory* 6 (1): 5–26.

Cashore, Benjamin W., Graeme Auld, and Deanna Newsom. 2004. *Governing through Markets: Forest Certification and the Emergence of Non-state Authority.* New Haven, CT: Yale University Press.

Cashore, Benjamin W., and Michael W. Stone. 2014. "Does California Need Delaware? Explaining Indonesian, Chinese, and United States Support for Legality Compliance of Internationally Traded Products." *Regulation & Governance* 8 (1): 49–73.

Certification Control Union. 2017. "Homepage." Accessed November 15, 2017. https://certifications.controlunion.com/en/about-us/history.

Cerutti, Paolo Omar, Richard Eba a Atyi, Edouard Essiane Mendoula, Davison Gumbo, Guillaume Lescuyer, Kaala Moombe, Tsangam Raphael, and Joanne Walker. 2018. "Sub-Saharan Africa's Invisible Timber Markets: ITTO Tropical Forest Update 26/1." Accessed February 20, 2018. https://www.cifor.org/publications/pdf_files/ articles/ACerutti1704.pdf.

CFTI. 2018. "Conflict-Free Tin Initiative: Homepage." Accessed February 20, 2018. https://solutions-network.org/site-cfti.

Chan, Sander, and Philipp Pattberg. 2008. "Private Rule-Making and the Politics of Accountability: Analyzing Global Forest Governance." *Global Environmental Politics* 8 (3): 103–121.

Chatham House. 2019. "Resource Trade Earth." Accessed July 15, 2019. https:// resourcetrade.earth/data?year=2016&importer=156&units=weight.

Chen Chen, L., and L. Xin Yi. 2016. "Post-IPOP: How Indonesia Can Lead in Palm Oil Sustainability." *Jakarta Post*, July 26, 2016. https://www.thejakartapost.com/ academia/2016/07/26/post-ipop-how-indonesia-can-lead-in-palm-oil-sustainability .html.

Chevriot, Roland. 1972. "Creation of an International Federation." Invitation letter. https://infohub.ifoam.bio/sites/default/files/page/files/founding_letter.pdf.

Cheyns, Emmanuelle. 2014. "Making 'Minority Voices' Heard in Transnational Roundtables: The Role of Local NGOs in Reintroducing Justice and Attachments."

Agriculture and Human Values 31 (3): 439–453. https://doi.org/10.1007/s10460-014 -9505-7.

Ching, Ooi Tee, and Noorsila Abd Majid. 2017. "Mah Calls EU Parliament Resolution on Palm Oil a Disappointment." *New Straits Times*, April 5, 2017. https:// www.nst.com.my/news/2017/04/227548/mah-calls-eu-parliament-resolution-palm-oil -disappointment.

CmiA. 2018. "Homepage: Cotton Made in Africa." Accessed May 15, 2017. https:// www.cottonmadeinafrica.org/en/about-us/the-initiative.

Counsell, Simon. 2006. *Forest Governance in the Democratic Republic of Congo: An NGO Perspective.* Brussels: FERN. Accessed December 10, 2016. https://loggingoff.info/wp-content/uploads/2015/09/84-1.pdf.

Cuff, Madeleine. 2016. "Palm Oil Giant IOI Group Regains RSPO Sustainability Certification." *Guardian*, August 8, 2016. https://www.theguardian.com/environment/ 2016/aug/08/palm-oil-giant-ioi-group-regains-rspo-sustainability-certification.

Czempiel, Ernst-Otto, and James N. Rosenau, eds. 1992. *Governance without Government: Order and Change in World Politics.* Cambridge: Cambridge University Press.

Dahl, Robert A. 1957. "The Concept of Power." *Behavioral Science* 2 (3): 201–215.

Damro, Chad. 2012. "Market Power Europe." *Journal for European Public Policy* 19 (5): 682–699.

Dauvergne, Peter. 2018a. "The Global Politics of the Business of 'Sustainable' Palm Oil." *Global Environmental Politics* 18 (2): 34–52. https://doi.org/10.1162/ glep_a_00455.

Dauvergne, Peter. 2018b. *Will Big Business Destroy Our Planet?* Cambridge: Polity Press.

Dauvergne, Peter, and Jane Lister. 2013. *Eco-business: A Big-Brand Takeover of Sustainability.* Cambridge, MA: MIT Press.

de Haan, Jorden, and Sara Geenen. 2016. "Mining Cooperatives in Eastern DRC: The Interplay between Historical Power Relations and Formal Institutions." *Extractive Industries and Society* 3 (3): 823–831.

Deitelhoff, Nicole. 2009. "The Discursive Process of Legalization: Charting Islands of Persuasion in the ICC Case." *International Organization* 63 (1): 33–66.

Demeter. 2018. "Demeter-International: History." https://www.demeter.net/what-is -demeter/history.

De Zutter, Elisabeth. 2010. "Normative Power Spotting: An Ontological and Methodological Appraisal." *Journal of European Public Policy* 17 (8): 1106–1127. https:// doi.org/10.1080/13501763.2010.513554.

Diaz-Chavez, Rocio, Emily Kunen, David Walden, Kevin Fingerman, Lalit Arya, Jessica Chalmers, Bettina Kretschmer, et al. 2013. *Mandatory Requirements in Relation to Air, Soil, or Water Protection: Analysis of Need and Feasibility*. ECOFYS, February 21, 2013. https://ec.europa.eu/energy/sites/ener/files/documents/2013_tasks3and4 _requirements_soil_air_water.pdf.

Dieter, Heribert, and Rajiv Kumar. 2008. "The Downside of Celebrity Diplomacy: The Neglected Complexity of Development." *Global Governance* 14 (3): 259–264.

Dietz, Thomas, Jennie Auffenberg, Andrea Estrella Chong, Janina Grabs, and Bernard Kilian. 2018. "The Voluntary Coffee Standard Index (VOCSI): Developing a Composite Index to Assess and Compare the Strength of Mainstream Voluntary Sustainability Standards in the Global Coffee Industry." *Ecological Economics* 150:72–87. https://doi.org/10.1016/j.ecolecon.2018.03.026.

Diez, Thomas. 2013. "Normative Power as Hegemony." *Cooperation and Conflict* 48 (2): 194–210.

Diez, Thomas, and Ian Manners. 2007. "Reflecting on Normative Power." In *Power in World Politics*, edited by M. J. Berenskoetter and Felix Williams, 137–188. New York: Routledge.

Digeser, Peter. 1992. "The Fourth Face of Power." *Journal of Politics* 54 (4): 977–1007.

Dings, Jos. 2016. "Briefing: Cars and Trucks Burn Almost Half of Palm Oil Used in Europe." Transport and Environment, May 2016. https://www.transportenvironment.org/ sites/te/files/publications/2016_05_TE_EU_vegetable_oil_biodiesel_market_FINAL _0_0.pdf.

Dingwerth, Klaus, and Philipp Pattberg. 2009. "World Politics and Organizational Fields: The Case of Transnational Sustainability Governance." *European Journal of International Relations* 15 (4): 707–743.

Donahue, Bill. 2018. "China Is Turning Ethiopia into a Giant Fast-Fashion Factory." *Bloomberg Businessweek*, March 2, 2018. https://www.bloomberg.com/news/features/ 2018-03-02/china-is-turning-ethiopia-into-a-giant-fast-fashion-factory.

Dove, Stacey. 2014. "Ethiopian Cotton and Land Grabs." *Ecotextile News*, November 5, 2014. https://www.ecotextile.com/2014110521132/features/photo-story-ethiopian -cotton-and-deforestation.html.

Du, Michael M. 2018. "The Regulation of Private Standards in the World Trade Organization." *Food and Drug Law Journal* 73 (3): 432–464.

Easterly, William. 2002. "How Did Heavily Indebted Poor Countries Become Heavily Indebted? Reviewing Two Decades of Debt Relief." *World Development* 30 (10): 1677–1696.

Efeca. 2016. "Economics, Climate and Environment: Comparison of the ISPO, MSPO and RSPO Standards." Accessed July 10, 2018. http://www.efeca.com/wp-content/uploads/2016/03/Efeca_PO-Standards-Comparison-.pdf.

EIA. 2012. "Ethiopian Investment Agency: Investment Opportunity Profile for Cotton Production and Ginning in Ethiopia." Accessed November 20, 2017. http://ethemb.se/wp-content/uploads/2013/07/Cotton-Production-Ginning-in -Ethiopia.pdf.

EIA and Grassroots. 2015. "Environmental Investigation Agency and Grassroots: Who Watches the Watchmen? Auditors and the Breakdown of Oversight in the RSPO." EIA, November 16, 2015. https://eia-international.org/report/who -watches-the-watchmen.

Elder, Sara D., and Peter Dauvergne. 2014. "Farming for Walmart: The Politics of Corporate Control and Responsibility in the Global South." *Journal of Peasant Studies* 42 (5): 1029–1046. https://doi.org/10.1080/03066150.2015.1043275.

Eliasoph, Nina. 2015. "Direct Action, Deliberation, and Diffusion: Collective Action after the WTO Protests in Seattle." *Contemporary Sociology* 44 (2): 282–284. https://doi.org/10.1177/0094306115570271mmm.

Engelkamp, Stephan, and Katharina Glaab. 2015. "Writing Norms: Constructivist Norm Research and the Politics of Ambiguity." *Alternatives: Global, Local, Political* 40 (3–4): 201–218.

Environmental Investigation Agency. 2013. *Liquidating the Forests: Hardwood Flooring, Organized Crime, and the World's Last Siberian Tigers.* Washington, DC: EIA. https://content.eia-global.org/posts/documents/000/000/609/original/EIA_Liquidating _the_Forests.pdf?1479504214.

Ernah, Priyanka Parvathi, and Hermann Waibel. 2016. "Adoption of Sustainable Palm Oil Practices by Indonesian Smallholder Farmers." *Journal of Southeast Asian Economies* 33 (3): 291–316.

Esty, Daniel C., and Andrew S. Winston. 2009. *Green to Gold: How Smart Companies Use Environmental Strategy to Innovate, Create Value, and Build a Competitive Advantage.* Rev. ed. Hoboken, NJ: Wiley.

EU FLEGT. 2018. "Homepage." Accessed February 20, 2018. http://www.euflegt .efi.int.

European Commission. 2009. "Directive 2009/28/EC of 23 April 2009 on the Promotion of the Use of Energy from Renewable Sources and Amending and Subsequently Repealing Directives 2001/77/EC and 2003/30/EC (Text with EEA relevance): Directive 2009/28/EC." Accessed August 10, 2016. http://eur-lex.europa.eu/legal-content/EN/TXT/PDF/?uri=CELEX:32009L0028&from=EN.

European Commission, ed. 2014. *Impact Assessment. Accompanying the Document Proposal for a Regulation of the European Parliament and of the Council Setting Up a Union System for Supply Chain Due Diligence Self-Certification of Responsible Importers of Tin, Tantalum and Tungsten, Their Ores, and Gold Originating in Conflict-Affected and High-Risk Areas: Brussels, Brussel, 5 March 2014*. Accessed June 15, 2018. https://eur-lex.europa.eu/resource.html?uri=cellar:b05a9c8f-a54d-11e3-8438-01aa75ed71a1.0001.01/DOC_1&format=PDF.

European Commission. 2015. "Legislative Resolution of 28 April 2015 on the Council Position at First Reading with a View to the Adoption of a Directive of the European Parliament and of the Council Amending Directive 98/70/EC Relating to the Quality of Petrol and Diesel Fuels and Amending Directive 2009/28/EC on the Promotion of the Use of Energy from Renewable Sources (10710/2/201 4–C8-0004/2015–2012/0288(COD)): P8_TA(2015)0100." Accessed June 15, 2018. http://www.europarl.europa.eu/sides/getDoc.do?type=TA&language=EN&reference=P8-TA-2015-0100.

European Commission. 2016. "Proposal for a Directive Amending Directive 2012/27/EU on Energy Efficiency: COM(2016) 761 Final." Accessed December 10, 2016. http://ec.europa.eu/energy/sites/ener/files/documents/1_en_act_part1_v16.pdf.

European Commission. 2018a. "Directive (EU) 2018/2001 of the European Parliament and of the Council of 11 December 2018 on the Promotion of the Use of Energy from Renewable Sources (Text with EEA Relevance.)." Accessed June 10, 2019. https://eur-lex.europa.eu/legal-content/EN/TXT/?uri=uriserv:OJ.L_.2018.328.01.0082.01.ENG&toc=OJ:L:2018:328:TOC.

European Commission. 2018b. "EU's Renewable Energy Directive & Its Impact on Palm Oil: Fact Sheet." European Commission, January 18, 2018. https://eeas.europa.eu/sites/eeas/files/20180118_red2_fact_sheet_en_0.pdf.

European Commission. 2019. "Voluntary Schemes." Accessed May 10, 2019. https://ec.europa.eu/energy/en/topics/renewable-energy/biofuels/voluntary-schemes.

European Parliament. 2015. "Briefing: EU Biofuels Policy: Dealing with Indirect Land Use Change." European Parliament, January 2015. http://www.europarl.europa.eu/RegData/etudes/BRIE/2015/545726/EPRS_BRI(2015)545726_REV1_EN.pdf.

Eyben, Rosalind, Colette Harris, and Jethro Pettit. 2006. "Introduction: Exploring Power for Change." *IDS Bulletin* 37 (6): 1–10.

Fairphone. 2017. "Homepage." Accessed August 20, 2017. www.fairphone.com.

Fairtrade. 2017. "Homepage: Fairtrade Deutschland." Transfair Baumwolle. Accessed November 16, 2017. https://www.fairtrade-deutschland.de/produkte-de/baumwolle/hintergrund-fairtrade-baumwolle.html.

FAO and ICAC. 2015. "Measuring Sustainability in Cotton Farming Systems." Accessed November 20, 2017. https://www.crdc.com.au/sites/default/files/pdf/SEEP _Sustainability%20Indicators_FINAL.pdf.

FAO and IFC. 2015. "Ethiopia: Irrigation Market Brief." Accessed November 20, 2017. www.fao.org/3/a-i5196e.pdf.

Feindt, Peter H., and Angela Oels. 2005. "Does Discourse Matter? Discourse Analysis in Environmental Policy Making." *Journal of Environmental Policy & Planning* 7 (3): 161–173.

FFL. 2018. "Homepage: Fair for Life." Accessed July 20, 2018. http://www .fairforlife.org.

FFP. 2018. "Forest Peoples Programme: Homepage." Accessed July 10, 2018. www .forestpeoples.org/en.

Fikade, Birhanu. 2018. "GMO Cotton Approved for Plantations." *Reporter*, June 9, 2018. https://www.thereporterethiopia.com/article/gmo-cotton-approved-plantations.

Finnemore, Martha, and Kathryn Sikkink. 1998. "International Norm Dynamics and Political Change." *International Organization* 52 (4): 887–917.

Fishman, Akiva, and Krystof Obidzinski. 2014. "European Union Timber Regulation: Is It Legal?" *RECIEL Review of European Community & International Environmental Law* 23 (2): 258–274. https://doi.org/10.1111/reel.12060.

FLA. 2017. "Fair Labor Association: History." Accessed July 20, 2017. http:// www.fairlabor.org/about-us/history.

FLO. 2015. *Monitoring the Scope and Benefits of Fairtrade*. Bonn: Fairtrade International. https://www.fairtrade.net/fileadmin/user_upload/content/2009/resources/2015-Monitoring_and_Impact_Report_web.pdf.

Forsberg, Thomas. 2011. "Normative Power Europe, Once Again: A Conceptual Analysis of an Ideal Type." *Journal of Common Market Studies* 49 (6): 1183–1204. https:// doi.org/10.1111/j.1468-5965.2011.02194.x.

Foucault, Michel. 1982. "The Subject and Power." *Critical Inquiry* 8 (4): 777–795.

Friedmann, Thomas. 2000. *The Lexus and the Olive Tree: Understanding Globalization*. Rev. ed. New York: Macmillan.

Fritzen, Florentine. 2010. "Changing the World with Müsli." *German Research* 31 (3): 11-14.

FSC. 2019. "Forest Stewardship Council: Homepage." Accessed April 20, 2019. https:// us.fsc.org/en-us.

Fuchs, D. 2007. *Business Power in Global Governance*. Boulder: Lynne Rienner Publishers, Inc.

FWF. 2017. "Fair Wear Foundation: About Us." Accessed July 20, 2017. https://www.fairwear.org/about/.

Gaard, Greta. 2010. "Women, Water, Energy: An Ecofeminist Approach." In *Water Ethics: Foundational Readings for Students and Professionals*, edited by Peter G. Brown and Jeremy J. Schmidt, 59–75. Washington, DC: Island Press.

Gabler, Melissa. 2010. "Norms, Institutions and Social Learning: An Explanation for Weak Policy Integration in the WTO's Committee on Trade and Environment." *Global Environmental Politics* 10 (2): 80–117.

Gebauer, Thomas. 2001. "'. . . Von niemandem gewählt!': Über die demokratische Legitimation von NGO." In *Nichtregierungsorganisationen in der Transformation des Staates*, edited by Ulrich Brand, Alex Demirovic, and Christoph Görg, 95–119. Münster: Westfälisches Dampfboot.

Geenen, Sara. 2012. "A Dangerous Bet: The Challenges of Formalizing Artisanal Mining in the Democratic Republic of Congo." *Resources Policy* 37 (3): 322–330. https://doi.org/10.1016/j.resourpol.2012.02.004.

Geenen, Sara. 2017. "Trump Is Right on Congo's Minerals, but for All the Wrong Reasons." *Conversation*, February 22, 2017. http://theconversation.com/trump-is-right-on-congos-minerals-but-for-all-the-wrong-reasons-73320.

GEPA. 2017. "Homepage: Geschichte." Accessed April 20, 2019. https://www.gepa.de/gepa/geschichte.html.

Gereffi, Gary, John Humphrey, and Timothy Sturgeon. 2005. "The Governance of Global Value Chains." *Review of International Political Economy* 12 (1): 78–104.

Göhler, Gerhard. 2009. "'Power to' and 'Power Over.'" In *The Sage Handbook of Power*, edited by Stewart R. Clegg and Mark Haugaard, 27–39. Los Angeles: Sage.

Goldstein, Judith L., and Richard H. Steinberg. 2009. "Regulatory Shift: The Rise of Judicial Liberalization at the WTO." In *The Politics of Global Regulation*, edited by Walter Mattli and Ngaire Woods, 211–241. Princeton, NJ: Princeton University Press.

GOTS. 2018. "Homepage: Global Organic Textile Standard." Accessed August 10, 2018. http://www.global-standard.org.

Green, Andrew. 2005. "Climate Change, Regulatory Policy and the WTO." *Journal of International Economic Law* 8 (1): 143–189. https://doi.org/10.1093/jielaw/jgi008.

Green, Jessica F. 2013. *Rethinking Private Authority: Agents and Entrepreneurs in Global Environmental Governance*. Princeton, NJ: Princeton University Press.

Greenpeace Africa. 2013. "Cut It Out: Illegal Logging in the Democratic Republic of Congo (DRC)." Accessed February 20, 2018. https://www.greenpeace.org/archive-africa/Global/africa/publications/forests/CutItOut.pdf.

Greenpeace International. 2018. "Greenpeace International to Not Renew FSC Membership." Greenpeace International, March 26, 2018. https://www.greenpeace.org/international/press-release/15589/greenpeace-international-to-not-renew-fsc-membership/.

Gulbrandsen, Lars H. 2014. "Dynamic Governance Interactions: Evolutionary Effects of State Responses to Non-state Certification Programs." *Regulation & Governance* 8 (1): 74–92.

Gupta, Aarti. 2008. "Transparency under Scrutiny: Information Disclosure in Global Environmental Governance." *Global Environmental Politics* 8 (2): 1–7.

Gupta, Aarti, and Michael Mason, eds. 2015. *Transparency in Global Environmental Governance: Critical Perspectives.* Cambridge, MA: MIT Press.

Guzzini, Stefano. 2007. "The Concept of Power: A Constructivist Analysis." In *Power in World Politics*, edited by Felix Berenskoetter and M. J. Williams, 23–42. New York: Routledge.

Habermas, Jürgen. 1998. *Between Facts and Norms: Contributions to a Discourse Theory of Law and Democracy.* Cambridge, MA: MIT Press.

Hagedorn, Gregor, Peter Kalmus, Michael Mann, Sara Vicca, Joke van den Berge, Jean-Pascal van Ypersele, Dominique Bourg, et al. 2019. "Concerns of Young Protesters Are Justified." *Science* 364 (6436): 139–140. https://doi.org/10.1126/science.aax3807.

Haufler, Virginia. 2003. "Globalization and Industry Self Regulation." In *Governance in a Global Economy: Political Authority in Transition*, edited by Miles Kahler and David A. Lake, 226–252. Princeton, NJ: Princeton University Press.

Haufler, Virginia. 2010. "Disclosure as Governance: The Extractive Industries Transparency Initiative and Resource Management in the Developing World." *Global Environmental Politics* 10 (3): 53–73.

Hilson, Gavin. 2014. "'Constructing' Ethical Mineral Supply Chains in Sub-Saharan Africa: The Case of Malawian Fair Trade Rubies." *Development and Change* 45 (1): 53–78.

Hilson, Gavin, Abigail Hilson, and James McQuilken. 2016. "Ethical Minerals: Fairer Trade for Whom?" *Resources Policy* (49): 232–247.

Ho, Ming-sho. 2014. "The Fukushima Effect: Explaining the Resurgence of the Anti-nuclear Movement in Taiwan." *Environmental Politics* 23 (6): 965–983.

Hoare, Alison. 2008. *Due Diligence Systems Analysis of Due Diligence Systems in Non-timber Sectors, and Lessons to Be Learnt for Their Introduction into the Timber and Timber Products Sector in the EU.* London: Chatham House. https://www.illegal-logging.info/sites/files/chlogging/uploads/DuediligencecomparisonsChathamHouse.pdf.

Holzinger, Katharina. 2007. "'Races to the Bottom' oder 'Races to the Top': Regulierungswettbewerb im Umweltschutz." *Politische Vierteljahresschrift Sonderheft* 37:177–199.

Holzscheiter, Anna. 2005. "Discourse as Capability: Non-State Actors' Capital Global Governance." *Millennium: Journal of International Studies* 33 (3): 723–746.

Hopkins, Terence K., and Immanuel Wallerstein. 1986. "Commodity Chains in the World-Economy Prior to 1800." *Review (Fernand Braudel Center)* 10 (1): 157–170.

Hoskins, Transy E. 2014. *Stitched Up: The Anti-Capitalist Book of Fashion*. London: Pluto Press.

Hospes, Otto, and A. Kentin. 2014. "Tensions between Global-Scale and National-Scale Governance: The Strategic Use of Scale Frames to Promote Sustainable Palm Oil Production in Indonesia." In *Scale-Sensitive Governance of the Environment*, edited by F. Padt, P. Opman, N. Polman, and C. Termeer, 203–219. Chichester, UK: Wiley.

Hospes, Otto, Carolien Kroeze, Peter Oosterveer, Greetje Schouten, and Maja Slingerland. 2017. "New Generation of Knowledge: Towards an Inter- and Transdisciplinary Framework for Sustainable Pathways of Palm Oil Production." *NJAS—Wageningen Journal of Life Sciences* 80:75–84. https://doi.org/10.1016/j.njas.2017.01.001.

Huliaras, Asteris, and Nikolaos Tzifakis. 2011. "Bringing the Individual Back In? Celebrities as Transnational Activists." In *Transnational Celebrity Activism in Global Politics: Changing the World?*, edited by Liza Tsaliki, Christos A. Frangonikolopoulos, and Asteris Huliaras, 7–24. Chicago: University of Chicago Press.

Hunsberger, Carol. 2010. "The Politics of Jatropha-Based Biofuels in Kenya: Convergence and Divergence among NGOs, Donors, Government Officials and Farmers." *Journal of Peasant Studies* 37 (4): 939–962.

Hyde-Price, Adrian. 2008. "A 'Tragic Actor'? A Realist Perspective on 'Ethical Power Europe.'" *International Affairs* 84 (1): 29–44. https://doi.org/10.1111/j.146 8-2346.2008.00687.x.

IFOAM. 2012. *Organic without Boundaries: IFOAM Celebrating 40 Years, 1972–2012*. Bonn: International Federation of Organic Agriculture Movement. http://www .ifoam.bio/sites/default/files/ifoam40thanniv_dg_web.pdf.

IFOAM. 2019. "Homepage." Accessed June 20, 2019. http://www.ifoam.bio.

Indonesian Civil Society. 2017. "Indonesian Civil Society Groups' Position Paper on Sustainable Palm Oil Industry in Indonesia." Accessed July 10, 2018. http:// fwi.or.id/english/wp-content/uploads/2017/03/Final-KERTAS-POSISI_09032017 _English_edit-MM.pdf.

Indonesian Palm Oil Pledge. 2016. "Press Release: IPOP Signatories Support Government of Indonesia's Efforts to Transform Palm Oil Sector towards Sustainability."

Accessed February 10, 2017. https://www.palmoilpledge.id/en/2016/07/ipop-signatories-support-government-of-indonesias-efforts-to-transform-palm-oil-sector-towards-sustainability.

International Networks Archive. 2003. "The Magic Bean Shop." Infographic. https://www.princeton.edu/~ina/infographics/starbucks.html.

IUCN. 2018. "Homepage: Water Pollution." Accessed July 30, 2018. https://www.iucnredlist.org/initiatives/freshwater/panafrica/threats.

IVN. 2018. "Homepage: Internationaler Verband der Naturtextilwirtschaft e.V." Accessed July 30, 2018. http://naturtextil.de/en/home/#.

Jacobs, Brian W., and Vinod R. Singhal. 2017. "The Effect of the Rana Plaza Disaster on Shareholder Wealth of Retailers: Implications for Sourcing Strategies and Supply Chain Governance." *Journal of Operations Management* 49–51 (3): 52–66. https://doi.org/10.1016/j.jom.2017.01.002.

Jakarta Post. 2017a. "Editorial: EU Policy Unjustifiable." *Jakarta Post*, March 24, 2017. https://www.thejakartapost.com/academia/2017/03/24/editorial-eu-policy-unjustifiable.html.

Jakarta Post. 2017b. "Indonesia Calls EU's Ruling on Palm Oil 'Discriminatory.'" *Jakarta Post*, April 10, 2017. http://www.thejakartapost.com/news/2017/04/10/indonesia-calls-eus-ruling-on-palm-oil-discriminatory.html.

Jakir, Vanda. 2013. "The New WTO Tuna Dolphin Decision: Reconciling Trade and Environment?" *Croatian Yearbook of European Law & Policy* 9 (1): 143–176.

Jänicke, Martin. 2005. "Trend-Setters in Environmental Policy: The Character and Role of Pioneer Countries." *European Environment* 15 (2): 129–142.

Jänicke, Martin. 2008. "Ecological Modernisation: New Perspectives." *Journal of Cleaner Production* 16 (5): 557–565.

Janusch, Holger. 2016. "Normative Power and the Logic of Arguing: Rationalization of Weakness or Relinquishment of Strength?" *Cooperation and Conflict* 51 (4): 504–521.

Jeffrey, Jeremy C. 2012. "Tungsten Is Forever: Conflict Minerals, Dodd-Frank, and the Need for a European Response." *New England Journal of International and Comparative Law* 18 (1): 503–514.

Jordan, Andrew, Dave Huitema, Mikael Hildén, Harro van Asselt, Tim J. Rayner, Jonas J. Schoenefeld, Jale Tosun, Johanna Forster, and Elin L. Boasson. 2015. "Emergence of Polycentric Climate Governance and Its Future Prospects." *Nature Climate Change* 5:977–982. https://doi.org/10.1038/nclimate2725.

Jordan, Grant. 2001. *Shell, Greenpeace and the Brent Spar*. New York: Palgrave MacMillan.

Kaag, Mayke, and Annelies Zoomers, eds. 2014. *The Global Land Grab: Beyond the Hype*. London: Zed Books.

Kahler, Miles, and David A. Lake. 2009. "Economic Integration and Global Governance: Why So Little Supranationalism?" In *The Politics of Global Regulation*, edited by Walter Mattli and Ngaire Woods, 242–276. Princeton, NJ: Princeton University Press.

Kaldor, Mary. 2003. "The Idea of Global Civil Society." *International Affairs* 79 (3): 583–593.

Kalfagianni, Agni. 2015. "'Just Food': The Normative Obligations of Private Agrifood Governance." *Global Environmental Change* 31 (1): 174–186.

Kalfagianni, Agni, Lena Partzsch, and Miriam Beulting. 2019. "Governance for Global Stewardship: Can Private Certification Move beyond Commodification in Fostering Sustainability Transformations?" *Agriculture and Human Values*, July 5, 2019. https://doi.org/10.1007/s10460-019-09971-w.

Kalfagianni, Agni, and Sophia Skordili, eds. 2019. *Localizing Global Food*. New York: Routledge.

Kelle, Udo. 2007. "Computer-Assisted Qualitative Data Analysis." In *Qualitative Research Practice*, edited by Clive Seale, David Silverman, Jaber F. Gubrium, and Giampietro Gobo, 443–460. Los Angeles: Sage.

Kelle, Udo. 2015. "Theorization from Data." In *The Sage Handbook of Qualitative Data Analysis*, edited by Uwe Flick, 554–568. London: SAGE Publications.

Kelle, Udo, and Susann Kluge. 1999. *Vom Einzelfall zum Typus*. Opladen: Leske + Budrich.

Kemper, Laura, and Lena Partzsch. 2018. "A Water Sustainability Framework for Assessing Biofuel Certification Schemes: Does European Hybrid Governance Ensure Sustainability of Palm Oil from Indonesia?" *Journal of Cleaner Production* 26 (192): 835–843.

Kemper, Laura, and Lena Partzsch. 2019. "Saving Water while Doing Business: Corporate Agenda-Setting and Water Sustainability." *Water* 11 (2): 297. https://doi.org/10.3390/w11020297.

Kim, Yong H. 2015. "Challenges for Global Supply Chain Sustainability: Evidence from the Conflict Minerals Reports." *Academy of Management Procedures* 2015 (1). https://doi.org/10.5465/AMBPP.2015.18647abstract.

Kim, Yong H., and Gerald F. Davis. 2016. "Challenges for Global Supply Chain Sustainability: Evidence from Conflict Minerals Reports." *Academy of Management Journal* 59 (6):1896–1916.

Kleinschmit, Daniela. 2015. "Internationale Waldpolitik—Prinzip Freiwilligkeit." In *Gesucht: Weltumweltpolitik: Jahrbuch Ökologie 2016*, edited by Heike Leitschuh, Gerd Michelsen, Udo E. Simonis, Jörg Sommer, and Ernst U. von Weizsäcker, 82–87. Stuttgart: Hirzel.

Kleinschmit, Daniela, Helga Pülzl, Laura Secco, Arnaud Sergent, and Ida Wallin. 2018. "Orchestration in Political Processes: Involvement of Experts, Citizens, and Participatory Professionals in Forest Policy Making." *Forest Policy and Economics* 89:4–15.

Koch, Dirk-Jan, and Sara Kinsbergen. 2018. "Exaggerating Unintended Effects? Competing Narratives on the Impact of Conflict Minerals Regulation." *Resources Policy* 57:255–263. https://doi:10.1016/j.resourpol.2018.03.011.

Koenig-Archibugi, Mathias, and Kate Macdonald. 2013. "Accountability-by-Proxy in Transnational Non-state Governance." *Governance: An International Journal of Policy, Administration, and Institutions* 26 (3): 499–522.

Kohl, Uta. 2014. "Corporate Human Rights Accountability: The Objectives of Western Governments to the Alien Tort Ttatute. *International and Comparative Law Quarterly* 63 (3): 665–697.

Kuchler, Magdalena, and Björn-Ola Linnér. 2012. "Challenging the Food vs. Fuel Dilemma: Genealogical Analysis of the Biofuel Discourse Pursued by International Organizations." *Food Policy* 37 (5): 581–588.

Kulovesi, Kati. 2014. "Real or Imagined Controversies? A Climate Law Perspective on the Growing Links between the International Trade and Climate Change Regimes." *Trade Law and Development* 6 (1): 55–92. https://www.tradelawdevelopment.com/index.php/tld/article/view/6%281%29%20TL%26D%2055%20%282014%29.

Larsen, Rasmus Klocker, Norman Jiwan, Arie Rompas, Johanes Jenito, Maria Osbeck, and Abetnego Tarigan. 2014. "Towards 'Hybrid Accountability' in EU Biofuels Policy? Community Grievances and Competing Water Claims in the Central Kalimantan Oil Palm Sector." *Geoforum*, no. 54: 295–305. https://doi.org/10.1016/j.geoforum.2013.09.010.

Lauber, Volkmar. 1997. "Austria: A Latecomer which Became a Pioneer." In *European Environmental Policy: The Pioneers*, edited by Michael Andersen Skou and Duncan Liefferink, 81–118. Manchester: Manchester University Press.

Lawson, Sam. 2014. *Illegal Logging in the Democratic Republic of the Congo*. London: Chatham House. https://www.chathamhouse.org/sites/files/chathamhouse/publications/research/201404DRC.pdf.

Le Billion, Philippe. 2013. *Wars of Plunder: Conflicts, Profits and the Politics of Resources*. Oxford: Oxford University Press.

Lederer, Markus. 2018. "External State Actors." In *The Oxford Handbook of Governance and Limited Statehood*, edited by Thomas Risse, Tanja Börzel, and Anke Draude, 191–210. Oxford: Oxford University Press.

Lefort, René. 2012. "Free Market Economy, 'Developmental State' and Party-State Hegemony in Ethiopia: The Case of the 'Model Farmers.'" *Journal of Modern African Studies* 50 (4): 681–706. https://doi.org/10.1017/S0022278X12000389.

Leipold, Sina. 2017. "How to Move Companies to Source Responsibly? German Implementation of the European Timber Regulation between Persuasion and Coercion." *Forest Policy and Economics* 82:41–51.

Leipold, Sina, Metodi Sotirov, Tina Frei, and Georg Winkel. 2016. "Protecting 'First World' Markets and 'Third World' Nature: The Politics of Illegal Logging in Australia, the European Union and the United States." *Global Environmental Change* 39:294–304.

Leipold, Sina, and Georg Winkel. 2016. "Divide and Conquer: Discursive Agency in the Politics of Illegal Logging in the United States." *Global Environmental Change* 36 (1): 35–45.

Lesniewska, Feja, and Constance L. McDermott. 2014. "FLEGT VPAs: Laying a Pathway to Sustainability via Legality Lessons from Ghana and Indonesia." *Forest Policy and Economics* 48:16–23. https://doi.org/10.1016/j.forpol.2014.01.005.

Levi, Margaret, and April Linton. 2003. "Fair Trade: A Cup at a Time?" *Politics & Society* 31 (3): 407–432.

Levidow, Les. 2013. "EU Criteria for Sustainable Biofuels: Accounting for Carbon, Depoliticizing Plunder." *Geoforum* 44 (1): 211–223.

Levy, David L., and Peter J. Newell, eds. 2004. *The Business of Global Environmental Governance: Global Environmental Accord: Strategies for Sustainability and Institutional Innovation*. Cambridge, MA: MIT Press.

Li, Tania Murray. 2014. *Land's End: Capitalist Relations on an Indegenious Frontier*. Durham, NC: Duke University Press.

Li, Tania Murray. 2017. "After the Land Grab: Infrastructural Violence and the "Mafia System" in Indonesia's Oil Palm Plantation Zones." *Geoforum*. https://doi.org/10.1016/j.geoforum.2017.10.012.

Lightfoot, Simon, and Jon Burchell. 2005. "The European Union and the World Summit on Sustainable Development: Normative Power Europe in Action?" *Journal of Common Market Studies* 43 (1): 75–95.

Lin, Jolene. 2012. "Governing Biofuels: A Principal-Agent Analysis of the European Union Biofuels Certification Regime and the Clean Development Mechanism." *Journal of Environmental Law* 24 (1): 43–73.

Lowder, Sarah K., Jakob Skoet, and Terri Raney. 2016. "The Number, Size, and Distribution of Farms, Smallholder Farms, and Family Farms Worldwide." *World Development* 87:16–29. https://doi.org/10.1016/j.worlddev.2015.10.041.

Lucier, Cristina A., and Brian J. Gareau. 2015. "From Waste to Resources? Interrogating 'Race to the Bottom' in the Global Environmental Governance of the Hazardous Waste Trade." *JWSR* 21 (2): 495–520. https://doi.org/10.5195/JWSR.2015.11.

Lukes, Steven. 1974. *Power: A Radical View.* London: Macmillan.

Lund, Emma. 2013. "Environmental Diplomacy: Comparing the Influence of Business and Environmental NGOs in Negotiations on Reform of the Clean Development Mechanism." *Environmental Politics* 22 (5): 739–759.

Macdonald, Kate. 2007. "Globalising Justice within Coffee Supply Chains? Fair Trade, Starbucks and the Transformation of Supply Chain Governance." *Third World Quarterly* 28 (4): 793–812.

Macdonald, Kate. 2014. *The Politics of Global Supply Chains.* Cambridge: Polity Press.

Macdonald, Laura. 1994. "Globalising Civil Society: Interpreting International NGOs in Central America." *Millennium: Journal of International Studies* 23 (2): 267–285.

Malets, Olga. 2015. "When Transnational Standards Hit the Ground: Domestic Regulations, Compliance Assessment and Forest Certification in Russia." *Journal of Environmental Policy & Planning* 17 (3): 332–359. https://doi.org/10.108 0/1523908X.2014.947922.

Malmström, Cecilia. 2017. "Debate in EP plenary on the reg. on conflict minerals. Will lead to responsible mineral supply chains. Good example of valued based trade." Twitter, March 15, 2017, 9:01 a.m. https://twitter.com/MalmstromEU/status/842043074998087680.

Manhart, Andreas, and Tobias Schleicher. 2013. *Conflict Minerals: An Evaluation of the Dodd-Frank Act and Other Resource-Related Measures.* Freiburg i.B: Öko-Institut e.V.

Manners, Ian. 2002. "Normative Power Europe: A Contradiction in Terms?" *Journal of Common Market Studies* 40 (2): 235–258.

Manners, Ian. 2015. "Sociology of Knowledge and Production of Normative Power in the European Union's External Actions." *Journal of European Integration* 37 (2): 299–318.

Maryudi, Ahmad. 2016. "Choosing Timber Legality Verification as a Policy Instrument to Combat Illegal Logging in Indonesia." *Forest Policy and Economics* (68): 99–104.

Mathews, Jessica T. 1997. "Power Shift." *Foreign Affairs* 76 (1): 50–66.

Matthysen, Ken, and Andrés Zaragoza Montejano. 2013. *"Conflict Minerals" Initiatives in DR Congo: Perceptions of Local Mining Communities*. Antwerp: International Peace Information Service. http://ipisresearch.be/wp-content/uploads/2013/11/20131112_HU.pdf.

Mattli, Walter, and Ngaire Woods. 2009. "In Whose Benefit? Explaining Regulatory Change in Global Politics." In *The Politics of Global Regulation*, edited by Walter Mattli and Ngaire Woods, 1–43. Princeton, NJ: Princeton University Press.

McDermott, Constance L., Lloyd C. Irland, and Pablo Pacheco. 2015. "Forest Certification and Legality Initiatives in the Brazilian Amazon: Lessons for Effective and Equitable Forest Governance." *Forest Policy and Economics* 1 (50): 134–142.

McNeely, Jeff. 2008. "Biofuels, Biodiversity and Energy Security: What Are the Environmental and Social Impacts?" Paper presented at the SCOPE Conference on Biofuels, Gummersbach, Germany, September 22–25, 2008. Accessed March 16, 2009. https://www.eeb.cornell.edu/howarth/SCOPEBiofuels_Germany2008.html.

Mehta, Lyla, Gert Jan Veldwisch, and Jennifer Franco. 2012. "Water Grabbing? Focus on the (Re)appropriation of Finite Water Resources." *Water Alternatives* 5 (2): 193–207.

Mekonnen, Y., and T. Agonafir. 2002. "Pesticide Sprayers' Knowledge, Attitude and Practice of Pesticide Use on Agricultural Farms of Ethiopia." *Occupational Medicine* 52 (6): 311–315.

Methmann, Chris, Delf Rothe, and Benjamin Stephan, eds. 2013. *Deconstructing the Greenhouse: Interpretive Approaches to Global Climate Governance*. London: Routledge.

Montouroy, Yves. 2016. "Power and Political Change within Global Forest Governance: The EU Flegtaction Plan as Recentralisation." *European Review of International Studies* 2-2016: 58–76. https://doi.org/10.3224/eris.v3i2.04.

Moravaridi, Behrooz. 2012. "Capitalist Philanthropy and the New Green Revolution for Food Security." *International Journal of Sociology of Agriculture & Food* 19 (2): 243–256.

Morin, Jean-Frédéric, and Sikina Jinnah. 2018. "The Untapped Potential of Preferential Trade Agreements for Climate Governance." *Environmental Politics* 27 (3): 541–565. https://doi.org/10.1080/09644016.2017.1421399.

Moser, Christine, Tina Hildebrandt, and Robert Bailis. 2014. "International Sustainability Standards and Certification." In *Sustainable Development of Biofuels in Latin America and the Caribbean*, edited by Barry D. Solomon and Robert Bailis, 27–69. New York: Springer.

Mukama, Kusaga, Irmeli Mustalahti, and Eliakimu Zahabu. 2012. "Participatory Forest Carbon Assessment and REDD+: Learning from Tanzania." *International Journal of Forestry Research* 1 (1): 1–14.

Mukherjee, I., and B. K. Sovacool. 2014. "Palm Oil-Based Biofuels and Sustainability in Southeast Asia: A Review of Indonesia, Malaysia, and Thailand." *Renewable and Sustainable Energy Reviews* 37:1–2. https://doi.org/10.1016/j.rser.2014.05.001.

Murphy, Andrea, Jonathan Ponciano, Sarah Hansen, and Halah Touryalai. 2019. "Global 2000: The World's Largest Public Companies." *Forbes*, May 15, 2019. https://www.forbes.com/global2000/#40359664335d.

Murphy, Craig N. 2000. "Global Governance: Poorly Done and Poorly Understood." *International Affairs* 76 (4): 189–203.

Narain, Sunita. 2010. "Keine gemeinsame Teilhabe an der Welt." *Aus Politik und Zeitgeschichte* (32–33): 3–7.

Nesadurai, Helen E. S. 2013. "Food Security, the Palm Oil–Land Conflict Nexus, and Sustainability: A Governance Role for a Private Multi-stakeholder Regime Like the RSPO?" *Pacific Review* 26 (5): 505–529. https://doi.org/10.1080/09512748.2013.842311.

Neuhoff, Daniel, Sonam Tashi, Gerold Rahmann, and Manfred Denich. 2014. "Organic Agriculture in Bhutan: Potential and Challenges." *Organic Agriculture* 4 (3): 209–221.

Niesen, Peter, and Benjamin Herborth, eds. 2007. *Anarchie der kommunikativen Freiheit: Jürgen Habermas und die Theorie der internationalen Politik.* Frankfurt a.M.: Suhrkamp.

NPC. 2016. *National Planning Commission of Ethiopia: The Second Growth and Transformation Plan (GTP II).* Addis Ababa, Ethiopia. Accessed December 30, 2016. https://ethiopia.un.org/sites/default/files/2019-08/GTPII%20%20English%20Translation%20%20Final%20%20June%2021%202016.pdf.

Nye, Joseph S. 2008. *The Powers to Lead.* New York: Oxford University Press.

Nye, Joseph S. 2011. "Power and Foreign Policy." *Journal of Political Power* 4 (1): 9–24.

Nygren, Anja. 2015. "Governance and Images: Representations of Certified Southern Producers in High-Quality Design Markets." *Environmental Values* 24 (3): 391–412.

Obidzinski, Krystof, Rubeta Andriani, Heru Komarudi, and Agus Andrianto. 2012. "Environmental and Social Impacts of Oil Palm Plantations and Their Implications for Biofuel Production in Indonesia." *Ecology and Society* 17 (25). https://doi.org/10.5751/ES-04775-170125.

OECD. 2012. *OECD Review of Agricultural Policies: Indonesia 2012.* Paris: OECD Publishing. https://www.oecd.org/publications/oecd-review-of-agricultural-policies-indonesia-2012-9789264179011-en.htm.

OECD. 2015. "Chinese Due Diligence Guidelines for Responsible Mineral Supply Chains." Accessed December 20, 2015. http://mneguidelines.oecd.org/chinese-due-diligence-guidelines-for-responsible-mineral-supply-chains.htm.

Oosterveer, Peter, Betty E. Adjei, Sietze Vellema, and Maja Slingerland. 2014. "Global Sustainability Standards and Food Security: Exploring Unintended Effects of Voluntary Certification in Palm Oil." *Global Food Security* 3 (3–4): 220–226. https://doi.org/10.1016/j.gfs.2014.09.006.

O'Rourke, Dara. 2003. "Outsourcing Regulation: Analyzing Nongovernmental Systems of Labor Standards and Monitoring." *Policy Studies Journal* 31 (1): 1–19.

Osborne, Hilary, and Hannah Jane Parkinson. 2018. "Cambridge Analytica Scandal: The Biggest Revelations So Far." *Guardian*, March 22, 2018. https://www.theguardian.com/uk-news/2018/mar/22/cambridge-analytica-scandal-the-biggest-revelations-so-far.

Ostrom, Elinor. 2010. "Polycentric Systems for Coping with Collective Action and Global Environmental Change." *Global Environmental Change* 20 (4): 550–557.

OTA. 2017. "Homepage: Organic Trade Association." Accessed October 20, 2017. https://www.ota.com/.

Otto Shopping. 2018. "Rundhalsshirt, aus Baumwolle." Accessed August 7, 2018. https://www.otto.de/p/rundhalsshirts-3-stueck-baumwolle-cotton-made-in-africa-112166181/?variationId=2422459#variationId=2422459.

Overdevest, Christine, and Jonathan Zeitlin. 2014. "Assembling an Experimentalist Regime: Transnational Governance Interactions in the Forest Sector." *Regulation & Governance* 23 (8): 22–48.

Oxfam. 2018. "History of Oxfam." Accessed August 7, 2018. http://www.oxfam.org.uk/what-we-do/about-us/history-of-oxfam.

Pacini, Henrique, Lucas Assunção, Jinke van Dam, and Rudinei Toneto. 2013. "The Price for Biofuels Sustainability." *Energy Policy* 59 (3): 898–903. https://doi.org/10.1016/j.enpol.2013.03.042.

PAN UK. 2017. "Pesticide-Free Cotton in Ethiopia." Pesticide Action Network UK, May 31, 2017. https://www.pan-uk.org/pesticide-free-cotton/.

Parsons, Talcott. 1963. "On the Concept of Political Power." *Proceedings of the American Philosophical Society* 107 (3): 232–262.

Partzsch, Lena. 2011. "The Legitimacy of Biofuel Certification." *Agriculture and Human Values* 28 (3): 413–425.

Partzsch, Lena. 2014. *Die neue Macht von Individuen in der globalen Politik: Wandel durch Prominente, Philanthropen und Social Entrepreneurs.* Baden-Baden: Nomos.

Partzsch, Lena. 2015. "The Power of Celebrities in Global Politics." *Celebrity Studies* 6 (2): 178–191.

Partzsch, Lena. 2017a. "Biofuel Research: Perceptions of Power and Transition." *Energy, Sustainability and Society* 17 (4): 1–10. https://doi.org/10.1186/s13705-017 -0116-1.

Partzsch, Lena. 2017b. "'Power with' and 'Power to' in Environmental Politics and the Transition to Sustainability." *Environmental Politics* 26 (2): 193–211.

Partzsch, Lena. 2017c. "Powerful Individuals in a Globalized World." *Global Policy* 8 (1): 5–13.

Partzsch, Lena. 2018. "The New EU Conflict Minerals Regulation: Normative Power in International Relations?" *Global Policy* 9 (4): 479–488.

Partzsch, Lena, and D. Fuchs. 2012. "Philanthropy: Power with in International Relations." *Journal of Political Power* 5 (3): 359–376.

Partzsch, Lena, and Laura Kemper. 2019. "Cotton Certification in Ethiopia: Can an Increasing Demand for Certified Textiles Create a 'Fashion Revolution'?" *Geoforum* 99 (February): 111–119. https://doi.org/10.1016/j.geoforum.2018.11.017.

Partzsch, Lena, and Martijn C. Vlaskamp. 2016. "Mandatory Due Diligence for 'Conflict Minerals' and Illegally Logged Timber: Emergence and Cascade of a New Norm on Foreign Accountability." *Extractive Industries and Society* 3 (4): 978–986.

Partzsch, Lena, Macy Zander, and Hannah Robinson. 2019. "Cotton Certification in Sub-Saharan Africa: Promotion of Environmental Sustainability or Greenwashing?" *Global Environmental Change* 57 (July). https://doi.org/10.1016/j.gloenvcha .2019.05.008.

Pattberg, Philipp. 2007. *Private Institutions and Global Governance: The New Politics of Environmental Sustainability*. Cheltenham: Elgar.

Pattberg, Philipp, M. M. Betsill, and Eleni Dellas, eds. 2011. "Agency in Earth System Governance." Special issue, *International Environmental Agreements: Politics Law and Economics* 11 (1).

Pattberg, Philipp, and Oscar Widerberg. 2016. "Transnational Multistakeholder Partnerships for Sustainable Development: Conditions for Success." *Ambio* 45 (1): 42–51.

Paull, John. 2010. "From France to the World: The International Federation of Organic Agriculture Movements (IFOAM)." *Journal of Social Research & Policy* 1 (2): 93–102.

PEFC. 2018. "Programme for the Endorsement of Forest Certification: Homepage." Accessed February 20, 2018. https://www.pefc.org.

Pesqueira, Luli, and Pieter Glasbergen. 2013. "Playing the Politics of Scale: Oxfam's Intervention in the Roundtable on Sustainable Palm Oil." *Geoforum* 45:296–304. https://doi.org/10.1016/j.geoforum.2012.11.017.

Piattoni, Simona. 2009. "Multi-level Governance: A Historical and Conceptual Analysis." *European Integration* 31 (2): 163–180.

Pitkin, Hanna Fenichel. 1972. *Wittgenstein and Justice: On the Significance of Ludwig Wittgenstein for Social and Political Thought*. Berkeley: University of California Press.

Pitkin, Hanna Fenichel. 1981. "Justice on Relating Private and Public." *Political Theory* 9 (3): 327–352.

Planel, Sabine. 2012. "Du bon usage de l'engrais en politique: Introduction à la modernisation agricole en Ethiopie." *Annales d'Ethiopie* (27): 261–281. https://hal.archives-ouvertes.fr/hal-01418320.

Ponte, Stefano. 2014. "'Roundtabling' Sustainability: Lessons from the Biofuel Industry." *Geoforum* (54): 261–271.

Ponte, Stefano, and Carsten Daugbjerg. 2015. "Biofuel Sustainability and the Formation of Transnational Hybrid Governance." *Environmental Politics* 24 (1): 96–114.

Pramudya, Eusebius Pantja, Otto Hospes, and C. J. A. M. Termeer. 2017. "Governing the Palm-Oil Sector through Finance: The Changing Roles of the Indonesian State." *Bulletin of Indonesian Economic Studies* 53 (1): 57–82. https://doi.org/10.1080/00074918.2016.1228829.

Prittwitz, Volker, ed. 1996. *Verhandeln und Argumentieren*. Opladen: Leske + Budrich.

Proforest. 2011. "An Overview of Legality Verification Systems: Briefing Note." Proforest, February 2011. https://www.proforest.net/proforest/en/files/an-overview-of-legality-verification-systems.pdf.

Quark, Amy. 2013. *Global Rivalries: Standards Wars and the Transnational Cotton Trade*. Chicago: University of Chicago Press.

Radke, Sabine. 2017. "Verkehr in Zahlen 2017/18." Accessed December 3, 2018. https://www.bmvi.de/SharedDocs/DE/Publikationen/G/verkehr-in-zahlen-pdf-2017-2018.pdf?__blob=publicationFile.

Radley, Ben, and Christoph Vogel. 2015. "Fighting Windmills in Eastern Congo? The Ambiguous Impact of the 'Conflict Minerals' Movement." *Extractive Industries and Society* 2 (2): 406–410.

Rainforest Alliance. 2018. "Homepage." Accessed February 20, 2018. https://www.rainforest-alliance.org/business/forestry/verification.

Rapunzel. 2014. *40 Jahre Rapunzel: Von der Landkommune zur erfolgreichen Naturkostmarke*. Legau: Rapunzel-Naturkost. Accessed July 20, 2017. http://www.rapunzel.de/download/40jahre-sonderheft.pdf.

Rathke, Gisa-Wilhelmine, and Wulf Diepenbrock. 2006. "Mit Biomasse zum 'Energie-Scheich'? Stand, Ertragspotenziale und Perspektiven." In *Deutsche Landwirtschafts-Gesellschaft: Zukunftsstandort Deutschland: Strategien für die Landwirtschaft*, edited by DLG. Frankfurt a.M.: DLG-Verlag.

Raynolds, Laura T., Douglas Murray, and Andrew Heller. 2007. "Regulating Sustainability in the Coffee Sector: A Comparative Analysis of Third-Party Environmental and Social Certification Initiatives." *Agriculture and Human Values* 24 (2): 147–163. https://doi.org/10.1007/s10460-006-9047-8.

Reijnders, L., and M. A. J. Huijbregts. 2008. "Palm Oil and the Emission of Carbon-Based Greenhouse Gases." *Journal of Cleaner Production* (16): 477–482.

REM. 2013. "Resource Extraction Monitoring: Independent Monitoring of Forest Law Enforcement and Governance (IM-FLEG) in the Democratic Republic of Congo." Accessed February 20, 2018. http://www.observation-rdc.info/documents/ REM_IMFLEG_2013_report_DRC.pdf.

Renckens, Stefan, Grace Skogstad, and Matthieu Mondou. 2017. "When Normative and Market Power Interact: The European Union and Global Biofuels Governance." *Journal of Common Market Studies* 55 (66): 1432–1448. http://dx.doi.org/10.1111/ jcms.12584.

Ribka, Stefani. 2017a. "Only 12% of Indonesia's Oil Palm Plantations ISPO Certified." *Jakarta Post*, April 11, 2017. http://www.thejakartapost.com/news/2017/04/12/only -12-of-indonesias-oil-palm-plantations-ispo-certified.html.

Ribka, Stefani. 2017b. "RI to Strengthen ISPO, Aims for Global Recognition." *Jakarta Post*, April 18, 2017. http://www.thejakartapost.com/news/2017/04/18/ri -strengthen-ispo-aims-global-recognition.html.

Richey, Lisa Ann, ed. 2016. *Celebrity Humanitarianism and North–South Relations: Politics, Place and Power*. New York: Routledge.

Risse, Thomas, Tanja Börzel, and Anke Draude, eds. 2018. *The Oxford Handbook of Governance and Limited Statehood*. Oxford: Oxford Universiy Press.

RMI. 2018. "Homepage: Responsible Minerals Iniatitive." Accessed February 10, 2018. http://www.responsiblemineralsinitiative.org.

Roth, Roland, Florian Semle, and Bernhard Pötter, eds. 2001. *Vom David zum Goliath: NGOs im Wandel*. München: Oekom.

RSB. 2016. "Roundtable on Sustainable Biofuels." Accessed August 10, 2016. http:// www.bioenergywiki.net/Roundtable_on_Sustainable_Biofuels.

RSPO. 2013. *Rountable on Sustainable Palmoil: Principles and Criteria for the Production of Sustainable Palm Oil*. Kuala Lumpur: RSPO. http://www.rspo.org/publications/ download/224fa0187afb4b7.

RSPO. 2019. "Homepage: Roundtable on Sustainable Palm Oil." Accessed April 10, 2019. www.rspo.org.

Ruggie, John. 2013. *Just Business: Multinational Corporations and Human Rights*. New York: Norton.

Ruysschaert, Denis, and Denis Salles. 2014. "Towards Global Voluntary Standards: Questioning the Effectiveness in Attaining Conservation Goals." *Ecological Economics* 107:438–446. https://doi.org/10.1016/j.ecolecon.2014.09.016.

Sachs, Wolfgang, and Tilman Santarius. 2007. *Fair Future: Resource Conflicts, Security, and Global Justice*. London: Zed Books.

Sahide, Muhammad Alif Kaimuddin, Sarah Burns, Agung Wibowo, Dodik Ridho Nurrochmat, and Lukas Giessen. 2015. "Towards State Hegemony over Agricultural Certification: From Voluntary Private to Mandatory State Regimes on Palm Oil in Indonesia." *Manajemen Hutan Tropica: Journal of Tropical Forest Management* 21 (3): 162–171.

SAI. 2017. "Homepage: Social Accountability International." Accessed July 20, 2017. http://www.sa-intl.org/.

Saltzmann, Rafael. 2010. "Establishing a 'Due Care' Standard under the Lacey Act Amendments of 2008." *Michigan Law Review First Impressions* 109 (1). Accessed March 20, 2018. http://repository.law.umich.edu/mlr_fi/vol109/iss1/1.

Sarfaty, Galit A. 2015. "Shining Light on Global Supply Chains." *Harvard International Law Journal* 56 (2): 419–463.

Sassen, Saskia. 2005. "The Ecology of Global Economic Power: Changing Investment Practices to Promote Environmental Sustainability." *Journal of International Affairs* 58 (2): 11–33.

Sassen, Saskia. 2009. *Territory, Authority, Rights: From Medieval to Global Assemblages*. Princeton, NJ: Princeton University Press.

Scharpf, Fritz W. 1999. *Governing in Europe: Effective and Democratic?* Oxford: Oxford University Press.

Schleifer, Philip. 2013. "Orchestrating Sustainability: The Case of European Union Biofuel Governance." *Regulation & Governance* 7 (4): 533–546.

Schleifer, Philip, Matteo Fiorini, and Graeme Auld. 2019. "Transparency in Transnational Governance: The Determinants of Information Disclosure of Voluntary Sustainability Programs." *Regulation & Governance* 88:543. https://doi.org/10.1111/rego.12241.

Schleifer, Philip, and Yixian Sun. 2018. "Emerging Markets and Private Governance: The Political Economy of Sustainable Palm Oil in China and India."

Review of International Political Economy 25 (2): 190–214. https://doi.org/10.108 0/09692290.2017.1418759.

Schnepf, Randy. 2013. "Renewable Fuel Standard (RFS): Overview and Issues." Congressional Research Service. Accessed April 20, 2018. https://fas.org/sgp/crs/misc/ R40155.pdf.

Schoneveld, George, and Maru Shete. 2014. "Modernizing the Periphery: Citizenship and Ethiopia's New Agricultural Investment Policies." In *The Global Land Grab: Beyond the Hype*, edited by Mayke Kaag and Annelies Zoomers, 17–35. London: Zed Books.

SCS Global Services. 2018. "Scientific Certification Systems: Homepage." Accessed February 20, 2018. https://www.scsglobalservices.com/.

Segerlund, Lisbeth. 2010. *Making Corporate Social Responsibility a Global Concern: Norm Construction in a Globalizing World*. Aldershot: Ashgate.

Shaffer, Gregory. 2015. "How the World Trade Organization Shapes Regulatory Governance." *Regulation & Governance* 9 (1): 1–15. https://doi.org/10.1111/rego.12057.

Sifonios, David. 2018. *Environmental Process and Production Methods (PPMs) in WTO Law*. Cham, Switzerland: Springer.

Silva-Castaneda, Laura. 2012. "A Forest of Evidence: Third-Party Certification and Multiple Forms of Proof—a Case Study of Oil Palm Plantations in Indonesia." *Agriculture and Human Values* 29 (3): 361–370.

Simonis, Udo E. 2006. "Die Reform der Umweltpolitik der Vereinten Nationen." In *Die Reform der Vereinten Nationen: Bilanz und Perspektiven*, edited by Johannes Varwick and Andreas Zimmermann, 229–241. Berlin: Duncker & Humblot.

Sneyd, Adam. 2011. *Governing Cotton: Globalization and Poverty in Africa*. Basingstoke: Palgrave MacMillan.

Sneyd, Adam. 2014. "When Governance Gets Going: Certifying 'Better Cotton' and 'Better Sugarcane.'" *Development and Change* 45 (2): 231–256.

Sneyd, Adam. 2015. "The Poverty of 'Poverty Reduction': The Case of African Cotton." *Third World Quarterly* 36 (1): 55–74. https://doi.org/10.1080/01436597.2015.976017.

Soil Association. 2017. "Homepage." Accessed June 28, 2017. https://www .soilassociation.org.

Solidaridad. 2017. "Homepage." Accessed November 20, 2017. https://www .solidaridadnetwork.org.

Stattman, Sarah, Aarti Gupta, Lena Partzsch, and Peter Oosterveer. 2018. "Toward Sustainable Biofuels in the European Union? Lessons from a Decade of Hybrid Biofuel Governance." *Sustainability* 10 (11): 4111. https://doi.org/10.3390/su10114111.

Strange, Susan. 1997. *The Retreat of the State: The Diffusion of Power in the World Economy*. Cambridge: Cambridge University Press.

Susanti, Ari, and Suseno Budidarsono. 2014. "Land Governance and Oil Palm Development: Examples from Riau Province, Indonesia." In *The Global Land Grab: Beyond the Hype*, edited by Mayke Kaag and Annelies Zoomers, 119–134. London: Zed Books.

Sustainable Leader. 2014. "Achieving a More Sustainable Supply Chain in the Democratic Republic of Congo." *Sustainable Leader* (blog), June 6, 2014. http://www.thesustainableleader.org/blog/2014/06/06/achieving-a-more-sustainable-supply-chain-in-the-democratic-republic-of-congo/.

Swilling, Mark, and Eve Annecke. 2012. *Just Transitions: Explorations of Sustainability in an Unfair World*. Claremont, Cape Town: UCT Press.

Tan, K. T., K. T. Lee, A. R. Mohamed, and S. Bhatia. 2009. "Palm Oil: Addressing Issues and towards Sustainable Development." *Renewable and Sustainable Energy Reviews* 13 (2): 420–427. https://doi.org/10.1016/j.rser.2007.10.001.

Textile Exchange. 2016. "Organic Cotton Market Report 2016." Accessed July 20, 2017. http://textileexchange.org/wp-content/uploads/2017/02/TE-Organic-Cotton-Market-Report-Oct2016.pdf.

Textile Exchange. 2017. "Homepage." Accessed July 30, 2017. http://textileexchange.org.

Thematic Working Group on Mining and Natural Resources. 2017. "An Appeal from the Civil Society Organisations of South Kivu in the Democratic Republic of Congo in Reaction to the Announcement Made by the Security and Exchange Commission (SEC) Regarding the Trump Administration's Decision to Issue an Executive Order Aiming at Suspending the Dodd-Frank Act ('the Obama Law')." South Kuvu Civil Society, February 17, 2017. https://www.sec.gov/comments/statement-013117/cll2-1597728-132417.pdf.

Tucker, Karen. 2014. "Participation and Subjectification in Global Governance: NGOs, Acceptable Subjectivities and the WTO." *Millennium: Journal of International Studies* 42 (2): 376–396.

UN SDG. 2019. "Sustainable Development Goals: Goal 1: End Poverty in All Its Forms Everywhere." Accessed May 15, 2019. https://www.un.org/sustainabledevelopment/poverty/.

UN Security Council. 2003. "Security Council Condemns Plunder of Democratic Republic of Congo's Resources, Requests New Six-Month Mandate for Investigative Panel." Press release, January 24, 2003. http://www.un.org/press/en/2003/sc7642.doc.htm.

UN Security Council. 2016. "Report of the Secretary-General on the Implementation of the Peace, Security and Cooperation Framework for the Democratic

Republic of the Congo and the Region." UN Security Council, March 9, 2016. https://www.securitycouncilreport.org/atf/cf/%7B65BFCF9B-6D27-4E9C-8CD3-CF6E4FF96FF9%7D/s_2016_232.pdf.

UN Security Council. 2017. "Final Report of the Group of Experts on the Democratic Republic of the Congo: S/2017/672." UN Security Council, August 10, 2017. https://www.un.org/ga/search/view_doc.asp?symbol=S/2017/672.

UNDP, MoA, and RSPO. 2015. *Joint Study on the Similarities and Differences of the ISPO and the RSPO Certification Systems.* Jakarta: United Nations Development Programme. https://www.undp.org/content/dam/gp-commodities/docs/ISPO-RSPO%20Joint%20Study_English_N%208%20for%20screen.pdf.

UNEP-MONUSCO-OSESG. 2015. *Experts' Background Report on Illegal Exploitation and Trade in Natural Resources Benefitting Organized Criminal Groups and Recommendations on MONUSCO's Role in Fostering Stability and Peace in Eastern DR Congo: Final Report.* UNEP-MONUSCO-OSESG. http://postconflict.unep.ch/publications/UNEP_DRCongo_MONUSCO_OSESG_final_report.pdf.

UNFCCC. 2019. "Paris Agreement." Accessed May 20, 2019. http://unfccc.int/paris_agreement/items/9485.php.

US Department of Justice. 2012. "Gibson Guitar Corp. Agrees to Resolve Investigation into Lacey Act Violations." US Department of Justice, August 6, 2012. https://www.justice.gov/opa/pr/gibson-guitar-corp-agrees-resolve-investigation-lacey-act-violations.

US Department of Justice. 2015. "Lumber Liquidators Inc. Pleads Guilty to Environmental Crimes and Agrees to Pay More than $13 Million in Fines, Forfeiture and Community Service Payments." US Department of Justice, October 22, 2015. http://www.justice.gov/opa/pr/lumber-liquidators-inc-pleads-guilty-environmental-crimes-and-agrees-pay-more-13-million.

van der Ven, Hamish. 2019a. *Beyond Greenwash? Explaining Credibility in Transnational Eco-labeling.* New York: Oxford University Press.

van der Ven, Hamish. 2019b. "Private Accountability in Global Value Chains." In *Global Environmental Governance and the Accountability Trap*, edited by Susan Park and Teresa Kramarz, 63–84. Cambridge, MA: MIT Press.

Voge, Ann-Kathrin, and Friedel Hütz-Adams. 2014. *Sustainable Palm Oil: Aspiration or Reality?* Berlin: Brot für die Welt. http://www.brot-fuer-die-welt.de/fileadmin/mediapool/2_Downloads/Fachinformationen/Analyse/Analyse_44_Palmoel_en.pdf.

Vogel, David. 1997. *Trading Up: Consumer and Environmental Regulation in a Global Economy.* Cambridge, MA: Harvard University Press.

Walk, Heike. 2008. *Partizipative Governance: Beteiligungsformen und Beteiligungsrechte im Mehrebenensystem der Klimapolitik.* Wiesbaden: VS Verlag für Sozialwissenschaften.

Wanshel, Elyse. 2016. "Norway Is the First Country to Ban Deforestation." *Huffington Post*, June 7, 2016. https://www.huffingtonpost.com/entry/norway-first-nation -zero-deforestation_us_57559b5be4b0eb20fa0e7b79.

WBGU. 2011. *Welt im Wandel: Gesellschaftsvertrag für eine Große Transformation*. Berlin: Wissenschaftlicher Beirat der Bundesregierung Globale Umweltveränderungen. https:// www.wbgu.de/de/publikationen/publikation/welt-im-wandel-gesellschaftsvertrag -fuer-eine-grosse-transformation.

Weber, M. (1922) 1978. *Economy and Society: An Outline of Interpretive Sociology*. Edited by R. Guenther and C. Wittich. Berkeley: University of California Press.

Wellesley, Laura. 2014. "Trade in Illegal Timber: The Response in China." Chatham House. December 10, 2014. https://www.chathamhouse.org/publication/trade-illegal -timber-response-china.

Wendt, Alexander. 1992. "Anarchy Is What States Make of It: The Social Construction of Power Politics." *International Organization* 46 (2): 391–425.

West, Darrell M., and Christian Lansang. 2018. "Global Manufacturing Scorecard: How the US Compares to 18 Other Nations." Brookings Institution, July 10, 2018. https://www.brookings.edu/research/global-manufacturing-scorecard-how-the-us -compares-to-18-other-nations/.

WFTO. 2017. "World Fair Trade Organization: Homepage." Accessed July 20, 2017. http://wfto.com/.

WHO and UNICEF. 2017. *Progress on Drinking Water, Sanitation and Hygiene: Update and SDG Baselines*. Geneva: WHO and UNICEF. https://data.unicef.org/wp-content/ uploads/2017/07/JMP-2017-report-launch-version_0.pdf.

Widiatedja, I. Gusti Ngurah Parikesit. 2019. "The Supremacy of the Dispute Settlement Mechanism (DSM) under the World Trade Organization (WTO)." *Brawijaya Law Journal* 6 (1): 60–75. https://doi.org/10.21776/ub.blj.2019.006.01.05.

Wight, Colin. 1999. "They Shoot Dead Horses Don't They? Locating Agency in the Agent-Structure Problematique." *European Journal of International Relations* 5 (1): 109–142.

Wijaya, Atika, and Pieter Glasbergen. 2016. "Toward a New Scenario in Agricultural Sustainability Certification? The Response of the Indonesian National Government to Private Certification." *Journal of Environment & Development* 25 (2): 219–246. https://doi.org/10.1177/1070496516640857.

Williamson, Stephanie. 2011. "Understanding the Full Costs of Pesticides: Experience from the Field, with a Focus on Africa." In *Pesticides: The Impacts of Pesticides Exposure*, edited by Margarita Stoytcheva, 25–48. Rijeka, Croatia: IntechOpen.

http://cdn.intechopen.com/pdfs/13221/InTech-Understanding_the_full_costs_of _pesticides_experience_from_the_field_with_a_focus_on_africa.pdf.

Winter, Joseph. 2006. "DR Congo Poll Crucial for Africa." *BBC News*, November 16, 2006. http://news.bbc.co.uk/2/hi/africa/5209428.stm.

WRI. 2018. "World Resource Institute: Democratic Republic of Congo Resources: Interactive Map." Accessed February 20, 2018. https://www.wri.org/publication/ interactive-forest-atlas-congo-atlas-forestier-interactif-du-congo-version-30.

WTO. 2015. "United States—Measures Concerning the Importation, Marketing and Sale of Tuna and Tuna Products: Dispute Settlement DS381." Accessed December 20, 2015. https://www.wto.org/english/tratop_e/dispu_e/cases_e/ds381_e.htm #bkmk381abrw.

WTO. 2018. *World Trade Statistical Review 2018*. Geneva: WTO. https://www.wto.org/ english/res_e/statis_e/wts2018_e/wts2018_e.pdf.

WTO. 2019. "Homepage: World Trade Organization." Accessed July 16, 2018. https://www.wto.org.

WWF. 2013. "Illegal Logging in the Russian Far East: Global Demand and Taiga Destruction." WWF, April 16, 2013. https://www.worldwildlife.org/publications/ illegal-logging-in-the-russian-far-east-global-demand-and-taiga-destruction.

WWF. 2019. "Homepage: World Wide Fund for Nature." Accessed May 15, 2019. https://wwf.panda.org.

Zelli, Fariborz, and Harro van Asselt, eds. 2013. "The Institutional Fragmentation of Global Environmental Governance: Causes, Consequences and Responses." Special issue, *Global Environmental Politics* 13 (3).

Zudrags, Maris, Shikin Rasikon, Jessie Ooi, and László Máthé. 2015. *Compliance Audit and Investigation Report*. Accreditation Services International, October 9, 2015. https://rspo.org/files/download/40cbe54823271bc.

Index

www.ingramcontent.com/pod-product-compliance
Lightning Source LLC
Chambersburg PA
CBHW031125270326
41929CB00011B/1493